The European Union's Democratization Agenda in the Mediterranean

Democracy promotion in the Middle East and North Africa (MENA) remains a central pillar of the foreign policy in the European Union (EU). Rather than concentrating on the relations between the incumbent authoritarian regimes and the opposition in the relevant countries, and on the degree to which these relations are affected by EU efforts at promoting democracy, human rights and the rule of law (an outside-in approach), this collection of chapters inverts the focus of such relationships and attempts to look at them 'inside-out'. While some contributions also emphasise the 'outside-in' axis, given that this continues to be analytically rewarding, the overarching thrust of this book is to provide some empirical substance for the claim that EU policy making is not unidirectional and is influenced by the perceptions and actions of its 'targets'. We thus focus on domestic political changes on the ground in the MENA and how they link into what the EU is attempting to achieve in the region. Finally, the self-representation of the EU and its (lack of a) clear regional role is discussed.

This book was published as a special issue of *Democratization*.

Michelle Pace is Senior Research Fellow and RCUK Fellow, POLSIS at the University of Birmingham. She is Principal Investigator on two large projects and has published widely on EU policies towards the wider Mediterranean.

Peter Seeberg is Associate Professor, Ph.D. Director of Studies at the Centre for Contemporary Middle East Studies, University of Southern Denmark. He has published on the EU and the Middle East, Arab nationalism, migration issues and ethnic minorities in Europe and Denmark.

The European Union's Democratization Agenda in the Mediterranean

Edited by Michelle Pace with Peter Seeberg

Routledge
Taylor & Francis Group
LONDON AND NEW YORK

First published 2010 by Routledge
2 Park Square, Milton Park, Abingdon, Oxon, OX14 4RN

Simultaneously published in the USA and Canada
by Routledge
711 Third Avenue, New York, NY 10017

Routledge is an imprint of the Taylor & Francis Group, an informa business

© 2010 Taylor & Francis

First issued in paperback 2013

Typeset in Times New Roman by Value Chain, India

British Library Cataloguing in Publication Data
A catalogue record for this book is available from the British Library

ISBN13: 978-0-415-55168-7 (hbk)
ISBN13: 978-0-415-84751-3 (pbk)

CONTENTS

Preface

At a time when the processes of political reform in the Mediterranean are going backwards rather than forwards, and when there are calls for strong voices in Europe, the US, and elsewhere to speak out and condemn the authoritarian regimes' tight reign on their populations in the MENA region, engagement with concrete alternatives on the ground are most urgent.

It is in this spirit that this book brings together an active group of academic researchers. The origins of this group lie in an *Encuentro*, a meeting of UK and Spanish specialists on the Mediterranean and the Middle East, held in Barcelona between 10–11 March 2006, sponsored by the British Council and coordinated by Richard Gillespie and Iván Martín. A guiding principle of this endeavour has been the need to address the needs of 'early career' researchers and, in particular, to facilitate the entry of PhD researchers, close to submitting their thesis, into the wider academic community. Besides that, the *Encuentro* made clear the need for longer term enhancement of research activity by establishing frameworks and infrastructures that will last, and that include close interaction with the policy-making community and the media. The need to promote interdisciplinary approaches and comparative studies in the EU-MENA region was also emphasised.

Thus, in April 2007, with the generous financial support of the University Association for Contemporary European Studies (UACES), the British International Studies Association (BISA) working group on International Mediterranean Studies, the Faculty for the Humanities & the Institute for History and Civilization (University of Southern Denmark), the Danish Ministry of Foreign Affairs, the Danish–Egyptian Dialogue Institute (Cairo) and the European Research Institute (Birmingham University), Peter Seeberg and I co-organized a workshop on the EU's democracy promotion in the Mediterranean region at the Centre for Contemporary Middle East Studies in Odense, Denmark. Our agenda was not just to have an academic discussion on the topic but to attempt to engage with the policy-making community: thus, the different panels offered a critical investigation of the recent emergence of socio-political movements in the wider Mediterranean and the EU's postcolonial legacy.

This book is the fruit of all the work that this team of new and older generations of researchers has put together since that workshop in the hope that our voices will contribute to a more nuanced and informed EU policy towards the MENA. Most of us have carried out extensive field research on the ground in this region and thus we also attempt to bring to our readers the recurring themes in the reflections of the people we interviewed and whose calls for a

Michelle Pace

more pluralistic society in their area we seek to represent. I wish to sincerely thank all those who were directly or indirectly involved in this project and can only hope that our policy recommendations find some sympathetic ears for action in the corridors of Brussels.

Finally, but not least, I would like to thank the British Academy and the Economic & Social Research Council for project grants which facilitated my own contribution to this project.

Michelle Pace, Birmingham, 15 October 2008.

The EU's democratization agenda in the Mediterranean: a critical inside-out approach

Michelle Pace[a], Peter Seeberg[b] and Francesco Cavatorta[c]

[a]Political Science and International Studies, University of Birmingham, Birmingham, B15 2TT, UK; [b]Centre for Contemporary Middle East Studies, University of Southern Denmark, Campusvej 55, 5230 Odense M, Denmark; [c]School of Law and Government, Dublin City University, Dublin 9, Ireland

Introduction

Democracy promotion in the Middle East and North Africa (MENA) remains a central pillar of the foreign policy of both the European Union (EU) and the United States (US), despite the failure of 'democracy by imposition' in Iraq. A recent relative military success in fighting insurgents still leaves a problematic political reality where war-lordism and a weak central government make democracy a difficult goal to achieve. Despite the embedding of the Iraqi government's control, the growing numbers of actors who seem prepared to take part in politics according to democratic norms /rules of the game may yet be outflanked by extremists. The fragmentation of Shi'a and Sunni communities into numerous sectarian political organizations and the reluctance of many Sunnis to participate in formal politics mean that some eschew violence while others perpetrate violence on a daily basis.[1] In addition, external actors plough on with democracy promotion efforts even though there are still significant contradictions between the objectives of the policy and its instruments.[2]

To a large extent, post-2003 American policy in Iraq has focused attention of both scholars and policymakers on the methods through which the EU attempts to export democracy in the MENA region, such as positive political engagement with authoritarian regimes, the promotion of economic reforms, and the strengthening of civil society activism.

Rather than concentrating on the relations between the incumbent authoritarian regimes and the opposition in the relevant countries, and on the degree to which these relations are affected by EU efforts at promoting democracy, human rights, and the rule of law (an outside-in approach), this book inverts the focus of such relationships and attempts to look at them 'inside-out'.[3] While some contributions also emphasize the 'outside-in' axis, given that this continues to be analytically rewarding, the overarching thrust of this book is to provide some empirical substance for the claim that EU policy-making is not unidirectional and is influenced by the perceptions and actions of its 'targets'. We thus focus on domestic political changes as they are happening at the time of writing (late 2008) on the ground in the MENA and how they link into what the EU is attempting to achieve in the region. Conceptually, the literature on democracy promotion takes it for granted that certain institutional structures are necessary to promote reform within existing institutions, in accordance with liberal-democratic and market-capitalist 'guidelines' for good governance. Rather than merely looking from the outside at how democracy promotion policies shape reform in the context of authoritarian regimes, or how regimes and opposition are induced toward a liberal democratic model, we invert the focus and look from the inside-out at *how* regimes and opposition groups can *induce* external actors to view and react to their situation as a viable exception to their preferred practices. Our reference to MENA countries as an 'exception' denotes, on the one hand, exception at a practical level where regimes rule over populations mainly unversed in democratic politics and, on the other hand, exception at a conceptual level where Islamists who accept democratic procedures aim to build a significantly different type of nation-state, which might challenge what European policy-makers would consider to be democratically acceptable (see Volpi in pp. 20–38). Finally, we discuss the self-representation of the EU and its (lack of a clear) regional role (see Pace in pp. 39–58).

The combination of strong regimes in weak states[4] and the reluctance of the EU to approach popular Islamist opposition groups in the MENA region creates a situation which – from an EU perspective – entails a very limited range of political options. Thus, while the EU promotes a liberal-democratic and capitalist type of governance that reflects its own experience and its own interests, it is also willing to compromise on what can be achieved in the region, especially in a context where MENA regimes and some secular opposition actors influence how the EU conceives both political change and, more importantly, stability. Thus, this book examines how MENA ruling elites encourage the EU to look at them as a 'special case' or as an exception in terms of the EU's preferred practices built around the notions of democratic accountability and human rights. Similarly, opposition actors, be they secular or Islamist, are not only influenced by the ways that the EU seeks to export its preferred norms, but also may contribute to the EU's preferred policies by virtue of their ideologies and policy positions. It follows that secular opposition parties and civil society movements tend to present themselves as the only genuine 'democratic' actors in the region in order to gain benefits from a privileged relationship with the EU and organize their political activities around the necessity of satisfying the requirements of this privileged relationship. This behaviour tends, however, to marginalize them in the domestic political game, as the wider population may not subscribe either to their tactics or proposed policies.[5] In the case of the Islamists, related parties and movements generally accept democratic procedures while at the same time wishing to construct a different type of nation-state, which may offer a conceptual exception for the EU and the way it conceives of nation-state building in terms of founding norms. Yet, while Islamist movements in the region have generally accepted the primacy of elections as one of the crucial founding moments of democracy-building, the EU has remained highly sceptical of their involvement in the electoral process. Thus, the move towards electoral politics that many Islamist parties consider to be extremely significant is paradoxically perceived to be very problematic by the EU because such moves are not usually accompanied by the adhesion of Islamists to the liberal values that the EU considers inseparable from democratic procedures and institutions. In addition, it should be borne in mind that Islamist parties have usually not changed their views with respect to a number of international issues that the EU deems important for international stability, such as the Arab–Israeli question or the occupation of Iraq. It is thus the ambition of this book to move beyond an exclusively normative or exclusively realist approach, and to adopt a combined approach to understanding relations between authoritarian MENA regimes and opposition groups in Middle Eastern societies within the framework of external democracy promotion efforts. In some ways, this work has already begun with the contributions of authors like Pace and Bicchi, who in their respective work use the concepts of discursive constructivism and ideational inter-governmentalism in order to capture the complex mixture of realist and normative concerns at the heart of EU external policy-making.[6] In this book, we assume such a mixture and examine in some detail how EU policy-making processes are informed by the feedback effects that the targeted domestic actors in the MENA generate. In other words, by highlighting the current reality on the ground in MENA, the book gives prominence to how local actors' actions themselves influence EU democracy promotion policies in the region.

Some claim that the whole idea of focusing on the EU's democracy promotion efforts is no longer enlightening. They suggest that the explicit focus on democracy promotion is in itself preventing new insights.[7] Schlumberger, for example, suggests that instead we should focus on the nature of MENA states, in particular, on the inter-relationship between rents, rent-seeking, and the prospects for economic and political transformation to a market economy and democratic governance:

> For current research, the key challenge is to increase our knowledge of the causes for Arab authoritarianism. This topic has only recently become a core area of research on Middle East politics. Donor strategies, in their turn, should follow research and be ready to enter the 'post-democratization era', take into account these causes and develop new ideas in order to explicitly address them ... Such ideas need to start from present authoritarian conditions in recipient countries rather than from ideal-type images of liberal democracies.[8]

But to our mind such claims still leave a research vacuum, which has thus far not been filled. In fact the underlying assumption of these critics is that a comprehensive, academic description and analysis of democracy promotion initiatives by the EU in the Mediterranean region and/or the wider Middle East has been achieved and nothing more needs to be said. While we agree on the focus on conditions in MENA countries, we endeavour to add MENA actors and their actions to the context. The contention here is that, in light of both scholarly and policy-making developments, a new form of analysis is necessary, particularly when the focus shifts from evaluating the policies of the EU to analysing *how* the targeted actors (MENA regimes and opposition actors) themselves react to and influence how such policies are designed and implemented.

From a scholarly point of view, the wider literature on democratization has now accepted the significant role that external actors can have in influencing processes of regime change, which were previously believed to be solely domestic affairs.[9] This means that more refined, theoretical tools can now be employed to understand *how* specific EU policies and actors affect the transitional game within targeted countries. This allows scholarship to move beyond discussions of the EU's attempts at exporting the model of liberal democracy to the MENA and seek instead an approach where the focus is on domestic actors and their possible contributions in shaping the perceptions of the region of external actors. Previous discussions largely focused on the notorious failures of progress in democratization processes in the region and on the internal contradictions that characterize EU policy-making.[10] From a policy-making point of view, much has changed since previous systematic analyses of the EU's relationship with the MENA,[11] because of the extremely important impact of the US-led 'war on terror', which has reconfigured both strategies and policy tools of action and led to the rise of security and stability goals. Although this is far from being empirically proven,[12] there is now, among US policy-makers in particular, the almost unquestioned assumption that democracy will contribute to reduce, if not eliminate, political violence.[13] The type of democracy that is envisaged by external actors for the MENA is one that, over time, will come to reflect the institutions and the values upon which Western democracies are built. Thus, while democracy might be an essentially contested concept in theoretical terms, at the practical and policy-making level a blueprint for what democracy should look like does exist, and it is not surprising that it mirrors the experience and the institutions of the leading Western powers. Western-style democracy is pursued as an objective partly because of its presumed beneficial international repercussions, associated with 'democratic peace theory'. We could hypothesize that the EU promotes democracy with vigour in the MENA region because it believes it to be crucial to international stability and security.[14] It might be logical to assume that EU democracy promotion policies would be strengthened and made more coherent and effective after 9/11. This, however, does not seem to be the case, as contradictions in EU policy regarding democracy promotion in the MENA region are still significant. This would seem to point to an understanding of the EU as a rationalistic and realist actor rather than a normative one.[15] Yet, this does not entirely capture what the EU 'does' in the region and does not fully explain how its policies are conceived and implemented by local actors on the ground. As Youngs[16] highlights, the EU pursues interests within an intensely normative framework and it is only through an understanding of this dynamic process that external policies can be analysed. When it comes to the MENA region, the normative value attached to democracy as a norm to be exported frames the manner in which specific interests are pursued because the EU has a very definitive image of what kind of outcome it wishes to see in the MENA region as a result of domestic political change: namely, European-style liberal democracy. Policies aimed at achieving this goal are both normative *and* realist. They are normative because any policy that aims to embed Western-style democracy can be justified as one defending freedom and democracy (the Algeria case is quite paradigmatic in this respect). The policies, however, are also realist because in the EU's conceptualization of stability, only Western-style liberal democracy can create a stable and friendly environment where Western material interests can be pursued. At the same time, EU actors have acknowledged that: (1) the 'Western' model does not necessarily work in the MENA, and (2) the EU must therefore adapt to local, regional, social, and religious settings in this region.[17] Norms and interests are thus inextricably linked. It is at this juncture that domestic actors in the region can signal to the EU what their preferences are, highlighting their position and 'values' in order to influence the ways in which EU policies, such as the Euro-Mediterranean Partnership (EMP, launched in 1995) and the European Neighbourhood Policy (ENP, launched in 2003), are then implemented in practice.

Scholars are generally engaged in explaining under which circumstances the promotion of liberal democracy systems is successful or, alternatively, under which conditions failures are to be expected. It follows that much of the literature, just as in the case of analyses of the EU's key policies towards the Mediterranean, namely the EMP and the ENP, and their successes and/or shortcomings in fulfilling the promises they contain on matters related to democracy, tends to look at how external democracy promotion of the Western, liberal kind influences both authoritarian regimes and opposition actors.

It is widely assumed that powerful external actors, including the EU, are the dominant partners in unequal relationships, whereby resources available to them fuel their pursuit of their objectives and interests. To a considerable extent this is the case, as the EU enjoys a predominant position in the Mediterranean by virtue of its economic power, but relationships with individual MENA countries and political actors are not unidirectional. In this book, we want to emphasize that MENA regimes have a number of strategic advantages, such as natural resources, as well as the growing populations and the spectre of radical Islamism. Collectively, these factors can be put to use to try to manipulate how external actors conceive of their role in the region, and can thus be potentially influential in shaping European attitudes. Domestic opposition political actors also have a role to play because they can provide knowledge and access to EU policy-makers and by virtue of their position, they can contribute to shaping the perceptions and views of the EU. Therefore, the apparent robustness of authoritarianism in the

MENA, which, among other things, leads to institutionalization of strong groups of elites in power[18] – and is a central paradox of weak MENA states[19] – becomes important as part of our analysis in this book. In particular, as explained earlier, this can enable regimes to persuade the EU to view their situation as an 'exception'. The region has a remarkable success rate of incumbent autocratic regimes remaining in power for long periods, in spite of sometimes significant challenges to their rule and widespread lack of popular legitimacy.

   The resilience and durability of the regimes in the MENA can be explained by various factors, as recent research has shown.[20] If we look at the many different attempts to explain authoritarian ability for survival or 'persistence', they span from orientalist/psychologically familiar assumptions about a special resistance of the Islamic mind,[21] via an extreme degree of state repression attached to Mediterranean regimes, to macro-sociological explanations taking their point of departure in the ability of the regimes to include or co-opt different forms of opposition groups.[22] Furthermore, there are also explanations based on assumptions that MENA political elites manage to stay in power by 'buying off' possible contestants to local hegemony. A distribution of significant amounts of symbolic or material resources to ethnic, religious or politically defined minorities (or majorities), makes it possible for often illegitimate regimes to survive, resisting demands for democracy and good governance from both inside and outside. In addition, they are able to convince external actors, including the EU, of the particular and exceptional circumstances on the ground.

   Focusing on political issues in the MENA highlights how the supposedly normative, long-running EU push for democracy in the MENA is at best a very slow work in progress, and at worst democracy is not advancing but retreating. Disappointment in this regard is in part due to inherent paradoxes and contradictions in the making of a policy with no clear, defined vision due to internal institutional problems of the EU structure itself. However, as this book highlights, the production of relevant policies and norms is not solely the realm of the EU, as the design and implementation of democracy promotion strategies is clearly influenced by the way the targeted actors react to them and transform them. This book is therefore specifically concerned with outlining *how* authoritarian MENA regimes and opposition actors induce external actors, and specifically the EU, to perceive and react to their respective situation. This approach marks a novel contribution to the study of democracy promotion, while permitting, at the same time, an examination of *how* the EU represents itself in the region and *how* it conceives its role. Some of the past critiques of EU democracy promotion strategies in the region tended to concentrate their attention on the tools, resources, and discourse of the EU in an attempt to explain the gap between the normative rhetoric and the disappointing reality.[23] Other critiques came from those scholars subscribing to a more realist interpretation of EU external policy-making.[24] What both approaches have in common is an exclusive focus on the EU as the 'leading agency or actor' in this process. This book, on the contrary, attempts to analyse what the EU does in the region in light of what the targeted actors hope to achieve and how they utilize EU resources in order to achieve their objectives. These factors are an important insight into how the EU formulates and implements policies because it is only through a thorough understanding of the complexities of individual domestic political arrangements in each MENA country that we can have a clearer theoretical picture of EU policy-making.

An agenda for inquiry

This book contains three separate but interconnected sections. The first section is informed by the academic debate about the current state of democratization studies. It seeks to frame conceptual arguments on the theme of EU democracy promotion and how this policy is read and affected by various political agents in the MENA. Thus, the first section deals with normative and discursive dimensions of EU democracy promotion efforts, how they influence domestic actors and, importantly, how they are influenced by them. This is a crucial aspect in explaining the so far failed democracy promotion efforts of the EU in the region.

The next two sections contain case studies covering the Mashrek and the Maghreb respectively. The overarching objective of these two sections is to illustrate the complex interaction that exists between the domestic actors and the EU on matters related to democracy promotion. Such interaction contributes to an understanding of the persistence of authoritarianism in the region, and analysis is furthered by examining how domestic actors position themselves in relation to EU policies. Specifically, the chapters in these two sections focus on different MENA polities and how they are influenced by the postcolonial legacy of the EU, with special reference to the role of opposition movements and parties, as well as how EU policy-making and implementation are in turn influenced by these domestic actors. Rather than once again outlining how EU efforts in the region fare, the goal is to examine MENA polities by concentrating on the recent emergence of socio-political movements, their role as opposition forces to authoritarian regimes in the region, and how the ruling elites exploit the emergence of Islamist movements to strengthen their hands *vis-à-vis* the EU.

Problems, paradoxes, and contradictions

Traditional views about the problems in promoting democracy and controlling political Islam are challenged in the first chapter by Frederic Volpi. Volpi discusses the democratizing potential of Islamist movements and parties and the challenges that they pose to basic assumptions about relations between liberalism and democracy. He points to the alternative of talking about 'grey areas' of democracy, suggesting a partial convergence between Islamist and liberal-democratic agendas. First, Volpi approaches the issue of political Islam and democracy as seen from an orientalist perspective with its dual philosophical and political sets of implications. He then discusses democracy in the Middle East after the cold war, looking at Iran and Turkey, as these countries have been analysed within many democratization studies. Drawing on Perthes and Lust-Okar, he also discusses how MENA elites have managed to co-opt their opponents and, at the same time, neutralize popular demands for democracy by manipulating and exploiting splits between opposition groups. Finally, he points to the neglect of detailed considerations of conceptual compromises that are needed for a meaningful dialogue between opposition and government. This might help explain the current lack of options for democracy promotion in the region. Volpi concludes by claiming that we need to move beyond functionalist explanations, which tend to dominate the field, and that the undermining of modernization theory has left a vacuum in contemporary explanatory frameworks of democratization in the Muslim world. He also criticizes 'civil society' explanations for their weaknesses, particularly that they view democratization processes as functional adaptations of Islamist movements to state repression: by being predicated upon a static political order, such explanations fail to consider democratization processes as engines of change. This conceptual exercise leads to an important theoretical outcome in highlighting the challenges 'political Islam' poses to international actors attempting to promote democratic transformation in the MENA. As Volpi points out:

> [A]lthough sometimes presented as an exception to the dominant realist paradigm, the activities of the EU, especially in this context ... had difficulties in moving beyond a sophisticated realist model for politics in the region, not least because the EU had difficulty conceiving what the Mediterranean should be as a region.

MENA authoritarian regimes are able to exploit the existing suspicion of the EU towards Islamist movements by highlighting their illiberal traits on issues such as women's rights and religious minorities, therefore presenting current elites as the only viable alternative to the Islamist project. The access that ruling elites enjoy at the EU level, through a multiplicity of channels set up under the EMP and the ENP, ensures that their input is taken into account at the EU level.

Michelle Pace takes this theoretical insight further by explaining the EU's diagnosis of the Mediterranean 'condition', which in turn highlights the logic behind the EU's prescription for liberal democratization in the MENA. The strategy of promoting democracy by the EU proved relatively successful in Central and Eastern Europe. This, however, has not been the case in the MENA. For years, theorists of international democracy have discussed why this is the case. Through a novel re-visitation of previous debates, Pace points to profound contradictions in EU democracy promotion in the Mediterranean. Specifically, Pace discusses the limits of EU normative power. She focuses on the interconnectedness between democratization on the one hand and stability and prosperity on the other. Pace takes the 1990s as her point of departure and the attempts by the EU to promote democracy and human rights in the Mediterranean as a counterweight to the unstable situation in the region. This was done in practice by signing a series of association agreements with the states south and east of the Mediterranean and by launching the EMP. Pace points to a problematic logic in much EU thinking, that is, that the promotion of economic development will automatically lead to democratization, and argues that the EU lacks a clear, long-term vision for democratic transformation in the MENA in particular and more generally in the South. Linking up with Volpi's arguments, Pace claims that the problems of modernization theory are particularly obvious in the MENA, where much of the struggle between sectors of the opposition and incumbent regimes is precisely about the very meaning and content of modernization. She also points to a tension between the EU's objectives of promoting democracy on the one hand and seeking to ensure security on the other. This refers to security in the economic sense, meaning oil and gas supplies, and, in the political sense, it implies relations with authoritarian regimes rather than opposition groups, including Islamist actors. Taking the relationship between Israel and the Palestinians as a case study, Pace discusses the paradoxes and contradictions inherent in EU efforts to promote democratic transformation. She concludes that the EU, by focusing primarily on external democracy promotion in the Mediterranean region, creates the impression that the concept of democracy in itself is external to the region. This marginalizes the domestic production of democratic norms because they do not seem to fit with European conceptualizations of how a polity should be governed or organized.

Case studies I: the Mashrek

The sections consisting of case-studies begin with Are Hovdenak's study on Palestine. Specifically, he analyses the challenges for democratic reform in Palestine with a focus on the political transformation process which the Islamic Resistance Movement (Hamas) recently underwent. Hovdenak examines the implications of Hamas's political role in relation to the prospects for democratic developments within the Palestinian Authority.

The international dimension is particularly relevant for Palestinian politics and outcomes that are contextualized in relation to the EU's activities in the region. Building on extensive fieldwork in Palestine, the chapter discusses the expectations on the part of Hamas of the possibilities for improving relations with European countries and the perspectives in the EU's policies towards the Palestinian Islamists. It discusses the role of the EU in connection with the international boycott of the Hamas government and the failure of the EU to respect the outcome of the democratic election among the Palestinians. Hovdenak concludes that EU democratization efforts have suffered a serious setback in the Palestinian case. The EU has been quite successful in presenting itself as a normative actor which pro-democracy movements can rely on for support, as the cases in the Balkans demonstrate. It was, therefore, expected that a more positive attitude towards Hamas would have been forthcoming given the democratic mandate the movement received and the 'distance' the movement had travelled from the very margins of Palestinian and international politics.[25] The normative credit that the EU had built up significantly diminished, when it decided to follow the US in its boycott of Hamas. The renewed authoritarianism of both the Fatah-led Palestinian Authority and of Hamas in their respective strongholds can be seen as being partly the outcome of a redistribution of resources that the EU initiated by responding negatively to the electoral outcome of the 2006 elections. The democratic step that Hamas believed it had taken was understood in a completely different manner in Europe, widening the gap not only between two political actors, but also between two conceptualizations of what constitutes a *democratic* order. While Hamas partly believed that it was making a choice that would fit in with the requirements and wishes of the international community and of the EU in particular, the effect that its victory had on the EU was extremely negative because it challenged the latter's normative tenets. This clearly demonstrates how MENA's domestic actors and developments are understood in the EU, with policies designed according to both normative values (a Hamas-led government is conceived to be un-democratic by definition because of the presumed illiberal positions of the movement) and realist necessities (the difficulty of dealing with, what is considered by the EU as, a much less flexible partner for peace).

Irrespective of political and doctrinal religious differences, Hezbollah of Lebanon offers a parallel to Hamas and the former's political strengthening is taken as the point of departure in the second chapter covering the Mashrek region. Peter Seeberg focuses on the EU's problematic role as a democracy promoter in this region. Seeberg describes the ongoing political turmoil in Lebanon and its background. Both the war between Hezbollah and Israel in the summer of 2006 and the protracted presidential election process of 2007 and 2008 deepened the political turmoil in Lebanon. Seeberg points to the relation between Lebanon's particularistic political system and the proclaimed support of the Lebanese elites for a consociational political system. He also points to the importance of taking this into consideration when analysing internal political configurations in Lebanon. Hezbollah is, in many ways, the entity around which regional interests revolve, not least because of the regional role of the movement, which is bolstered by Iran's foreign policy. The EU has been reluctant to engage with Hezbollah and has instead chosen a low-level dialogue with its leaders. Seeberg analyses the ENP Action Plan with Lebanon as an EU democracy promotion tool, through which the EU seeks to reaffirm its normative commitment to democracy. Despite this, Seeberg concludes that from the EU's perspective, the Action Plan is a rather defensive initiative. It represents another rather incoherent policy towards the MENA. The vagueness and inconsistency of EU policies in Lebanon are partly explained by tactical considerations. It also suggests that the EU pursues a realist agenda via normative policies while not officially engaging with a movement that, despite holding on to its weapons, has made a significant move towards democratic politics. More than normative policies, political expediency and political disagreements on the geopolitics of the region seem to dictate the EU's refusal to engage consistently with Hezbollah. Lebanese opponents of Hezbollah make matters worse, as they successfully present themselves to international actors as an alternative to Hezbollah by emphasizing their own democratic and liberal credentials, thereby turning the Lebanese political scene into a contest for the exclusive label of 'democratic group' that they hope will bring both material benefits and legitimacy.

The next two contributions deal with the case of Egypt. First, Sarah Wolff discusses the so-called 'revolt of the judges' as a test case for the EU in engaging non-state actors and movements without specific political-ideological programmes. Second, Thomas Demmelhuber presents a wider analysis of the EU's role in Egypt by examining the difficult reform process within this country.

The three-stage election in Egypt during November and December 2005 to determine the composition of the People's Assembly occurred two months after the country's first multi-candidate, presidential elections. The ruling National Democratic Party (NDP) maintained its majority and control of the Assembly, but gains were made by others at the expense of the NDP. Wolff gives a detailed analysis of the election in 2005 with a specific focus on the 'Judges' Revolt', widely covered in the world media. Judges wanted to emphasize their important electoral supervisory role, as detailed in Egypt's constitution. She claims that, despite intimidations, the judges were successful in advancing the rule of law in Egypt. Given the normative and legalistic nature of the judges' protest, it could have been expected that the EU would have tried to seize the opportunity to influence domestic political events by forcefully supporting the judges in the name of democracy and accountability. Yet the EU failed to support the judges. The Egyptian government managed quickly to defuse the issue through its privileged access to European policy-makers, successfully presenting itself as a reluctant strong ruler trying to modernize and liberalize in the face of widespread radical hostility from domestic actors. The privileged position the Egyptian government enjoys with EU policy-makers thus affected how the judges' revolt was understood at the apex of the EU.

Demmelhuber takes as his point of departure the succession issue in the Egyptian republic, where it appears that the ageing President Hosni Mubarak is trying to manoeuvre his son Gamal into position to succeed him as ruler. Gamal Mubarak plays an important role in Egyptian reform processes, which mainly focus on economic relations, but also, to some degree include political reforms. These reforms do not solely arise from external pressures but can, according to Demmelhuber, be seen as the ruling elites' answer to the challenges of a changing domestic and international environment. The composition of Egyptian reform actors is of significance for European efforts at addressing the challenges arising from Egypt. Demmelhuber analyses the role of various political actors in Egypt, categorizing them in terms of the 'Gamal-group', the Muslim Brotherhood, various syndicates and associations, the secular opposition, and the Kifaya; in sum, a varied and complex group of actors. In addition, Demmelhuber points to weblogs and various non-governmental organizations (NGOs) as informal yet important expressions of interest (and thereby also being potential reform actors) within the Egyptian public sphere. Demmelhuber claims that what unites all opposition actors is what he terms the 'variety-capability gap'. Moreover, they are all up against the Egyptian state, 'the type of state that allows a relative freedom of expression, but not freedom of action'. Demmelhuber acknowledges that the EU finds it difficult to respond adequately to Egypt's political realities. Echoing Pace's contribution, Demmelhuber argues that the EU's long-term goal may be to support democratization in Egypt. In the short-term, however, the EU prioritizes stability and cooperation with the incumbent regime as necessary for its achievement. Demmelhuber claims that despite the EMP and the ENP, there remains 'an incremental need for practicable instruments and partners'. His analysis has its foundations in a well-known fact: the EU privileges realist objectives to the detriment of normative ones, for example, by providing resources for authoritarian actors, rather than engaging opposition actors that the EU may regard as lukewarm democrats at best. Demmelhuber claims that the 'Muslim Brotherhood should not be considered as part of the problem but more as part of the solution for the sake of Egypt's long-term stability'. Consequently, he avers that the EU should encourage the gradual insertion of the Brotherhood into the political process, not permanently exclude it, as this will only destabilize the country.

Case studies II: the Maghreb

The last part of the book discusses issues related to the EU's attempts at promoting democracy in the Maghreb. Two contributions focusing on Morocco commence the coverage, followed by chapters on Algeria and Tunisia. Morocco has, for several reasons, including its proximity to Europe and its importance as a large-scale source of migrants, been subject to significant European political and economic attention. In his contribution, Francesco Cavatorta discusses the lack of unity within the Moroccan opposition and explores the reasons for this. He explains that the opposition groups in Morocco do not pool their resources to pressurize the regime in the direction of meaningful political reforms. Rather, there is competition among the various opposition groups, especially between secular and Islamist groups. The EU influences Morocco's political contestation by highlighting perceived ideological and tactical differences between Islamist and secularist political actors. The EU appears unwilling to conceive of the possibility that an alternative might exist to liberal democracy, which is what Islamists believe. For Islamist parties, the focus is on elections and accountability of officials (a corollary to their anti-corruption campaigns) and democracy is simply taken to mean catering to the collective needs of the people. Political Islam does not emphasize the liberal aspect of governance, which is crucial to Western democratic political thinking. By promoting a specific form of *liberal* democracy, to which only secular and liberal Moroccans might adhere, the EU helps reinforce the divide between opposition groups. In turn, the divisions within the opposition help secure the continuity of the regime through a 'divide and conquer' strategy, as the secular opposition subscribes to values that render it a privileged partner of the EU, while political moves by Islamists are regarded with suspicion. The EU's normative values are not sufficiently flexible and the phenomenon of 'Islamic democracy' is regarded as a type of 'non-democratic confrontational regime', leading to what Bicchi has called 'cognitive uncertainty'.[26] This, in turn, leads to policy choices that, in the eyes of Islamists and of much public opinion in the MENA, run contrary to the EU's stated pro-democracy policies. In this context, it is no surprise that in their struggle against Islamism for political influence in society, secular movements play up their liberal and democratic credentials in order to extract benefits from the EU.

Islamists are also at the centre of Eva Wegner and Miquel Pellicer's contribution. Their focus is specifically on the ideological moderation of the Islamist movements in Morocco. They define the concept of moderation as 'becoming more flexible towards core ideological beliefs'. Their point is that this understanding of moderation is feasible because it does not presume that Islamists are, by definition, anti-democratic. This potentially offers a way out of the problematic in regard to EU perceptions of Islamist movements in the MENA. Their chapter commences by analysing the relationship between the Parti de la Justice et du Développement (PJD) and the Mouvement Unité et Réforme (MUR) during 1992–2007, with the most recent parliamentary elections in Morocco occurring in 2007. The process of gaining autonomy informs the development of moderation which the PJD appears to pursue while, at the same time, gaining strength as both social movement and political party. Wegner and Pellicer claim that the EU's policy towards Islamists can be seen as a policy of avoidance of engagement with them. The PJD's recent moderation was not met with a response of political liberalization from the regime. In addition, the authors claim that the EU, consistently supportive of the governing regime in Morocco, has not yet developed a consistent stance towards Morocco's Islamists.

The preferences and political decisions of the political elite are crucial for understanding the conditions for democracy promotion in Algeria. The background for the discrepancy between the political objectives of the EMP/Barcelona Declaration and the actual practices of EU policies in Algeria can be understood by focusing on the contradictions between the ruling elite in the country, which has been able to sustain non-democratic governing structures, and the Islamic opposition, which was denied electoral victory and kept from power by the suspension of the elections and army intervention in 1992. This situation laid the foundation for the tragedy of Algeria in the 1990s. Ayşe Aslıhan Çelenk interprets the Algerian reality within the framework of a 'misfit model' claiming that:

> When the costs of responding to EU pressure for change are higher, domestic political actors tend to resist EU-level pressure ... the colonial legacy, perceptions about political Islam and the preferences of the military and the president as the major political actors are the domestic determinants of the way in which EU democracy promotion policies affect the country.

The EU, once again, preferred stability over the promotion of democracy and the authoritarian regime was accepted by the international community, given the alternative of an Islamist regime. Çelenk demonstrates this by referring to MEDA funding, which was never suspended even though steps toward democratization were not taken in Algeria. In her concluding remarks, Çelenk claims that security priorities and the concerns of the EU about political and economic stability led to it abstaining from pressuring for democratization in Algeria. The EU instead chose to support and cooperate with the incumbent political elite, leaving others out. Thereby, the EU contributed to consolidating the power of the authoritarian political elite in Algeria, and did not contribute to democratization in Algeria.

The issue of identity and political change in Tunisia is analysed in the last chapter covering the Maghreb sub-region. Brieg Powel takes recent political developments in Tunisia as his point of departure, and examines how the EU presents them as a success story of its programmes of democratic assistance. Powell investigates the notion of normative power in connection with a discussion about the nature of the EU as an international actor. He claims that the inclusion by the EU of Tunisia within a discursive 'Mediterranean' construction associates the Tunisian state and society with signifiers which may actually only be of relevance to other parts of the region. He also examines the role of political Islam in the Tunisian context. Tunisia is, in its rhetoric and practice, securitizing Islamists. As a result, Islamist political parties, such as the Nahda party, are hounded by the security forces. There is little understanding amongst EU officials of differences between the Islamist groups in Tunisia, and it is shown that, seen from the EU perspective, democracy promotion and security issues are linked, hence contributing to the sidelining of the Islamists by the Tunisian regime. Powel concludes that Tunisia represents a challenge to the conceptualization of the EU as a normative power. Contrary to the EU claiming democracy promotion as its primary ambition, Powel shows that, together with the incumbent regime, the EU first and foremost pursues stability in Tunisia, and in so doing contributes to delegitimizing non-regime, Islamist actors and discourses. Finally, Powel concludes that this has implications not only for the role of the EU as a democracy promoter, but for the concept of democracy itself.

Conclusion

It is our claim that by taking an inside-out approach in our case studies, as well as seeking to combine realist and normative approaches, we can usefully generate new insights into relations between the EU and other external actors and authoritarian regimes in the MENA. We also argue that in choosing not to interact or engage with other actors in the MENA, the EU holds a very limited and blurred understanding of the specificities of each country in the region as well as of the region as a whole. By focusing in particular on Islamist groups in the MENA, the contributors in this book are not claiming that these groups are necessarily 'democratic': no such group has so far been given the opportunity to take part in a 'liberal political system'. Attempting to understand the exact political nature of Islamist groups without taking into account their surrounding institutional environments does not usefully help us understand how they might operate in democratic political systems.[27] Instead, we have highlighted how internal actors in the MENA have read the EU's efforts at promoting its particular model of liberal democracy and how they, in turn, have attempted to respond to the EU. We have also attempted to highlight how marginal groups, including Islamist movements in the MENA, are characterized by their own agency and are not merely subject to EU programmes and policies. Moreover, such groups can help shape what the EU attempts to do in the region. We have also emphasized how these agents play a specific political role in relation to the particular structures of MENA authoritarian regimes and how such governments seek to initiate and develop political systems characterized by what might be called 'staged democracy' in order ultimately to retain power. Often ignoring such manipulative tactics, the EU typically continues to support authoritarian regimes in the MENA. This does not necessarily mean that the EU's policies have failed, but it does suggest that the EU's policies have serious unintended consequences. Although normatively, the EU's political endeavours at promoting democracy in the MENA may seek a positive image of the EU, it is unclear how local populations understand such initiatives. It may be that the EU is losing its credibility as well as its legitimacy as an external actor and as a result what may happen in the MENA is a move to more extreme and violent reactions from disgruntled groups.

Acknowledgements

The guest editors of this special issue, Michelle Pace and Peter Seeberg, would like to thank the editors of *Democratization*, Jeff Haynes and Gordon Crawford, for their constructive comments and suggestions.

Earlier versions of the articles of this special issue were presented at the workshop held at the University of Southern Denmark on 21–22 April 2007. The guest editors are very thankful for their generous support in setting up the workshop to the following institutions: the Danish Ministry of Foreign Affairs, the British International Studies Association (BISA) Working Group on International Mediterranean Studies, the Faculty for the Humanities and the Institute for History and Civilization as well as the Centre for Middle East Studies (University of Southern Denmark), the University Association for Contemporary European Studies (UACES), the Danish-Egyptian Dialogue Institute (Cairo), RAMSES (a Network of Excellence on Mediterranean Studies, Oxford), and the European Research Institute (Birmingham University).

Notes

1. Springborg, 'Political Islam and Europe'.
2. Cofman Wittes, *Freedom's Unsteady March*.
3. The authors are very grateful to Frédéric Volpi for teasing out the 'inside-out' framework of analysis.
4. Migdal, *Strong Societies and Weak States*.
5. The weakness of established secular political parties and civil society organizations has been in evidence for some time. For the weakness of secular parties see for instance Willis, 'Political Parties in the Maghreb'; for the weakness of secular civil society see Cavatorta, 'Civil Society, Democracy Promotion and Islamism'.
6. Pace, *The Politics of Regional Identity*; Bicchi, *European Foreign Policy Making*.

7. Schlumberger, 'Dancing with Wolves'.
8. Ibid., 53.
9. See the special issue of *Democratization* 12 (2005).
10. Youngs, 'European Approaches to Security' and Olsen, 'The EU: An Ad Hoc Policy'. For a thorough overview of the EU's key policies towards the Mediterranean, namely the Euro-Mediterranean Partnership and the European Neighbourhood Policy, see Pace, 'Norm Shifting from EMP to ENP'.
11. See the special issue of *Democratization* 9 (2002).
12. Dalacoura, 'US Democracy Promotion in the Arab World'.
13. Hasan, 'Bush's Freedom Agenda'.
14. See the strong emphasis on democratic governance in the EU Security Strategy. Available in English at http://www.consilium.europa.eu/uedocs/cmsUpload/78367.pdf
15. Hyde-Price, 'Normative Power Europe'.
16. Youngs, 'Normative Dynamics and Strategic Interests'.
17. Confidential communication between Michelle Pace and an EU policy-maker, Brussels, April 2008.
18. Bellin, 'The Robustness of Authoritarianism'.
19. Migdal, *Strong Societies and Weak States*.
20. Jung, *Democratization and Development*.
21. Tibi, *Islam and the Cultural Accommodation;* Kedourie, *Democracy and Arab Political Culture*.
22. Smith, 'Life of the Party'; Smith, 'The Wrong Kind of Crisis'.
23. Philippart, 'The Euro-Mediterranean Partnership'.
24. Cavatorta et al., 'EU External Policy-Making'.
25. Gunning, *Hamas in Politics*.
26. Bicchi, *European Foreign Policy Making*.
27. Brumberg, 'Islamists and the Politics of Consensus'.

Bibliography

Bellin, Eva. 'The Robustness of Authoritarianism in the Middle East: Exceptionalism in Comparative Perspective'. *Comparative Politics* 36 (2004): 139–57.
Bicchi, Federica. *European Foreign Policy Making Toward the Mediterranean*. New York: Palgrave Macmillan, 2007.
Brumberg, Daniel. 'Islamists and the Politics of Consensus'. *Journal of Democracy* 13 (2002): 109–15.
Cavatorta, Francesco. 'Civil Society, Democracy Promotion and Islamism on the Southern Shores of the Mediterranean – Review Article'. *Mediterranean Politics* 13 (2008): 109–19.
Cavatorta, Francesco, Raj Chari, Sylvia Kritzinger, and Arantza Gomez. 'EU external policy-making: "Realistically" Dealing With Authoritarianism? The Case of Morocco'. *European Foreign Affairs Review* 13 (2008): 357–76.
Cofman Wittes, Tamara. *Freedom's Unsteady March*. Washington DC: Brookings Institution Press, 2008.
Dalacoura, Katerina. 'US Democracy Promotion in the Arab World since September 11 2001: A Critique'. *International Affairs* 81 (2005): 963–79.
Gunning, Jeroen. *Hamas in Politics*. London: Hurst & Company, 2007.
Hasan, Oz. 'Bush's Freedom Agenda: Between Democracy and Domination'. Paper presented at the launch meeting of the EU Democracy Promotion Efforts in the Middle East working group, University of Birmingham, 6, August 2008.

Hyde-Price, Adrian. 'Normative Power Europe: A Realist Critique'. *Journal of European Public Policy* 13 (2006): 217–34.

Jung, Dietrich, ed. *Democratization and Development. New Political Strategies for the Middle East*, New York: Palgrave Macmillan, 2006.

Kedourie, Elie. *Democracy and Arab Political Culture.* Washington DC: Washington Institute for Near East Policy, 1994.

Migdal, Joel. *Strong Societies and Weak States: State-Society Relations and State Capabilities in the Third World.* Princeton: Princeton University Press, 1989.

Olsen, Rye G. 'The EU: An Ad Hoc Policy with a Low Priority'. *Exporting Democracy; Rhetoric Vs. Reality*, ed. Paul Schraeder. London: Lynne Rienner, 2002.

Pace, Michelle. 'Norm Shifting from EMP to ENP: The EU as a Norm Entrepreneur in the South?'. *Cambridge Review of International Affairs* 20 (2007): 657–73.

Pace, Michelle. *The Politics of Regional Identity. Meddling with the Mediterranean.* Oxford: Routledge, 2006.

Philippart, Eric. 'The Euro-Mediterranean Partnership: A Critical Evaluation of an Ambitious Scheme'. *European Foreign Affairs Review* 8 (2003): 201–20.

Schlumberger, Oliver. 'Dancing with Wolves: Dilemmas of Democracy Promotion in Authoritarian Contexts'. In *Democratization and Development. New Political Strategies for the Middle East*, ed. Dietrich Jung, 33–60. New York: Palgrave Macmillan, 2006.

Smith, Benjamin. 'Life of the Party: Origins of Regime Breakdown and Persistence under Single Party Rule'. *World Politics* 57 (2005): 421–51.

Smith, Benjamin. 'The Wrong Kind of Crisis: Why Oil Booms and Busts Rarely Lead to Authoritarian Breakdown'. *Studies in Comparative International Development* 40 (2006): 55–76.

Springborg, Robert. 'Political Islam and Europe. Views from the Arab Mediterranean States and Turkey'. In *Political Islam and European Foreign Policy. Perspectives from Muslim Democrats of the Mediterranean*, ed. Michael Emerson and Richard Youngs, 160–84. Brussels: Centre for European Policy Studies, 2007.

Tibi, Bassam. *Islam and the Cultural Accommodation of Social Change.* Boulder: Westview Press, 1990.

Youngs, Richard. 'European Approaches to Security in the Mediterranean'. *Middle East Journal* 57 (2003): 414–31.

Youngs, Richard. 'Normative Dynamics and Strategic Interests in the EU's External Identity'. *Journal of Common Market Studies* 42 (2004): 415–35.

Willis, Michael. 'Political Parties in the Maghreb: The Illusion of Significance'. *Journal of North African Studies* 7 (2002): 1–22.

Political Islam in the Mediterranean: the view from democratization studies

Frédéric Volpi

School of International Relations, University of St. Andrews, St. Andrews, KY16 9AX, Scotland

Contemporary perceptions of, and responses to, the growth of political Islam on the southern shores of the Mediterranean are still heavily influenced by traditional orientalist views on 'Islam' and by realist notions of regional security. This situation contributes to the formation of predominantly state-centric responses to what is perceived to be a monolithic Islamist threat. The issues of democratization and democracy promotion are downplayed in the face of security concerns. When addressed, liberal-inspired views of democracy and civil society are nonetheless problematically deployed in a social and political context that does not duplicate well the conditions met in previous 'waves' of successful democratization elsewhere. The prospects for democratization are linked to a situation where moderate Islamist movements are expected to endorse liberal-democratic values – albeit reluctantly and by default – and where state-imposed constraints on political liberalization can only slow down the process of implementation of electoral democracy. Far too little attention is paid to the alternative forms of participation that are devised locally by Islamists, as well as to the relevance of standard electoral processes in the context of refined authoritarian systems.

Introduction: influences on the study of democratization in the Middle East and North Africa (MENA)

Over the last few decades, the issue of the absence of recognizable forms of liberal democracy in most Muslim-majority countries has been at the centre of much debate in both political science and foreign policy. In the preceding decades, political Islam was not deemed to be a research topic worthy of much social science inquiry and was seen as something better left to orientalist scholars with regional interests. The most emblematic Islamic political movement of the twentieth century, the Muslim Brotherhood, hardly featured on the political science landscape until the 1960s.[1] In practice, political science studies on Islamic movements, when they existed, received little attention before the 1979 Iranian revolution. Then, in the space of two decades, political Islam moved from being viewed as an anachronism to being considered one of the leading features of political life and institutional change in the region.[2] From the mid-1980s onward, there has been an exponential growth of two comparatively new bodies of literature attempting to explain political change in the Muslim world: democratization studies and studies of Islamism. These two types of expertise met after the end of the cold war in the so-called 'third wave' of democratization, when many believed that authoritarian regimes worldwide would quickly disappear to be replaced by Western-style, liberal democracies.[3]

Due to the largely disappointing results of democratization in most Muslim-majority polities, and in particular in the Middle East and North Africa, scholars and policy-makers have concentrated their attention on what might cause the continuing absence of substantial democratic reforms in those parts of the world.[4] Repeatedly, the most conspicuous answers to the lack of 'progress', liberalism, and democracy in Muslim polities have been that it is a consequence of the intrinsically regressive and authoritarian precepts of Islam as a system of belief(s) and social organization, and/or a result of the political and socio-economic backwardness of these countries. These issues became a global concern in the post-9/11 period when the radical edge of political Islam began to present itself as a new international security challenge for the dominant state actors.

At about the same time, many analyses of democratization began to shift the grounds of their inquiries toward more empirical methods of political assessment. They refocused their attention to practical dilemmas about political Islamization and democratization, rather than meta-questions about Islam and democracy.[5] These analyses became concerned with the issue of the practical role played by Islamist movements as institutional actors for political mobilization, and not with the more diffuse cultural and religious underpinnings of social identification. In the years of the 'war on terror', democracy and democracy promotion were reaffirmed in connection with the dominant institutions and practices of 'really existing' liberal democracies. Serious considerations on what might constitute viable, democratic alternatives to this prevailing model receded into the background.

In the following, I analyse the above mentioned trends in order to highlight the internal dynamics of the study of democratization in Muslim polities, particularly those on the southern shores of the Mediterranean, and how this is relayed into the field of policy-making. In the first section, I look at the heritage of orientalism and its role in constructing Islam and, later, political Islam as unitary objects of analysis in the region. In the second section, I examine the 'realist' legacy of the Cold War, as a power-focused, state-centric set of narratives, and its influence on the growth of democratization studies from the mid-1980s onwards. In the third section, I assess the debates on civil society that are prevalent in the 'third wave' of democratization and outline how this idea (and ideal) is deployed in connection to political Islam in MENA polities. In the fourth section, I detail

the mechanisms that are commonly invoked to explain how and why democratization is currently caught up in a 'grey zone' in the Muslim world, and particularly
on the southern shores of the Mediterranean.

Legacies of orientalism

It is instructive first to approach the issue of political Islam and democracy in the
Muslim context from an orientalist perspective. By orientalism, I mean an
approach to Islam that tries to build a comprehensive and systematic picture of
an Islamic civilization, with its own logic and system of values.[6] Admittedly,
this Islamic narrative is being analysed and explained through the lenses of
western concepts and methodologies. Yet, as long as these concepts and methods
are presented as rational universals, orientalist accounts have no particular difficulty
in making their case. They are firmly in the lineage of the positivist social sciences
of the nineteenth century and have a clear, realist epistemology. There is an object
out there called 'Islam', or the 'Muslims', which can be the object of systematic
study; and the task of orientalist scholarship is precisely to contribute, little by
little, to providing the grand picture of the internal workings of this phenomenon
or society.

As both critiques and proponents of this scholarship have argued repeatedly,
there is little doubt that traditional orientalists had (and in some cases have) a sophisticated knowledge of many aspects of the fields that they studied. Indeed, in the
early days of social science investigation of the Middle East, it seemed difficult to
move beyond orientalism. Manfred Halpern's approach in the 1960s is a clear
illustration of this trend.[7] Rather than directly questioning the narratives put
forward by traditional orientalists, he attempted to supplement them with more
empirical analyses of political behaviour in the postcolonial states of the region.
Reviewing the orientalist scholarship of the 1950s, Halpern stated unambiguously
that in his view, 'it would be quite impossible for students of political modernization to do any sensible work without, for example, drawing upon the works
of H.A.R. Gibb, Gustave von Grunebaum, or Wilfred Cantwell Smith'.[8] Hence,
he was concerned with developing a 'new orientology', more attuned to the
paradigms of modern political science and based more in quantitative methods
of analyses than was previously the case. Halpern did not see a fundamental
contradiction between these two approaches; rather, he envisioned a complemen-
tary relationship – one that fully appreciated the orientalist heritage. Indeed, social
and political science experts in the 1960s and 1970s, from Leonard Binder to
Dankwart Rustow, would mainly provide more empirically grounded elaboration
of traditional, 'ex cathedra' orientalist arguments about the dynamics of the political culture of the MENA.[9]

For those authors in the political science tradition, the main legacy of orientalism has a dual philosophical and political set of implications. First, from a
philosophical perspective, orientalist scholarship seeks to (re)construct a paradigmatic reading of Islam that structures the freedom of action of Muslim social and

political actors; what they can or cannot do and say, what they should or should not do and say. This is contrasted to a similarly rigid account of liberal democratic principles that cannot accommodate, or be accommodated by, the Islamic tradition in some of its most fundamental characteristics. While traditional orientalism focused on religious and theological exegesis, contemporary, 'neo-orientalist' analysts concentrate instead on the politicized pronouncements of various Islamic ideologues, as well as the performative media dimension of their discourse. Second, from a political perspective, orientalist approaches are connecting these philosophical/theological interpretations directly to political practice. This perspective argues that because this is what the leaderships of Islamist movements think, this is how politics will be organized by an Islamist regime, therefore, this is what foreign policy and international alignment will be like, and so on. This (neo-)orientalist take on Islam accommodates itself well to, and is also constitutive of, a traditional realist (or neorealist) account of power construction and projection in international relations theory.

Seen from outside the region, political Islam was, for most of the Cold War, merely a dependent variable of political change. In MENA settings, where 'realist' theories of international relations appear to be quite adequate to account for external state behaviour, and where modernization theory was meant to encapsulate the direction of societal change internally. In this context, for decidedly orientalist scholars like Elie Kedourie or Bernard Lewis, the democratization debate is a non-starter, both because of the weight of the Islamic tradition and because Islamist ideologues and leaders repeatedly speak openly against the idea of democracy.[10] Such analyses emphasize the utilization of key theological resources of Islam to undermine the basic concepts of democratic organization, like popular sovereignty. As such, these approaches are attempting to frame the domestic and international politics of Muslim-majority societies in relation to a fairly unitary notion of 'national interest', defined on the basis of Islamist ideology.

For more political science-minded authors, the merging of orientalist scholarship and the study of political behaviour remains largely under-scrutinized and/or is waved away as commonsensical. Thus, in an often-consulted textbook about Middle Eastern politics from the 1970s and 1980s, James Bill and Carl Leiden could argue that 'despite all the differences that separate Middle Eastern leaders and elites, there are in the Muslim world a number of deep seated and persisting similarities in rule'.[11] They suggested that these similarities 'have existed throughout Islamic history and can be traced to the days of the Prophet Muhammad, himself the model par excellence of political leadership'. Thus Bill and Leiden could conclude that since 'millions of Muslims continue to pattern their lives after his, it is not surprising, therefore, that twentieth-century Muslim political leaders often have styles and use strategies that are very similar to those instituted by the Prophet Muhammad in Arabia some 1,400 years ago'.[12] These 'commonsense' approaches to political culture in the MENA were not, in fact, proposing an analysis of political elites and of the institutional organization of the postcolonial state in the region. Yet, there were already accounts, such as Michael Hudson's study of the legitimization crisis in the Arab world, which actually did provide this kind of detailed and careful explanation of political order (and its failures) in the region.[13] Nor did these narratives propose a more historically-construed investigation into the survival and modernization of tribal and religious modes of governance, which various studies of 'neo-*asabiyya*' processes provided.[14] Rather, what was invoked in the kind of analyses that Bill and Leiden (and many others) proposed at that time was a set of culturalist assumptions, which are at best supported by tenuous historical correlations. For example, how does the above-mentioned argument apply to secularized, modernist Middle Eastern elites, who only make perfunctory and rhetorical uses of the examples set by the Prophet? Alternatively, how is one able to specify what constitutes a specifically Islamic model of leadership: Is it to be a reference to the constitution of Medina? Is it the entire life of the Prophet himself? Does it include the time of the first few caliphs (the so-called Golden Age of Islam)? And so on.

For domestic politics, because the notion that modernization and secularization of institutions and, more generally, of social life was the preferred, developmental paradigm for Muslim polities, a comparison of these transformations with democratic developments in the 'West' was not only useful for understanding what was happening, but was, in fact, necessary to explain it. Resistance to the secularization and modernization of social and political life was deemed largely futile before the 1979 Iranian revolution. As Daniel Lerner's well-known comment indicated it appeared to be a straightforward choice between 'Mecca and mechanization'.[15] In effect, it was not even a choice at all since Lerner and many others fully anticipated that the religious glue of Muslim societies would be dissolved by modernization. Some less sanguine observers, like Abu-Lughod, noted however, that since these processes were often forcefully implemented by authoritarian regimes, a return of the repressed social and political forces, particularly Islamic ones, was likely to happen at some point and provide a corrective to this trend.[16] By and large, however, this corrective was not actually deemed to be significant enough to warrant much research and thinking on the topic at that time. It was not until well after the Iranian revolution that scholars began to consider the overstretching of the modernization/secularization theory, especially when it was applied to largely under-studied social forces in Muslim-majority countries.[17]

Ending the Cold War: democracy as a peculiar dilemma of Middle Eastern politics

At a substantive level, interpretations of political Islam remained on the whole a second order tool of analysis for most of the 1980s since the bipolar dynamics of the Cold War were viewed as the first order *explanandum* in the (greater) Middle Eastern context. In international relations, the specificities of Muslim-majority countries were for a long time subsumed under a regionalist approach to Middle East politics.[18] This area-study perspective was, in turn, structured for a long time by the dominant (neo)realist paradigms of the Cold War. Even when supplemented by a dose of neo-liberal analyses, such a 'realist' take on the Muslim world is key to understanding the evolution of the democratization debates from the mid-1980s onwards. Illustrative of this situation are the views on the 'third wave' of democratization that Samuel Huntington presents in his analysis of the Middle Eastern/Islamic democratization conundrums. From his 1984 article 'Will More Countries Become Democratic' to his 1991 book *The Third Wave*, Huntington views the spread of liberal democracy to the Middle East and the Muslim world as a problematic process, but not for conceptual reasons.[19] He does not see Islamism as providing a concrete and realistic alternative to liberal democratic institutional models for the region. He warns against a particularly difficult set of structural factors stacking up against a smooth and rapid democratization sequence in many key Muslim-majority countries. Yet, he argues that this situation only points to a quantitatively bigger problem rather than to a qualitatively different democratization dilemma.[20] Huntington's account from the 1980s (like his civilizational narrative in the 1990s) proposes some 'obvious' generalizations about Muslim politics, underpinned by orientalist scholarship, that rely on very little else than correlations; and these correlations remain to be explained since they do not constitute explanations in themselves.

This strand of thinking, as well as the tendency to merge *explanan* and *explanandum*, continues unabated after the Cold War when it comes to analysing Muslim polities. Many democratization specialists do not seriously revise their positions regarding the Muslim world and one notices instead an increased polarization between approaches to democratization in the region.[21] This polarization is informed by the debate in the sociology of religion that emphasizes the (partial) deprivatization of religion.[22] The undermining of the edifice of modernization theory that many analysts had used to frame their understanding of social and political change in the MENA, led to even more exceptionalist explanations of Muslim exceptionalism. In particular, there is a new set of more pessimistic interpretations of the prospects for liberal democratization in the Muslim world shaped by the idea of the emergence of a political order based on political Islam. In Huntington's narrative, this is illustrated by the revision of his argument about quantitative resistances into a qualitative clash of 'civilizations'.[23] In a not too dissimilar mould, Adrian Karatnycky's review of the Freedom House Survey trends in 2001 stresses that Muslim-majority societies remain the most resistant to the spread of democracy and, quoting Lewis approvingly on the paucity of the democratic lexicon in Arabic and Persian, refers back to the idea that it simply takes time and efforts for democratic principles to take root in an Islamic political culture.[24] This over-reliance on some vague notion of 'Islamic political culture' as a generic explanation provides a common thread between modernization accounts of the 1950s and 1960s, the realist analyses of the Cold War, and the post-Cold War narratives about Muslim democratic exceptionalism.[25]

Up to the end of the Cold War, such loose references to political Islam only served to buttress a state-centric narrative about Middle Eastern politics as *realpolitik* in a realist/neorealist regional order. Immediately after the collapse of the USSR and the rise of Islamic militancy in Central Asia, the notion of a 'Greater Middle East' even gained popularity as a means of bringing the new Central Asian republics within a known frame of reference. This meant that explanations emphasized traditional security practices, such as the role of military alliances with nationalist autocrats to secure oil resources and hold Islamism in check.[26] Although sometimes presented as an exception to the dominant realist paradigm, the activities of the European Union (EU), especially in relation to the Euro-Mediterranean Partnership, had difficulties in moving beyond a sophisticated realist model for politics in the region. This is due not least to the fact that the EU had difficulty conceiving what the Mediterranean should be as a region.[27] As Pace indicates in this special issue, the EU has considerable difficulties not only in turning theory into practice, but also in thinking through a coherent, conceptual approach for its multiple policy initiatives at the regional level. EU officials generally wish to emphasize a 'soft power' approach to reforming institutions and practices in the region instead of imposing some new rules of the game. Yet, they do resort to arm-twisting tactics whenever the circumstances appear to demand it (for example, in trade negotiations, in the recognition of Hamas). This 'realist' tendency has been more visible in EU policies after 9/11 as the dynamics of securitization became more prominent within both the EU zone and the Mediterranean region, especially when Islamist movements are involved, since they remain an unknown quantity for EU institutions.[28]

Fred Halliday noted how, in the post-Cold War context, the debates about political Islam in the Middle East became polarized between 'essentialist' and 'contingencist' strands of arguments.[29] Essentialists develop an argument with a strong orientalist flavour that posits that the 'fundamentals' of Islam are the reason for systemic and systematic clashes with western notions of liberal democracy. Contingencists, on the other hand, argue that, like any other religious doctrine, Islam is malleable enough to be conceptually and practically interpreted in such a way that the areas of frictions with liberal notions of democracy are minimal in the right circumstances. Such polarized views remain common mainly because analysts in each 'camp' have embarked upon rather different kinds of intellectual endeavours that cannot be unified by mere reference to the 'data'. From an international relations perspective, various neo-orientalist and neorealist approaches repeatedly try to establish a causal link between (liberal) democracy and political Islam (or Islam *tout court*) in order to show the incompatibility (or occasionally compatibility) of these two organizing principles of social and political life. Meanwhile, their post-orientalist and constructivist opponents engage with them on those same terms. For the former, the task is to construct a usable framework for constructing/representing 'national interests' from the discourse on political Islam and, therefore, to find unity in diversity. For the latter, the task is to unmask the alternative articulations of Islamic discourses and show where and when the resources of the Islamic tradition can be re-articulated synergistically with other resources, including those from the liberal democratic tradition.

These opposing perspectives parallel the disagreements in democratization studies between, on the one hand, those agency-based, transitology studies in the fashion of Guillermo O'Donnell and Phillipe Schmitter that became fashionable in the mid-1980s and, on the other hand, those slightly older, structure-based accounts of democratization that have their roots in modernization theory.[30] For essentialist-minded writers, the core characteristics of the Islamic and liberal-democratic tradition are simply too dissimilar to ever allow individuals to build a polity that would satisfy both sets of skills and expectations; no matter how much *fortuna* and *virtu* one may have. For contingencist-minded authors, given the right circumstances, individuals and groups can find interpretations of their religious principles that interact synergistically, rather than conflict with, liberal-democratic practices and institutions. Evidently, the mere possibility of a convergence does not imply that it will necessarily happen in practice. Some of the key post-orientalist narratives of the 1990s, from Kepel's *The Revenge of God* to Roy's *The Failure of Political Islam*, did in fact emphasize a sizeable chasm between the two traditions, as well as the continuing relevance of an 'Iranian model' or an 'Algerian scenario' type of Islamist takeover.[31] As ever, simply referring to the 'facts of life' in the region does not provide a way of resolving such a dilemma. Because of the limited numbers of examples and counter examples invoked in each instance, what counts as meaningful generalization and what is meant to be an exception is strongly determined by the type of explanation that the analysts want to put forward in the first instance.

Democratization in Turkey can be used as a useful illustration of how either narrative can be supported by political transformations in a polity. For analysts attributing a benign role to political Islam, the fact that the country has been governed by political parties with strong Islamist inclinations in 1996–1997 and since 2002 is a clear indication that democratization can proceed smoothly even in the presence of a substantial Islamic political discourse. Yet Turkey also proclaims its republican credentials loud and clear, and it promotes its own brand of republicanism, Kemalism, as the state ideology. On the basis of the latter aspects of the political evolution of Turkey, some authors are able to articulate developmentalist and primordialist arguments about the relationship between Islamism and modern liberal democracies. Lewis has long argued that there is a prior requirement for a radical change in frames of reference for the conduct of democratic politics, since even words such as 'citizen' and 'citizenship' had, until recently, no direct equivalent in the Arabic, Persian or Turkic languages.[32] From this perspective, the current situation in Turkey is not an example of Islamic moderation, but an illustration of the successes of political secularization. Even though one may agree with some of the historical points made by orientalist scholars, it should be noted that such a developmentalist approach is linked to the construction of an 'oriental' approach to modern liberal democracy. 'Contingencists' might reply that actual words are less important than the meanings that they acquire politically over time. Clearly, the western political lexicon has long possessed those terms, but their political meaning has been changed and recreated from the Enlightenment onwards to resonate with the new practices corresponding to the modern liberal democratic ethos.[33]

To avoid such conceptual dilemmas, some comparative studies within political science have attempted to leave semantic issues behind and simply to take into account political and social preferences in the contemporary context. From the mid-1990s onward, there has been an increasingly fashionable strand of survey-based studies that investigate the attitudes of 'Muslims' toward 'democracy' in order to assess the degree of compatibility between the two. A wide array of more or less well-designed surveys, as well as more rigorous political analyses, outline how the religious beliefs held by the citizenry in various parts of the Muslim world do not in themselves seem to preclude people from taking an interest in 'democracy'.[34] Although this approach has the advantage of avoiding the pseudo-philosophical problems that flourished in the earlier debates by focusing on what a substantial number of people actually say, it faces a different kind of definitional problem. Repeatedly the notion of democracy is taken to be not only a fixed concept, but also a self-evident one. Hence, these analyses do not particularly focus on what respondents actually mean when they use the words that are put in front of them by researchers. Rather, a very malleable notion of liberal democracy is alluded to in connection to a set of basic social and political preferences that are put forward for consideration by the surveys' respondents. Because of the very nature of data obtained, these analyses do not and cannot describe the deliberative processes that produce a substantive account of what a word such as 'democracy' actually means. The lack of characterization of these key concepts undermines the explanatory powers of the analyses, regardless of their descriptive capabilities. Clearly, 'democracy' and 'democratization' are far more fashionable political terms than they were 20 years ago. Yet the mere presence of a practical interest in democratization throughout the Muslim world today does not allow analysts to make many direct political forecasts.

Beyond the 'democratization paradigm' for political Islam in the MENA

Trying to measure 'really existing democracy' in the Muslim world has created a new set of dilemmas. Two types of related, but distinct, contemporary debates have emerged to address these new issues, as illustrated by the contributions to this volume. The first set of arguments is attuned to the development of democratization studies in the 1980s and 1990s and focuses on civic activism and the role of civil society in political transformations. The second type of debate has a longer tradition in development studies and focuses on the structural impediments to democratization, primarily from socio-economic and politico-military perspectives.

There are evidently different types of 'civil society' or 'civil sphere' in different parts of the Muslim world, but the debates have commonly been polarized between those who view the MENA region as just another setting for the kind of civil society revival that was witnessed in Latin America and in Eastern and Southern Europe, and those who emphasize the distinctiveness of the Muslim and/or MENA context. Thus, for the followers of Ernest Gellner's *Conditions of Liberty*, whatever associative life there may exist in Muslim polities, they are not of the 'right' kind and, therefore, unpropitious to the emergence of a genuine liberal democratic order.[35] By contrast, those influenced by the work of Augustus Norton and his collaborators in *Civil Society in the Middle East* emphasize the presence of a recognizably liberal civil society impulse, even when it remains the project of a small but active minority.[36] The debates to date on the practical and conceptual developments in civil society in the Muslim world remain tentatively optimistic, but proponents of a progressive 'civil society' paradigm advance their argument with extreme prudence.[37] In the cases of Latin America and Eastern Europe, there had been a tendency to let one's own normative preferences and teleological inclinations brush aside some serious inconsistencies of the process of democratic consolidation.[38] For these particular democratic transitions, such conceptual lapses appear not to have had significant consequences because the voluntarist drive of the analyses, more often than not, reflected the views of the civil society groups and political counter-elites that were on the ascendancy in those polities at that time. In most of the Muslim world, however, similar assumptions about the liberal nature of civil society and of the political counter-elite cannot be taken for granted today.

In effect, even for those scholars who do not endorse Gellner's negative assessment of the prospect for civil society in the region, the common view appears to be that civil society cannot play the role of a dominant democratization paradigm in the Muslim context in the same way that it could be invoked in the 1980s and 1990s in Latin America and Eastern Europe.[39] Only in a few specific cases is this factor being invoked as one of the main explanatory tools for democratic transition, as in Robert Hefner's analysis of the Indonesian case.[40] From this perspective there are fewer opportunities for the authoritarian elites to hand over power 'gracefully' on the model of the Latin American 'pacted' transitions because of the ideological positions of the most powerful Islamist opposition movements in the MENA countries. The situation in Southeast Asia might have been the most propitious for such a process; but elsewhere in the Muslim world, only the better-run parliamentary monarchies, like Morocco or Jordan, appear to provide the kind of exit strategy for the ruling elite that might avoid a brutal democratic transition.

Yet, as the articles on Morocco by Cavatorta and by Wegner and Pellicer-Gallardo in this special issue illustrate, even in a reforming authoritarian system, the opportunities for full democratization are dependent upon the goodwill of the monarchy. Whatever incentives a powerful regional player like the EU can devise, the limits of its effectiveness are principally dictated by the willingness of the regime to allow a degree of political pluralism. In other cases, clearly, what emboldens the determination of the ruling elite to stay in power is simply the perception that dramatic consequences would follow were they to relinquish power to the Islamist opposition, as the Algerian scenario illustrates. The contributions by Wolff and by Demmelhuber in this volume, regarding the situation in Egypt, exemplify quite well the inadequacy of EU incentives in the face of a regime that places survival and continuity at the core of its system of governance. Optimistically, one could view this situation as creating reserves of good democratic practices in civil and political society, waiting only for a weakening of authoritarian institutions in order to come out in the open and reshape domestic and regional politics.[41] A less sanguine assessment would be that not only democratic skills are being built up and refined, but also authoritarian views and practices. Hence, were a specific authoritarian system to go bust, democratic alternatives would not be the only ones available on the ground for political entrepreneurs.[42]

In many countries of the Muslim world, the limited liberal democratic civil society impulse contributes to creating an enduring situation of stalled transitions, which analysts then evaluate in connection to more structural, socio-economic, political and security factors. As Thomas Carothers points out,

> what is often thought of as an uneasy, precarious middle ground between full-fledged democracy and outright dictatorship is actually the most common political condition today of countries in the developing world and the post-communist world. It is not an exceptional category to be defined only in terms of its not being one thing or the other; it is a state of normality for many societies, for better or worse.[43]

From a functional/instrumental perspective, these pseudo-democratic systems actively produce a political order that tries to look like a liberal democracy in order to make domestic and international gains, without actually trying to become one.[44] This predicament is one of the main features of the democratization conundrums of the Muslim world, where the nature of political opposition generates an additional strain on the processes of democratic transition.

In the MENA region, three sets of structural issues appear to be particularly problematic. Because of the apparent weakness of civil society, scholars have been keen to stress the particular organization of state power in the (greater) Middle East. Analysts including Marsha Posusney and Eva Bellin emphasize the role played by the authoritarian elite, arguing that the strength of the coercive apparatus in the Arab world is the principal inhibitor of democracy change.[45] This line of argumentation is also invoked in conjunction with references to the notion of *asabiyya* (either regarding reconstructed tribes or clans, or regarding new military and technocratic cliques) as a key *explanan* in the politics of the (greater) Middle East.[46] Some commentators, like Akbar Ahmed, have even suggested that a notion of 'hyper-*asabiyya*' could also be used in order to understand the new security dynamics post-9/11.[47] On the more political (as opposed to securitarian) side of the argument, analysts including Volker Perthes and Ellen Lust-Okar stress how elites have managed to co-opt their opponents, as well as to exploit and manipulate the splits between opposition groups (especially the secular-Islamist divide), so that they can neutralize demands for democracy from the masses.[48] This trend is reinforced by the fact that, historically, the MENA countries are generally latecomers to the democratization process. Everywhere, autocrats learn from past mistakes, and the rise of more competitive forms of authoritarianism in relation to liberal democracy is a noticeable trend at the beginning of the twenty-first century. Unsurprisingly, efforts to liberalize and democratize the political system of Muslim countries in recent years have often been equivalent to the refinement of the euphemized, authoritarian skills of the ruling elite.[49] Finally, as Raymond Hinnebusch indicates, explanations focusing on structural state power find additional support for their case by incorporating a political economy perspective that shows how oil wealth in the contemporary international context reduces the necessity to liberalize politically.[50]

Rethinking democracy and its promotion
The problem that Islamic movements and parties create for common explanations of democratization on the southern shores of the Mediterranean is that their mobilizing potential challenges some basic assumptions about the relationship between contemporary forms of liberalism and democracy. For quite some time, analysts on the 'clash' side of the debate have maintained that all the discrete cases of opposition between Islamist views and 'western' liberal or democratic views are only the surface manifestations of a deeper and all-inclusive, illiberal and undemocratic worldview. This is a view that has been well conveyed to policy circles, despite its obvious problems of over-generalization. Opponents of the 'clash' primarily point out that there exists a more benign alternative, and emphasize the impact of the more 'democratic' and 'liberal' forms of political Islam.[51] Yet, what is commonly missing from these analyses are detailed considerations of what conceptual compromises are needed for a meaningful dialogue between opposition and government (both domestically and internationally). This void may help to explain, to some degree, the current lack of options for (liberal) democracy promotion at the policy level. The lack of a cogent conceptual framework for assessing the role of Islamists in the Mediterranean, and for engaging adequately with them, is stressed by most of the contributors to this special issue as one of the key flaws of the EU approach(es) to the region.

Because of this impoverished conceptual perspective, it is usually the case that any deviation from the liberal democratic model in the Muslim context is perceived to favour the emergence of what Fareed Zakaria calls 'illiberal democracies'.[52] An alternative to the illiberal democracy scenario is to talk about 'grey areas' of democracy, thereby suggesting the partial convergence of Islamist and liberal-democratic political agendas. This is a policy approach that is well developed in connection to US democracy promotion, with scholars including Nathan Brown, Amr Hamzawy and Marina Ottaway providing sophisticated analyses of these processes. For them, a key difficulty in the region is that the ethos of political and civil society needs to be reformed alongside the institutional setting.[53] Yet, their notion of convergence is generally viewed as a prelude to the full acceptance of existing liberal democratic models of governance, without much discussion of the flaws of these models. This is the kind of incrementalist scenario that is also most favoured by the EU when it comes to democracy promotion on the southern shores of the Mediterranean.

What remains understated in these analyses of the 'grey zone' is that the clarity which has been achieved in established liberal democracies is not merely a process of Rawlsian or Habermasian enlightenment, where legally backed, discursive processes ensure that an acceptable consensus on individual rights and collective duties is reached. It is also a more pragmatic assessment of the ability of political entrepreneurs to deliver material and ideological goods in an attractive and sustainable fashion. The choices of Palestinian voters regarding Fatah and Hamas in the 2006 parliamentary elections provided a clear illustration of that point. For all their merits, the above-mentioned analyses of democratization do not reflect upon the alternative political realities that Islamist movements are constructing, both ideologically and socially, and how far these models constitute locally viable and acceptable versions of 'democracy'.[54] Clearly, the construction of an alternative pro-democratic project is not a straightforward process. Charles Hirschkind's study of discursive interactions between Islamists and non-Islamists in Egypt illustrates the coercive undertone of apparently communicative dialogues.[55] In addition, as I indicated elsewhere, it may also be the case that, while Islamist players may welcome political liberalization as leading one step closer to their preferred model of democracy, once they reach the tipping point beyond which 'their' democracy is no longer compatible with the liberal-democratic standard currently promoted by the international community, then they may themselves settle for pseudo-democratic governance.[56] Yet, even when Islamists propose discourses and practices which are not opposed to liberal-democratic perspectives, the international community may still fail to recognize such an opportunity, as the EU's lack of involvement with key Islamic movements in the Mediterranean region illustrates today.[57]

Conclusion

As the postcolonial literature emphasizes, it is conceptually hazardous to equate democratization with secularization and westernization. Talal Asad stresses that modernity is a set of interlinked projects for the institutionalization of principles such as constitutionalism, moral autonomy, democracy, human rights, civil equality, industry, consumerism, a free market, and secularism.[58] This idea of modernity encapsulates what western policy-makers and public opinion usually understand by a modern democracy. In practice, democratization may entail curtailing some of the prerogatives of the demos for the benefit of a liberal constitutional ideal. The kind of democratic order that had become the norm at the end of the twentieth century proposes a democracy that is designed to place restraints on majority rule, with the view to protect very specific individual rights and civil liberties.[59] In most parts of the Muslim world, though, the process of democratic reinvention and institutionalization of 'a-liberal' Islamic practices is harnessed to the diffusion of a specific ethos that portrays them as virtuous components of a political project.

Islamist approaches blur the distinction between the public and the private, which is central to the functioning of contemporary liberal democratic institutions and introduce a more positive definition of liberty, which is couched in terms of religious law.[60] This observation does not imply that one should view a 'state versus church' power struggle as the sole, or even the main, bone of contention in Muslim politics when it comes to democratization in the region. As Alfred Stepan noted, 'the "lesson" from Western Europe, therefore, lies not in the need for a "wall of separation" between church and state, but in the constant political construction and reconstruction of the "twin tolerations".'[61] The ongoing reconfiguration of the secular-religious divide is bound to involve periods of crisis and confrontations. In this context, the bottom-up Islamic democratic construction of these ideological and institutional arrangements poses problems for traditional interpretations of democratization and democracy promotion, which are built on western, liberal perspectives.

To understand the new trends in democratization studies in the MENA region, there is a need to look beyond the functionalist explanations that currently dominate the field. The collapse of much of modernization theory, particularly in relation to secularization, which underpinned linear accounts of democratic transitions over the last two decades, has left a vacuum in the contemporary explanatory frameworks of democratization (or its lack thereof) in the Muslim world in general, and the MENA region in particular. Overall, the weakness of 'civil society'-based explanations opened the way for analyses based on structural factors, such as the role of security apparatuses and oil revenues, which form the backbone of accounts of the slow pace of political change in the region. Internationally, democratization processes continue to be viewed mainly as a dependent variable in a 'realist' geostrategic balance of power, with oil being a key *explanan*. Domestically, these processes are viewed mainly as a functional adaptation of Islamist movements to state repression and as their tactical adoption of a democratic discursive repertoire. Both sets of narratives are predicated upon a fairly static political order and fail fully to consider the process of democratization as an engine of change in domestic and international processes; hence the limited (and shrinking) interest in democracy promotion. As the historical trends in scholarship indicate, this situation is partly caused by the polarization of the debates about the direction of political change in the region. The contributors to this volume illustrate that there are many more aspects of democratization in the Mediterranean that need to be taken into consideration in order to have a more meaningful understanding of the contemporary political transformation – one that can truly inform policy-making.

Notes

1. Mitchell, *The Society of the Muslim Brothers*.
2. See for example Salamé, *Democracy without Democrats?*; Ayubi, *Political Islam*; Zubaida, *Islam, the People and the State*; Arjomand, *From Nationalism to Revolutionary Islam*.
3. See Diamond and Plattner, *The Global Resurgence of Democracy*; Esposito and Voll, *Islam and Democracy*.
4. Fish, 'Islam and Authoritarianism'; Tessler, 'Islam and Democracy in the Middle East'.
5. Eickelman and Piscatori, *Muslim Politics*.
6. For an interesting postcolonial perspective on this theme, see Sayyid, *A Fundamental Fear*.
7. Halpern, *The Politics of Social Change in the Middle East and North Africa*.
8. Halpern, 'Middle Eastern Studies', 111.
9. See Binder, *The Ideological Revolution in the Middle East*; Rustow, 'Turkey: The Modernity of Tradition'.
10. Kedourie, *Democracy and Arab Political Culture*; Lewis, *The Political Language of Islam*.
11. Bill and Leiden, *Politics in the Middle East*, 133.
12. Ibid.
13. Hudson, *Arab Politics*.
14. In the modern context *asabiyya* is a solidarity group founded on personal allegiances that derives directly or indirectly from clan-based or tribal solidarity networks and that displays a distinct 'group-spirit' or *esprit-de-corps*. See Khoury and Kostiner, *Tribes and State Formation in the Middle East*; Roy, 'Patronage and Solidarity Groups: Survival or Reformation'.
15. Lerner, *The Passing of Traditional Society in the Middle East*.
16. Abu-Lughod, 'Retreat from the Secular Path?'.
17. For an early (and not altogether committed) illustration of this trend see Binder, *Islamic Liberalism*.
18. This is despite many attempts to introduce more fully regional specialisms in the larger social science debates. See for example, Tessler, Nachtwey, and Banda, *Area Studies and Social Science*.
19. Huntington, 'Will More Countries Become Democratic'; Huntington, *The Third Wave*.
20. In his 1984 article, the only Islamic studies specialist that Huntington refers to in order to back his argument that Islamic political culture is an obstacle to democratic principles is the orientalist and political activist Daniel Pipes.
21. For a trenchant critique see Sadowski, 'The New Orientalism and the Democracy Debate'.
22. See Casanova, *Public Religions in the Modern World*.
23. Compare Huntington, 'The Clash of Civilizations?' with Huntington, *The Third Wave*.
24. Karatnycky, 'The 2001 Freedom House Survey'.
25. This is not to say that notions of 'political culture' cannot be deployed usefully in the region – particularly to provide accounts of political change that avoid various forms of socio-economic determinism. See Hudson, 'The Political Culture Approach to Arab Democratization'.
26. See Perthes, 'America's "Greater Middle East" and Europe', and compare Bilgin, 'Whose "Middle East"?'
27. See Adler et al., *The Convergence of Civilizations*; Pace, *The Politics of Regional Identity*.

28. See Emerson and Youngs, *Political Islam and European Foreign Policy.*
29. Halliday, 'The Politics of Islam'.
30. O'Donnell and Schmitter, *Transitions from Authoritarian Rule.*
31. Roy, *The Failure of Political Islam*; Kepel, *The Revenge of God.* Both Kepel and Roy would later add a corrective to their earlier narratives on the development of Islamism.
32. Lewis, *The Emergence of Modern Turkey*; Lewis, *The Political Language of Islam.*
33. On Turkey see, Yavuz, *Islamic Political Identity in Turkey.* More generally see Terence Ball, James Farr, and Russell L. Hanson, *Political Innovation and Conceptual Change.*
34. See for example the online outputs of the Pew Global Attitudes Project, http://pewglobal.org and World Values Survey, http://www.worldvaluessurvey.org. See also Tessler, 'Islam and Democracy in the Middle East'; Fattah, *Democratic Values in the Muslim World.*
35. Gellner, *Conditions of Liberty.*
36. Norton, *Civil Society in the Middle East.*
37. See Hawthorne, 'Middle Eastern Democracy'; Eickelman and Salvatore, 'The Public Sphere and Muslim Identities'.
38. O'Donnell, *Counterpoints.*
39. Yom, 'Civil Society and Democratization'.
40. Hefner, *Civil Islam.*
41. See Adler et al., *The Convergence of Civilizations.*
42. See Volpi, 'Pseudo-Democracy in the Muslim World'.
43. Carothers, *Critical Mission*, 164.
44. Diamond, 'Thinking about Hybrid Regimes', 24.
45. Posusney, 'Enduring Authoritarianism'; Bellin, 'The Robustness of Authoritarianism in the Middle East'.
46. See Roy, 'Patronage and Solidarity Groups'; Collins, 'The Political Role of Clans in Central Asia'.
47. Ahmed, *Islam under Siege.*
48. Perthes, *Arab Elites;* Lust-Okar, *Structuring Conflict in the Arab World.*
49. Brumberg, 'The Trap of Liberalized Autocracy'; Volpi, 'Algeria's Pseudo-Democratic Politics'.
50. Hinnebusch, 'Authoritarian Persistence, Democratization Theory and the Middle East'.
51. Salvatore and Eickelman, *Public Islam and the Common Good*; Esposito and Voll, *Islam and Democracy.*
52. Zakaria, *The Future of Freedom.*
53. See Brown, Hamzawy, and Ottaway, 'Islamist Movements and the Democratic Process in the Arab World'.
54. For some interesting recent works doing just that, see Yavuz, *Islamic Political Identity in Turkey*; Mahmood, *Politics of Piety.*
55. Hirschkind, 'Civic Virtue and Religious Reason'.
56. See Volpi, 'Pseudo-Democracy in the Muslim World'.
57. This situation evidently contributes to fostering of a mutual lack of recognition. See Emerson and Youngs, *Political Islam and European Foreign Policy.*
58. Asad, *Formations of the Secular.*
59. See Tully, *Strange Multiplicity.*
60. The case of Shi'a governance in Iraq might prove to be an interesting case in point. See Gleave, 'Conceptions of Authority in Iraqi Shi'ism'; Cole, 'The Ayatollahs and Democracy in Iraq'.
61. Stepan, 'Religion, Democracy and the "Twin Tolerations"', 42.

Bibliography

Abu-Lughod, Ibrahim. 'Retreat from the Secular Path? Islamic Dilemmas of Arab Politics'. *The Review of Politics* 28 (1966): 447–76.

Adler, Emanuel, Beverly Crawford, Federica Bicchi, A. Raffaella Del Sarto, eds. *The Convergence of Civilizations: Constructing a Mediterranean Region*, Toronto: University of Toronto Press, 2006.

Ahmed, Akbar. *Islam under Siege: Living Dangerously in a Post-Honor World*. Cambridge: Polity Press, 2003.

Arjomand, Said Amir, ed. *From Nationalism to Revolutionary Islam*, Albany: State University of New York Press, 1985.

Asad, Talal. *Formations of the Secular: Christianity, Islam, Modernity*. Stanford: Stanford University Press, 2003.

Ayubi, Nazih. *Political Islam: Religion and Politics in the Arab World*. London: Routledge, 1991.

Ball, Terence, James Farr, and Russell L. Hanson, eds. *Political Innovation and Conceptual Change*, Cambridge: Cambridge University Press, 1989.

Bellin, Eva. 'The Robustness of Authoritarianism in the Middle East: Exceptionalism in Comparative Perspective'. *Comparative Politics* 36 (2004): 139–57.

Bilgin, Pinar. 'Whose "Middle East"? Geopolitical Inventions and Practices of Security'. *International Relations* 18 (2004): 25–41.

Bill, James, and Leiden Carl. *Politics in the Middle East*. 2nd ed. Boston: Little, Brown, 1984.

Binder, Leonard. *The Ideological Revolution in the Middle East*. Chicago: University of Chicago Press, 1964.

Binder, Leonard. *Islamic Liberalism: A Critique of Developmental Ideologies*. Chicago: University of Chicago Press, 1988.

Brown, Nathan, Amr Hamzawy, and S. Marina Ottaway. 'Islamist Movements and the Democratic Process in the Arab World: Exploring Gray Zones'. *Carnegie Paper*, 67 March 2006.

Brumberg, Daniel. 'The Trap of Liberalized Autocracy'. *Journal of Democracy* 13 (2002): 46–68.

Carothers, Thomas. *Critical Mission: Essays on Democracy Promotion*. Washington, DC: Carnegie Endowment for International Peace, 2004.

Casanova, José. *Public Religions in the Modern World*. Chicago: University of Chicago Press, 1994.

Cole, Juan. 'The Ayatollahs and Democracy in Iraq'. *ISIM Paper* 7 (2006).

Collins, Kathleen. 'The Political Role of Clans in Central Asia'. *Comparative Politics* 35 (2003): 171–90.

Diamond, Larry. 'Thinking about Hybrid Regimes'. *Journal of Democracy* 13 (2002): 21–35.

Diamond, Larry, and Marc F. Plattner, eds. *The Global Resurgence of Democracy*, Baltimore: Johns Hopkins University Press, 1996.

Eickelman, Dale F., and Piscatori James. *Muslim Politics*. Princeton: Princeton University Press, 2004.

Eickelman, Dale F., and Salvatore Armando. 'The Public Sphere and Muslim Identities'. *Archives Européennes de Sociologie* 43 (2002): 92–115.

Emerson, Michael, and Richard Youngs, eds. *Political Islam and European Foreign Policy: Perspectives from Muslim Democrats of The Mediterranean*, Brussels: Centre for European Policy Studies, 2007.

Esposito, John L., and John O. Voll. *Islam and Democracy*. Oxford: Oxford University Press, 1996.

Fattah, Moataz A. *Democratic Values in the Muslim World*. Boulder: Lynne Rienner, 2006.

Fish, M. Steven. 'Islam and Authoritarianism'. *World Politics* 55 (2002): 4–37.

Gellner, Ernest. *Conditions of Liberty: Civil Society and its Rivals.* London: Hamish Hamilton, 1994.

Gleave, Robert. 'Conceptions of Authority in Iraqi Shi'ism'. *Theory Culture and Society* 24 (2007): 59–78.

Halliday, Fred. 'The Politics of Islam: A Second Look'. *British Journal of Political Science* 25 (1995): 399–417.

Halpern, Manfred. 'Middle Eastern Studies: A Review of the State of the Field with a Few Examples'. *World Politics* 15 (1962): 108–22.

Halpern, Manfred. *The Politics of Social Change in the Middle East and North Africa.* Princeton: Princeton University Press, 1963.

Hawthorne, Amy. 'Middle Eastern Democracy: Is Civil Society the Answer?'. *Carnegie Paper* no. 44. March (2004).

Hefner, Robert W. *Civil Islam: Muslims and Democratization in Indonesia.* Princeton: Princeton University Press, 2000.

Hinnebusch, Raymond. 'Authoritarian Persistence, Democratization Theory and the Middle East: An Overview and Critique'. *Democratization* 13 (2006): 373–95.

Hirschkind, Charles. 'Civic Virtue and Religious Reason: An Islamic Counterpublic'. *Cultural Anthropology* 16 (2001): 3–34.

Hudson, Michael C. *Arab Politics: The Search for Legitimacy.* New Haven: Yale University Press, 1977.

Hudson, Michael C. 'The Political Culture Approach to Arab Democratization: The Case for Bringing It Back, Carefully'. *Political Liberalization and Democratization in the Arab World: Theoretical Perspectives*, ed. Korany Bahgat, Rex Brynen, and Paul Noble, 61–76. Boulder: Lynne Rienner, 1995.

Huntington, Samuel P. 'The Clash of Civilizations?'. *Foreign Affairs* 72 (1993): 22–49.

Huntington, Samuel P. *The Third Wave: Democratization in the Late Twentieth Century.* Norman: University of Oklahoma Press, 1991.

Huntington, Samuel P. 'Will More Countries Become Democratic'. *Political Science Quarterly* 99 (1984): 193–218.

Karatnycky, Adrian. 'The 2001 Freedom House Survey: Muslim Countries and the Democracy Gap'. *Journal of Democracy* 13 (2002): 99–112.

Kedourie, Elie. *Democracy and Arab Political Culture.* Washington, DC: Washington Institute for Near East Policy, 1992.

Kepel, Gilles. *The Revenge of God: Resurgence of Islam, Christianity and Judaism in the Modern World*, trans. A. Braley. Cambridge: Polity Press, 1993.

Khoury, Philip S., and Joseph Kostiner, eds. *Tribes and State Formation in the Middle East*, Berkeley: University of California Press, 1990.

Lerner, Daniel. *The Passing of Traditional Society in the Middle East.* New York: Free Press, 1958.

Lewis, Bernard. *The Emergence of Modern Turkey.* Oxford: Oxford University Press, 1968.

Lewis, Bernard. *The Political Language of Islam.* Chicago: Chicago University Press, 1988.

Lust-Okar, Ellen. *Structuring Conflict in the Arab World: Incumbents, Opponents, and Institutions.* Cambridge: Cambridge University Press, 2007.

Mahmood, Saba. *Politics of Piety: The Islamic Revival and the Feminist Subject.* Princeton, NJ: Princeton University Press, 2005.

Mitchell, Richard P. *The Society of the Muslim Brothers.* Oxford: Oxford University Press, 1969.

Norton, Augustus R. *Civil Society in the Middle East.* Leiden: Brill, 1995–1996.

O'Donnell, Guillermo. *Counterpoints: Selected Essays on Authoritarianism and Democratization.* Notre Dame, IN: University of Notre Dame Press, 1999.

O'Donnell, Guillermo, and Philippe C. Schmitter. *Transitions from Authoritarian Rule: Tentative Conclusions about Uncertain Democracies.* Baltimore: Johns Hopkins University Press, 1986.

Pace, Michelle. *The Politics of Regional Identity: Meddling with the Mediterranean.* London: Routledge, 2006.

Perthes, Volker, ed. 'America's "Greater Middle East" and Europe: Key Issues for Dialogue'. *Middle East Policy* 11 (2004): 85–97.

Perthes, Volker. *Arab Elites: Negotiating the Politics of Change*, ed. Volker Perthes. Boulder, CO: Lynne Rienner, 2004.

Posusney, Marsha Pripstein. 'Enduring Authoritarianism: Middle East Lessons for Comparative Theory'. *Comparative Politics* 36 (2004): 127–38.

Roy, Olivier. *The Failure of Political Islam*, trans. C. Volk. Cambridge, MA: Harvard University Press, 1996.

Roy, Olivier. 'Patronage and Solidarity Groups: Survival or Reformation'. *Democracy Without Democrats? The Renewal of Politics in the Muslim World*, ed. G. Salamé, 270–81. London: I.B. Tauris, 1994.

Rustow, Dankwart A. 'Turkey: The Modernity of Tradition'. *Political Culture and Political Development*, ed. L.W. Pye and S. Verba, 171–98. Princeton: Princeton University Press, 1965.

Sadowski, Yahya. 'The New Orientalism and the Democracy Debate'. *Middle East Report* 183 (July–August 1993): 14–21.

Salamé, Ghassan, ed. *Democracy without Democrats? The Renewal of Politics in the Muslim World*, London: IB Tauris, 1994.

Salvatore, Armando, and Dale F. Eickelman, eds. *Public Islam and the Common Good*, Leiden: Brill, 2006.

Sayyid, B.S. *A Fundamental Fear: Eurocentrism and the Emergence of Islamism.* London: Zed Books, 2003.

Stepan, Alfred. 'Religion, Democracy and the "Twin Tolerations"'. *Journal of Democracy* 11 (2000): 37–57.

Tessler, Mark. 'Islam and Democracy in the Middle East: The Impact of Religious Orientations on Attitudes Toward Democracy in Four Arab Countries'. *Comparative Politics* 34 (2002): 337–54.

Tessler, Mark A., Jodi Nachtwey, and Anne Banda, eds. *Area Studies and Social Science: Strategies for Understanding Middle East Politics*, Bloomington: Indiana University Press, 1999.

Tully, James. *Strange Multiplicity: Constitutionalism in an Age of Diversity.* Cambridge: Cambridge University Press, 1995.

Volpi, Frédéric. 'Algeria's Pseudo-Democratic Politics: Lessons for Democratization in the Middle East'. *Democratization* 13 (2006): 442–55.

Volpi, Frédéric. 'Pseudo-Democracy in the Muslim world'. *Third World Quarterly* 25 (2004): 1061–78.

Yavuz, M. Hakan. *Islamic Political Identity in Turkey.* New York: Oxford University Press, 2003.

Yom, Sean L. 'Civil Society and Democratization'. *Middle East Review of International Affairs* 9 (2005): 14–33.

Zakaria, Fareed. *The Future of Freedom: Illiberal Democracy at Home and Abroad.* New York: WW Norton, 2003.

Zubaida, Sami. *Islam, the People and the State: Essays on Political Ideas and Movements in the Middle East.* London: Routledge, 1989.

Paradoxes and contradictions in EU democracy promotion in the Mediterranean: the limits of EU normative power

Michelle Pace

Political Science and International Studies, University of Birmingham, Birmingham, B15 2TT, UK

Disciplinary debates about the challenge of liberal democracy in the Mediterranean suggest that the underlying constraints in the region, such as the nature of authoritarian regimes, economic underdevelopment, and the nature of rentier states, pose severe tests for external actors like the European Union (EU) seeking to encourage political reform. These debates have, however, failed to address the question of how and why liberal democracy per se achieved normative status. This article seeks to take this debate forward by examining the substance of the EU's efforts at democracy promotion in the Mediterranean. It does this first by explaining the EU's diagnosis of the Mediterranean 'condition', which highlights the logic behind the EU's prescription for democratization specifically in the Middle East and North Africa (MENA) region. This sheds light, second, on the inherent paradoxes and contradictions in the EU's push for democracy in the MENA. The article concludes by arguing that EU actions limit any potential for normative impact in the MENA because of the lack of coherence in EU policy.

Introduction

Since the 1990s, in the post-cold war context of the collapse of communist rule, the EU has been pursuing an almost messianic quest for the internationalization of liberal democracy abroad, as a key foreign policy instrument in its external relations. The European model of *liberal democracy* has been taken as a necessarily 'good' thing and its pursuit supposedly as a primary goal in and of itself. The often cited argument is that processes of *political liberalization and democratization* have served to bring about peaceful co-existence within Europe and that these successful processes can be emulated elsewhere. Although this policy has, to some extent, been successful in the case of former communist states in Central and Eastern Europe,[1] it has proven rather challenging in the case of the EU's efforts at exporting the model of liberal democracy to the Mediterranean.[2] Theorists of international democracy have asked the question: why is the introduction of liberal democracy in this region so difficult? The answers from both academics and policy-makers often highlight underlying constraints in the Mediterranean,[3] including: the nature of authoritarian regimes[4] and of rentier states,[5] economic underdevelopment,[6] and the alleged incompatibility of Islam with democracy (given that most MENA states are majority Muslim countries).

More broadly, scholars working within the international relations discipline, political theorists, comparative politics specialists, and historical sociologists have all attempted to theorize about international democracy and its promotion.[7] These debates have, however, failed to answer the question of how and why liberal democracy has achieved normative status, a taken for granted state of affairs, a 'naturalism'. Some with a flair for pragmatism would argue that it is still the best extant system,[8] and there is general consensus that liberal democracy is better than authoritarianism or dictatorship. Although it is understood that every political system has its weaknesses and that no functioning liberal democracy is perfect, it is important to question why liberal democracy is perceived as *the* model to be exported to undemocratic regions, including the MENA. In the case of the EU, while much of the literature on democracy promotion has looked at the EU's normative foundations for exporting democracy, little has been done by way of analysing what is 'normative' about the EU's democratization policy. Although there remains considerable concern about the apparent lack of a strong commitment to democracy in the Mediterranean, there is a lack of reflection, both in academic debates as well as in policy-making circles, as to what exactly the EU seeks to export to the region. An exception to this is Hazel Smith's edited collection,[9] which offers a critical and dynamic research agenda for all those concerned with the problematic practices of those seeking to export democracy to other areas of the world.

This article seeks to take this work further by examining the EU's efforts at democracy promotion in the Mediterranean. The first section uncovers the EU's diagnosis of the Mediterranean's 'disease'. The following section looks at the logic behind the EU's prescription for democratization in the MENA. This leads to a further section on the paradoxes and contradictions inherent in the EU's push for democracy in the MENA. It concludes by arguing that *because* there is no coherence in EU policy, the goal of EU efforts at democracy promotion remains problematic. Thus, the EU limits itself in a policy area where it could potentially have normative impact.

The 1990s: EU diagnosis of the Mediterranean 'condition'

In November 1993, the Treaty on European Union (TEU) highlighted development and consolidation of 'democracy and the rule of law, and respect for human rights and fundamental freedoms' as an objective of the EU's Common

Foreign and Security Policy. It also stipulated that the EU's policy in the sphere of development cooperation must contribute to developing and consolidating democracy and the rule of law, and respect of human rights and fundamental freedoms. The EU draws on a wide range of instruments to promote democratization objectives in its external relations. Some of these are tools of traditional diplomacy and foreign policy, such as declarations, *demarches* (through diplomatic representations to third countries), as well as resolutions and interventions within the United Nations framework. In addition, the EU promotes human rights and democratization through various co-operation and assistance programmes it implements with third countries and through the political dialogues that it conducts with them. In doing so it uses a specific legal basis, a 'human rights clause', that is incorporated in nearly all EU agreements with third countries, as an *essential* element.

By the mid-1990s, the political situation in the MENA region was so unstable to European eyes that the EU sought to introduce a series of measures to address them. The principal 'threat' seemed to emanate from North Africa, where attacks by Islamic extremists threatened the stability of both Algeria and Egypt, with potential spillovers onto Europe. Conflict in these Mediterranean neighbours was thought potentially to challenge the fragile Middle East Peace Process (MEPP) involving Israel and the Palestinians. The situation became worse in Algeria between 1992 and late 1994. During this time, instability and concern over insecurity in the Maghreb, rooted in demographic and economic trends, worsened. The Algerian economy had suffered ever since oil prices started to drop in the mid-1980s, (although there was a rise in the mid-1990s). The country's situation was complicated by a swift growth in population, with 70% of the population aged under 30 years and with male unemployment for those between the ages of 18 and 24 rising to 70–75%.[10] Following the victory by the Islamic Salvation Front (FIS) in the first round of the 1992 elections, the army cancelled the second round and forced President Chadli Benjedid to resign.[11] The extreme horror of some of the state attacks on militants that followed, combined with the rhetoric of extremist militants, fed the worst stereotypes of the Islamic world in the West.[12] Terrorist attacks in France, where over 1.5 million people of Algerian descent lived, during the mid-1990s, fuelled concerns about a spread of the violence to Europe. The growing alarm about developments in the Mediterranean led the EU to sign (or at least initiate) a series of association agreements with Tunisia (1995), Israel (1995), Morocco (1996), Jordan (1997), the Palestinian Authority (Interim Agreement 1997), Egypt (2001), Algeria (2002), Lebanon (2002), and Syria (initialled 2004), and to launch the Euro-Mediterranean Partnership (EMP) in 1995 (giving Libya observer status). This drive stressed the need to safeguard Europe's southern sphere, a key source of inward migratory flows. Developments in the Mediterranean also affected other security concerns not only in terms of economic security (vital energy sources) but also in terms of ideological challenges from political Islam. Dialogue along three pillars (political, economic, and social) with the EU's Mediterranean partners was deemed crucial to provide for an exchange of information and discussion of subjects of common concern. This dialogue framed EU–Mediterranean relations in terms of principles, including respect for human rights and democracy and the use of peaceful means for the settlement of disputes. Thus, through the EMP's institutionalized framework, the EU committed itself to democracy promotion and Mediterranean partners signed up to '[D]evelop the rule of law and democracy in their political systems'.[13]

The 1 May 2004 enlargement and further growth possibly to include Turkey in the future, prompted the EU to rethink its relations with neighbouring countries on both southern and eastern borders. The possibility of having borders with Syria, Iran, and Iraq led the EU to launch the European Neighbourhood Policy (ENP) in 2003. Now, fear of mass (in)migration, remains an important aspect of ongoing processes of socio-spatial bordering in and by the EU.[14] On paper, the ENP's Action Plans make up the declared 'common' values and interests 'shared' between EU member states and their neighbours. The principles of democracy, human rights, rule of law, market economy, sustainable development, stability, security, prosperity, joint response to common challenges (border management, prosperity gaps, crime, environment, health, terrorism, etc.) have been further institutionalized through the 2003 (ENP) instrument.

Normative-power prescription for democratization in the MENA. What is the EU trying to do?

EU instruments exist for a serious engagement in political, economic, and social reform processes in the Mediterranean. However, the EU's democratization orthodoxy shows signs of flaws when unpacked and exposed to empirical enquiry. If by generally pursuing liberal democracy, the EU believes that it will lead to the expansion of zones of peace and thereby security and stability for all, why is it that, in the case of the Mediterranean, the situation is far from secure and stable? Rather than democratic progress, the region is more characterized by a *lack* of democratic governance, with increasing tensions between regimes and opposition forces; in effect, a lack of implementation of political reforms in the MENA.[15]

This article argues that, in seeking to claim the status of a 'normative power', the EU's democracy promotion efforts follow a (mistakenly) sequential logic. The 'normative' dimensions of this policy include the EU's favouring of some specific norms for export to other regions, including the MENA, such as democracy, rule of law, respect for human rights, liberty, and peace.[16] In the EU's own words:

> The EU doesn't believe in imposing reform, but we do want to do all we can to support *the region's own reforms* quite simply because we believe that democracy, good governance, rule of law, and gender equality are *essential for stability and prosperity*. This has always been an objective of the Barcelona process and it is the cornerstone of the Neighbourhood Policy.[17]

This telling quote highlights the fact that democracy in itself is not envisioned as an ultimate goal in EU eyes, but as one of the means to another objective – stability and prosperity. This EU narrative constructs a relational triad between economic prosperity, stability, and peace. Arab regimes which have signed agreements with the EU (association agreements under the EMP and Action Plans under the ENP) also share an economic interest in such cooperation, knowing that the EU has thus far never used any sanctions against regimes which violate international principles. MENA governments have invested a lot of political capital into selective 'reform' (or 'managed democracy'). Although some would argue that a focus on economic development reflects a pragmatic realization of what is possible for the EU in the area of promoting reform in the Mediterranean, the general consensus among key societal actors in the Mediterranean region is that there is a problematic logic in the EU's thinking that the promotion of economic development will automatically lead to democratization.[18] This article argues that crucial bases of democratization – including, the rule of law and well-functioning states – are not taken seriously by EU actors. Instead, as regional commentators argue, these core attributes should be in place *before* a society seeks to embark on a politically transformative process.

In Egypt, for example, President Hosni Mubarak's authoritarian rule is being challenged by a wide spectrum of discontented segments of Egyptian society, including the Egyptian Movement for Change, known as 'Kifaya' (Enough) which emerged in August 2004, accompanied by a consolidated National Rally for Democratic Transition, which has given itself the task of drafting a new constitution, and the Muslim Brotherhood (MB), the main and oldest Islamist opposition movement, which had significant successes in Egypt's elections late in 2005. However, because of Mubarak's authoritarian rule, Egypt still suffers from a lack of genuine democratization that impedes development of the rule of law. The problem is exacerbated by external actors such as the government of the USA and the EU which, given their priorities for 'stability' and counter-terrorism cooperation, tread very carefully in their relations with Mubarak. Egypt is closely watched by the international community not least in terms of political, economic, and cultural developments. Egypt has a long-standing regional reputation as the 'mother' of the MENA region. Moreover, it is the coordinator of the Arab group in the EMP as well as a venue of choice for a succession of important Euro-Mediterranean events – including at the highest level. This Mashrek country is also the home of the Euro-Med Anna Lindh Foundation for dialogue and is known for its mediating role in the MEPP. It also exerts cultural influence on the rest of the region. The Mubarak government's decision to allow multi-candidate elections in 2005 was widely interpreted as the regime's means of simply pre-empting pressure for meaningful political liberalization: nominations to stand against Mubarak were still controlled by the National Democratic Party, while the main opposition group, the MB, was still denied official recognition. In fact, during the early months of 2005, nearly 2,000 supporters of the MB were arrested and Kifaya-led demonstrations were strictly controlled. Despite some official EU complaints, there was no serious pressure to change the Mubarak government's familiar tactics of manipulation and voter intimidation. There seems to be a shared understanding among EU member states that if they push Arab-Mediterranean regimes, such as that of Mubarak, too hard on political reform issues (respect for human rights, rule of law, etc.) then their likely replacements (in Egypt, potentially the MB if the latter were to have official recognition) might seriously challenge the status quo of EU–MENA cooperation on counter-terrorism strategies and 'stability and peace' policies.[19]

When, in January 2008, the European Parliament (EP) issued a critical resolution on the situation of human rights in Egypt, the Egyptian government was quick to respond that the EP was interfering in Egypt's domestic affairs.[20] In spite of vowing not to yield to Egyptian pressure, just a few weeks later, EU lawmakers went ahead and signed a Memorandum of Understanding agreement regarding the National Indicative Programme (NIP, 2007–2010) with Egypt.[21] This 'assistance' package totals €558 million.[22] In sum, it appears that there is a clear tension between the EU's stated objective of promoting democracy in MENA, on the one hand, and ensuring 'security' (economic security in terms of oil and gas supplies; political security in terms of relations with authoritarian regimes rather than Islamist actors, etc.), on the other.

This brings us to the related issue of the role of a vibrant civil society which is crucial for a well-functioning democratic state. Although the EMP highlighted the role of civil society within the third chapter, and given that the Barcelona Declaration was adopted *unanimously* by all Euro-Mediterranean partners, there was much difference in opinion on how to put such a civil society dialogue into practice. On the one hand, northern EU member states such as Germany, Sweden, and Denmark wished to encourage relatively free and self-sustained interaction between a variety of civil society actors across the Mediterranean. On the other, southern EU governments, such as Spain and France, insisted that it was necessary to try to control civil society development in MENA, due to fears of terrorist groups and other unsuitable political opposition. Using the EU's own language on 'countering terrorism threats', North African and Middle Eastern governments managed to get southern EU member states on their side, culminating in a fudged 'compromise' for a very 'timid and gradual' opening for growing civil liberties over an unspecified period of time. The EU seemed happy to oblige in such contexts as when, in 2003, the Commission withdrew funding that had already been approved for civil society projects in Egypt, at the insistence of the country's authorities that some of the actors involved in these projects were linked to Islamic terrorism.[23] As Menon argues, if the EU will not admit how its member states' priorities influence its external policies, then at least there should be a clear incentive for these actors to decide and clearly state which objectives they prefer to prioritize.[24] This is another key paradox in EU democracy promotion, which highlights the limits of what the EU can actually do when national (member states') politics supersede those of the European political community. This often leads to grandiose political declarations, initiatives, and statements made by individual, or a group of, leaders from the 'core' of the EU's member states which commit the EU to promises it actually cannot keep. This was the case, for example, when in November 2006 Spain, France, and Italy unveiled a

Middle East peace plan amid frustration over developments between Israelis and Palestinians.[25]

So, although EU actors declare that the EU pursues democratization in the MENA region, there is no coherent EU policy driven by a unified consensus on the strategy. As one Commission official from the European Commission delegation in Rabat, Morocco put it:

> When it comes to supporting newly arising, reform agents in this region, we struggle to respond in a proactive and flexible manner because calls for proposals and selection procedures of democracy related projects are decided in Brussels. [In turn] . . . local agents for change complain about the complexity of application procedures, long lead times, onerous financial management and reporting requirements, without the necessary training for local actors to fit the bill.[26]

The EU's so-called democratization agenda for the MENA region is flawed on at least two counts: its ultimate objective not being *clearly* and *explicitly* democracy in itself (that is, rather than having political transformation in the MENA as the core objective of EU policy, there is most concern with stability and security goals) and the timing of the democratization efforts. If the situation in Mediterranean societies is not acceptable to the EU and if it thereby seeks to order, modify, improve, and re-arrange the current state of affairs in the region, then it should seriously reflect upon what it has been doing all along. There is a plethora of EU policy instruments supposedly aimed at 'democracy promotion in the MENA'. These include individual EU member states' initiatives,[27] and, at the EU level, the 1995 EMP with its association agreements, the 2003 strategy paper on the Arab world,[28] the ENP with its reform-oriented 'action plans', and the 2005 European Initiative on Democracy and Human Rights (EIDHR). However, the ultimate objective of these initiatives is securing the EU's own concerns about (in)migration, security, and stability rather than 'transformation' in the MENA.[29]

In order to examine further this crucial aspect of EU democratization policy in the Mediterranean, the following section seeks to draw out further key paradoxes and contradictions inherent in this aspect of the EU's external relations.

Further paradoxes and contradictions inherent in EU efforts at democracy promotion in the MENA region

Until at least January 2006, the EU's understanding of 'democracy' seemed to follow, on the one hand, the view of comparative politics specialists such as Huntington, Pridham and Vanhanen, Remmer, Schmitter, and Whitehead (who argue that democracy is electorally based with some allowances for freedoms of the press and of association)[30] and on the other hand, the position of modernization theorists including Boix and Stokes, Lipset et al., and Przeworski and Limongi (who stipulate that the prevalence of economic inequality requires a push for economic prosperity which will lead to progress, stability, and eventually peace and democratization).[31] EU actors also seem to be influenced by the democratic peace proposition that liberal democratic states are inherently unlikely to go to war with each other and that, due to the transnational connections between domestic, political, and economic structures and international politics in a globalized world, the EU should encourage democracy in order to secure, stable orders in and around its borders.[32] Some analysts also consider the EU's pursuit of exporting its model of liberal democracy for stability as a realist conceptualization of stability, security, and order. We can add to this the constructivist argument that norms constitute EU action: the EU is embedded in social rules and conventions (treaties) that constitute its identification processes and which can give reasons for the ideas that motivate EU actors. But all these interpretations of liberal democracy were seriously challenged following the Palestinian elections of January 2006. In this case, a nation in its fortieth year under military occupation produced a fair, free, and transparent process, which was confirmed as such by the EU's own mission. The organization, however, reacted by freezing direct aid to the Palestinian Authority, since the elected Hamas was on the EU's black list of outlawed terrorist organizations.[33]

The EU is the biggest aid donor to the Palestinian territories. However, its decision to freeze funds to the Hamas-led administration was circumvented through the setting up of a 'temporary' financial mechanism, which provides aid to public institutions, such as hospitals and the poorest inhabitants, while seeking to evade control by Hamas officials. During 2006, the sum amounted to €700m, which was €200m more than was provided before the crisis. Officials expect this system to remain in place until the conditions of both the EU and the wider international community are met, that is until the Hamas group moves more 'significantly' towards reconciliation with Israel.[34] Tanya Reinhart summed up this series of events (as regards the embargo imposed on the Palestinians since the election of a Hamas government) in this way: 'Europe chose not to force Israel to respect its obligations under international law.'[35]

This action was also interpreted by most Palestinians and other observers in the MENA as a sign of the EU ignoring the democratic expression of the Palestinian people (even though it had made democracy one of the conditions for its aid) and depriving many Palestinians of their livelihood: in effect a contradiction – although Hamas had a legal mandate to govern through a fair, free, and transparent vote, it is considered as a terrorist organization by the EU and US.[36] So, paradoxically, while the democratically elected, Islamist Hamas government in Palestine has been boycotted by the EU, the authoritarian Mubarak-government in Egypt receives continued support – arguably for the sake of security – in spite of obvious, fundamental, democratic shortcomings in Egypt. As Youngs points out, the conditions imposed on Hamas have nothing to do with the standards of democratic governance or issues of civil rights within Palestinian territories, issues of considerable concern to many Palestinians.[37] Therefore, although Palestinians appeared to take their first steps toward a process of democratization, the EU's reactions to the electoral victory by Hamas stand in stark contrast to EU actors' self-construction of the EU as a normative power in the region and its associated reform agenda for the Middle East.[38] At the same time, the EU is strengthening the perception that there is a permanent double reasoning when it comes to reform and democratization in the Middle East. So, while full democratization requires both competitiveness and inclusion, the success of certain (Islamist) parties does not seem to feature on the EU's democratization radar.[39] The EU as an international backer of reform in the MENA region nevertheless has an astonishingly short-term focus, a highly personalized view of the process, and a very instrumental view of reform, leading to a key paradox in the context of Palestine: the EU harshly turned against the achievements of the Palestinian reform movement when it brought unexpected results![40] As one interviewee put it: 'The EU likes the ideal of democracy but they do not like its result'.[41] From the Israeli perspective, the fact that Israel, albeit via a third party, has engaged with Hamas over a ceasefire, however imperfect, is tacit recognition by the Israeli government that Hamas does represent a legitimate expression of a substantial percentage of the Palestinian people.[42]

Moreover, this action was interpreted by most Palestinians as the EU not being prepared to put equal pressure on Israel to recognize United Nations resolutions and Palestinian rights (as well as pressure on Hamas to renounce violence, recognize Israel, and accept all previous agreements between Israel and the Palestinian Authority). Added to this is an EU path dependency approach towards Israel: continued support for Israel even though this becomes a major burden at times.[43] At the June 2008 EU–Israel Association Council meeting in Luxembourg, the EU announced its decision to upgrade its political and economic relations with Israel. Slovenia's Foreign Minister Dimitrij Rupel, whose country was then holding the rotating EU presidency, and who chaired the EU-Israel Association Council meeting, the body overseeing the relationship, stated that the EU and Israel are 'elevating' their relations to a new level of 'more intense, more fruitful, more influential cooperation'. Israel has now been granted the highest level of relations available to a non-member state.[44] Thus, EU–Israeli relations continue to improve despite increasing facts on the ground which damage peace talks with the Palestinians, such as, new housing units built in Israeli settlements on occupied Palestinian land.[45]

Liberal democratic theory reminds us of the moral significance of the aspirations of human beings for 'life, liberty and property'. The Palestinians' democratic right to live in an independent country remains absent from the EU's 'democratization' efforts – apart from some repetitive statements about the EU's aim at a Palestinian state in the context of the MEPP.[46]

However, the occupation itself is hardly ever described (at least officially) as a violation of democratic and human rights, despite Israeli schemes to create facts on the ground as mentioned above (the 'partition wall', settlements, checkpoints, curfews, de-linkage of the economies of Israel and Palestine, separate road systems set up by Israel) and to prevent the emergence of a Palestinian state.[47] These Israeli measures, in turn, are profoundly in contradiction to the EMP principles which aim to foster links at a political, social, economic, and cultural level between Mediterranean signatories to the Barcelona declaration. Thus, if, since the end of the cold war, the EU has sought to inscribe a normative value to its liberal democracy agenda globally as a 'good thing', it needs to abide more convincingly to the very same international norms that it seeks to export elsewhere in the world.

It is, therefore, a further contradiction to have policies like the EMP, which omit direct reference to the MEPP (although EMP fora do facilitate regional dialogue and bring all the partners together)[48] and through which the EU is supposed to encourage political reform in the region.[49]

This article contends that meaningful political reform in MENA requires a political resolution of the Middle East conflict. As Brown points out, Palestinian activists have, from an early date, insisted that their state be born reformed, avoiding authoritarian features common to Arab regimes in the Middle East.[50] Thus, if Palestinians are freed from occupation, if they establish their own sovereign state, and if democratization ensues in Palestine, there would likely be more pressure for neighbouring countries to reform politically.[51] Privately, Council officials endorse this analysis:

> Those with responsibility for the Middle East and North Africa (including myself) need to put forward a more persuasive argument in favour of focusing on the root issues of democratization including peacemaking. We have missed many windows of opportunity to negotiate a comprehensive peace in the Middle East. If such negotiations are successful, the outcome would have a profound effect on the whole region. Authoritarian regimes in the Arab-Mediterranean parts would no longer be able to use the excuse of the conflict with Israel to delay political and economic reforms in their respective countries ... But, there are some EU member states which fear the destabilizing impact that pressure for political reform would generate in such traditional and repressive societies. Pushing hard for political change might work against vital EU member states' interests ... Therefore the EU cannot exert significant pressure for domestic change in these Mediterranean countries.[52]

This brings us to yet another paradox in the EU's democratization agenda for the Mediterranean.

There appears to be an inherent tendency in EU efforts to universalize from the particular circumstances of Western Europe and the ensuing logic is that what worked for Europe will surely work for the MENA region, as it did for the Central and Eastern European countries.[53] Thus the EU envisions something that would do to the Mediterranean what Monnet and Schuman did to Europe in the 1950s: a bold initiative that transforms a war-torn zone into a peaceful, democratic, secure and stable space.

The underlying assumption in EU democracy promotion in the MENA, namely that a set of experiences peculiar to Western and Central and Eastern Europe is universal, needs further examination. The experience of Western Europe after the Second World War and of the Central and Eastern European countries after communism contrasts with the experiences of Mediterranean countries, colonized by European powers. Post-war, the logic of economic development, linked to peaceful relations and liberal democracy and stability, worked to some extent for western Europe. In addition, it was logical that liberal democracy would follow communism in much of Central and East of Europe. For the MENA, we need to inquire into the nature of regional states, as well as the political legacy from former colonial powers. This appears in many cases to hinder democratic aspirations of those living in the region. Europe's perspective of democracy draws from (European), liberal philosophy and therefore a specific set of cultural and historical dynamics.

Conclusion

The supposedly normative, long-running EU push for democracy in the MENA is at best a very slow work in progress, at worst a regression. Its slow advance is in part due to inherent paradoxes and contradictions in the making of a policy with no clear, defined vision. The stubborn position of some of the core EU member states remains that they have other prioritized interests – security and economic – such that cooperation with authoritarian regimes on antiterrorism enforcement actions and ensuring secure access to oil prevail. Moreover, EU member states remain wary of unpredictable and possibly rapid, political change driven by non-state actors in the region because EU member states are risk averse.[54] Political transformation anywhere, but particularly in the MENA, is a high-risk strategy for external actors. Norway, a non-EU European state, was among the first few external actors to seek engagement with the Hamas leader (and prime minister until the events in Gaza of June 2007) Ismail Haniyeh. Raymond Johansen, Norway's deputy foreign minister, called on other governments to follow suit. Most European countries refuse officially to claim that they are engaging with the political leadership of Hamas.[55] In such a limited vision of democratic politics, important forms of social exclusion are overlooked and the careful analysis and engagement with the conditions of possibility of democracy are placed to one side.[56] Politics is about grasping such possibilities and the international community needs to acknowledge the lost opportunity which was momentarily open for positive steps towards democratic transformation in the Palestinian territories (the formation of a Palestinian unity government was no mean diplomatic achievement. Palestinian unity could have offered a potent source of international legitimacy).[57]

This article has thus attempted to highlight some of these paradoxes and contradictions in EU efforts at democracy promotion in the Mediterranean. In doing so, it focused on the agents that the EU deals with (namely government elites and co-opted non-governmental organizations), the structures and instruments at its disposal (economic incentives, aid funding and (lack of) political conditionality) as well as the process the EU follows along the path to stability rather than democracy in the MENA (sequential rather than gradual). This analysis opens up the space for further research on the security/stability-economic development/prosperity-democracy-peace nexus which may help analysts and policy-makers better understand the European relational narrative: about how the EU aims to promote pluralism in its southern neighbourhood and how these policies are perceived in the region – inter alia against the background of European colonialism in the Middle East and North Africa in parts of the nineteenth and twentieth centuries.

Moreover, because overall EU policies include significant work, interests, and blockages at the member state level, coherence in EU democracy promotion efforts in the Middle East is made more complicated. Europeans thus opt to look at the 'problem' in the MENA region as a set of technical issues and tend to go for political positions that skew the intended outcome towards Western interests and that will pursue a course of least resistance from the EU's member states. This norm is a legacy of European experience of the Western nation state.[58]

If contemporary Southern expressions are understood as social struggles, then we may need to probe further the moral universalism of international projects of democratization in the Mediterranean/Middle East and North African region. Such an insight is of major relevance within the disciplinary confines in which this article is located, and also amongst a wider European/Middle Eastern Studies audience.

In recent years, there has been a hegemonic discourse of the liberal democratic order. Even Islamist movements have started to position themselves in a way which does not contradict this order of things. As Youngs suggests: 'Even in Saudi Arabia some detect[ed] the emergence of more reformist Salafi currents. Such trends [are being] interpreted as part of Islamists' "return to modernism".'[59]

Democratic accountability in the MENA region can only be assured as long as the general public is included and those that represent the people respond to their rights. As Alastair Cooke, former special Middle East adviser to the European Union's Foreign Policy Chief, Javier Solana, and adviser to the International Quartet, noted about his 'town hall meetings' (in the Palestinian Occupied Territories) initiative:

> It was like holding a sort of *shura* – people would come and make their points ... Usually there was little we could do to resolve the issues, but it was important to be there and to listen to the problems, actual problems and realities faced on the ground.[60]

For the EU, this requires political drive and a well thought-out and long-term approach to enhancing democratic accountability. By focusing primarily on external democracy promotion, the impression is created that democracy is a political concept external to the Mediterranean region. However, given the significant number of actors advocating democracy from within the Arab world (albeit for diverse reasons), such a focus may be perceived as ignoring such internal dynamics, thereby invoking a false image of an unbridgeable cultural rift between the European and the MENA sides in which democracy is framed as a Western concept. As Sadiki notes:

> The litmus test is the extent to which difference is tolerated, singularity and fixity of power opposed, and a fluid space of contingency, allowing for the renewal and opening up new possibilities of being, doing and thinking, is permitted.[61]

Thus, we need further conceptual reflection on the linkage and contradictions between domestic and external democracy promotion policies (actors, mechanisms, etc.). From the EU's side, this calls for more careful observation and monitoring procedures of its activities which pertain to address political reform in the MENA, a tougher line, through conditionality, on authoritarian regimes and a careful analysis of the integrity of the civil society actors it engages with. If the EU is to measure up to its image as a 'force for good', its agents need to address the constant pressure they feel to side-step 'difficult' issues in the interest of achieving a political 'success'.[62]

A broadened view of EU democracy promotion in the Mediterranean must address the core processes of political contestation and open up to many forms of activities triggered within civil society, especially by regional younger generations. The contemporary reality of Mediterranean societies is one where a devolution of the public sphere is gradually developing and in which political debates are being expressed in novel ways – particularly through spontaneous processes of communication including weblogs or 'blogging' and other internet facilities such as Facebook.[63] These subsystems within MENA political systems require a more coherent, consistent, and communicative focus by the EU as they play a crucial role in enhancing any democratic openings by providing ongoing sources of resistance to the always-contestable, coercive power of the regimes in the region. The meaning of democracy will remain a contested field, but what we observe in the MENA regional space today leads us at least to start by locating the essence of 'the political' in human agency. This is what the empirical articles in this special issue highlight, in particular, by focusing on the agency of Islamist movements in the MENA and their role in the transformation processes across this region. Thus, the focus here is inverted and contributors look from the inside-out, rather than from the outside-in: that is, rather than merely looking from the outside at how democracy promotion policy shapes 'reform' in authoritarian regimes or how regimes and opposition are induced toward a liberal democratic model, we look at the agents of change themselves *within* MENA, particularly at how they induce external actors to view and react to their situation as a viable exception to their preferred practices.

Notes

1. Schimmelfennig and Sedelmeier, *The Europeanization of Central and Eastern Europe*; Vachudova, *Europe Undivided*.
2. Baracani, 'From the EMP to the ENP'; Emerson et al., *Democratisation in the European Neighbourhood*; Gillespie and Youngs, *European Union and Democracy*

Promotion; Kelley, 'New Wine in Old Wineskins'; Stetter, 'Democratization without Democracy?'; Tocci, 'Does the EU Promote Democracy in Palestine '; Youngs, *European Union and the Promotion of Democracy.*

3. The term 'Mediterranean region' traditionally signifies the countries around the Mediterranean Sea, including southern Europe (Malta, Cyprus, and at least parts of Turkey), the Arab states of North Africa (or the Maghreb, that is Algeria, Libya, Morocco, Tunisia, and Mauritania, the latter referred to as a marginal state) and the Levant (or Mashrek, or Middle Eastern countries of Egypt, Israel, the Occupied Palestinian Territories, Jordan, Lebanon, and Syria). However, standard terminology – for example, of European Union policy – tends to separate what it refers to as the 'Mediterranean' countries from the rest of the Middle East, mainly the Arabian peninsula and the Gulf. More recently, however, the EU has acknowledged that it cannot have an approach to the Mediterranean littoral countries in isolation from their strategic links with the Middle East. Yet, it remains unclear how broadly the 'Mediterranean' and 'Middle East' regions can be defined, depending on context and often policy area. Although I find such debates about terminology fascinating in terms of discursive constructions, for the purposes of this article I take the Mediterranean region to refer to the Middle East and North African (MENA) countries. For further definitional discussions on the Mediterranean see Pace, *The Politics of Regional Identity.*
4. Ibrahim, *Egypt, Islam and Democracy.*
5. Commission of the European Communities, *Report on the Implementation.*
6. Pool, 'The Links Between Economic and Political Liberalization'.
7. Diamond, Linz, and Lipset, *Democracy in Developing Countries*; Grugel, *Democracy without Borders*; Pridham, *Encouraging Democracy*; Pridham, *Designing Democracy*; Rueschemeyer, Stephens and Stephens, *Capitalist Development and Democracy*; Schmitz, *Transnational Mobilization and Domestic Regime Change.*
8. See for example Rorty, *Philosophy and Social Hope.*
9. Smith, *Democracy and International Relations.*
10. Quoted in Moss, 'Europe, the Mediterranean and the Middle East'.
11. Yacoubian, *Algeria's Struggle for Democracy.*
12. While the army began its crackdown on Islamic groups, scholars, journalists, and commentators were debating whether the foreseeable victory of FIS justified the army's annulment of the elections and its subsequent coup. See Malmvig, *State Sovereignty and Intervention.*
13. Euro-Mediterranean Conference, *Barcelona Declaration.*
14. Van Houtum and Pijpers, 'The European Community as a Gated Community'.
15. National Endowment for Democracy, 'Backsliding on Reforms in the Middle East'. According to Freedom House scores, the overall level of freedom in the Middle East has declined since the 1970s. See *Freedom in the World 2008*. Specific country reports may be found at: http://www.freedomhouse.org/template.cfm?page=363& year=2008. For a detailed account of how the limits to political opening in the MENA have become so apparent see Youngs, *Europe and the Middle East*, 12–18.
16. On a further detailed examination of the 'normative dimensions' of this EU policy towards MENA, see the article by Brieg Tomos Powel in this issue. See also Manners, 'Normative Power Europe' and 'Normative Power Europe reconsidered'; Lucarelli and Manners, *Values and Principles*; Meyer and Vogt, *A Responsible Europe?* amongst others. In Manners' elucidation of the EU's normative power, he spells out how the EU seeks to shape conceptions of the 'normal' which are linked to constitutionalized values and which are bound by international institutions. On this see Diez and Pace, 'Normative Power Europe and Conflict Transformation'.
17. Ferrero-Waldner, 'The Middle East in the EU's External Relations'. Emphasis added.

18. Author's interviews with, among others, Larabi Jaidi (President of the Abderrahim Bouabid Foundation) in Rabat, Morocco, 2004; Andreas Radtke (Council of the European Union), in Brussels, January 2005; Mahdi F. Abdul Hadi (Head of PASSIA), Khalil Shikaki (PSR, Palestinian Center for Policy and Survey Research), George Giacaman (Palestinian Institute for the Study of Democracy), and Nasr El-Din Sha'r in the West Bank; Basem Naim (Ministry of Health) and Ahmed Yousef (Office of the Prime Minister) in Gaza, September 2007; and Bahgat Korany (American University, Cairo), Diaa Rashwan, Amr El Shobky, and Mohamed Kadry Said (Al Ahram Center) in Cairo, March 2008. See also International Crisis Group, *Reforming Egypt* and *Egypt's Muslim Brothers* as well as *Ruling Palestine I: Gaza Under Hamas*.
19. Youngs, *Europe and the Middle East.*
20. Agence France Presse, *EU Lawmakers.* On the specific case of Egypt, see the articles by Sarah Wolff and Thomas Demmelhuber in this issue.
21. European Parliament, *Resolution of 17 January.* See also Amnesty International, 'EU-Egypt Association Council Meeting'.
22. Fourth Meeting of the EU-Egypt Association Council.
23. Johansson-Nougés, 'Civil Society in Euro-Mediterranean Relations', 4, 8.
24. Menon, *Europe.*
25. EUobserver, 'EU Trio Takes London By Surprise'.
26. Author's interview, European Commission delegation, Rabat, Morocco 2002 and author's confidential telephone interview with a European Commission official, DG Development, 19 March 2007. See also University of Liverpool, Report on 'The EU and Civil Society'.
27. These include the British government's Arab reform strategy, Denmark's Wider Middle East Initiative for democratic reform programmes, Sweden's governance allocation into its Middle East and North Africa programme, Spain's new strategy for democracy assistance projects, France's enhanced democracy assistance scheme, and reform work by German political party foundations in the Arab world.
28. Commission of the European Communities, *Strengthening the EU's Relations with the Arab World.*
29. See also European Communities, *The European Union: Furthering Human Rights.*
30. See, for example, Huntington, *The Third Wave*; Pridham and Vanhanen, *Democratization in Eastern Europe*; Pridham, *Designing Democracy*; Pridham and Gallagher, *Experimenting with Democracy*; Pridham, *The Dynamics of Democratisation*; Remmer, 'New Theoretical Perspectives on Democratization'; Schmitter, 'The Influence of the International Context upon the Choice of National Institutions and Policies in Neo-Democracies'; and Whitehead, *The International Dimensions of Democratization.*
31. Interviews with officials from the Commission, Council and European Parliament, held by the author in Brussels, January 2004, February 2005, and April 2008. See, for example, Boix and Stokes, 'Endogenous Democratization'; Lipset, Kyoung-Ryung, and Torres, 'A Comparative Analysis'; Przeworski and Limongi, 'Modernization: Theories and Facts'.
32. Interviews with officials from the Commission, Council, and European Parliament, held by the author in Brussels, January 2004, February 2005, and April 2008.
33. Hamas had also received much international condemnation for using suicide attacks to pursue its resistance strategy. In the eyes of the EU, Hamas challenges the notion of a democratic political party.
34. Kubosova, 'EU Moves to Resume Talks With Palestinians'.
35. Brittain, 'Obituary. Tanya Reinhart', 40.
36. Interviews held by the author in the West Bank and Gaza, September 2007 and in Cairo, March 2008.

37. Youngs, 'The European Union and Palestine'.
38. Pace, 'The Construction of EU Normative Power'.
39. Although Hamas was not vilified for being Islamist but for being a 'terrorist organiz-
     ation' – due to the movement's use of 'suicide bombings' and rockets fired into north-
     ern Israel – which would not accept the right of Israel to exist. When asked
     specifically about this latter point, Hamas officials came back with the question:
     which borders of Israel would the international community like us to recognize?
     Interviews held by the author in Gaza and Nablus, September 2007.
40. Brown, *Requiem For Palestinian Reform*.
41. Author's interview, Ramallah, 4 September 2007.
42. I thank Clive Jones for our discussion on this issue. See McCarthy, 'Israel and Hamas
     Agree Ceasefire'.
43. Interviews conducted by the author in the West Bank and Gaza, September 2007.
44. Israel Ministry of Foreign Affairs, 'The European Union Upgrades Its Relations With
     Israel'.
45. Pace, 'Notions of Europe'.
46. See http://ec.europa.eu/comm/external_relations/mepp/index.htm
47. Bennis, 'Democratising the Unborn State', 172.
48. Euro-Mediterranean Conference, *Barcelona Declaration*.
49. Ibid.
50. Brown, 'Requiem for Palestinian Reform'.
51. Interviews held by the author in the West Bank and Gaza, September 2007 and in
     Cairo, March 2008.
52. Author's interviews, Council of the European Union, Brussels, February 2005 and
     April 2008.
53. Author's telephone interview with a European Commission official, DG Develop-
     ment (Brussels: AIDCO F.5, Relations with civil society and non state actors), 19
     March 2007.
54. Author's interview, Council of the European Union, Brussels, January 2004.
55. While many Western officials are against official talks with Hamas, it is a fact that EU
     and Western diplomats have been privately talking with representatives from the
     movement. Author's confidential interviews in Gaza and Nablus, September 2007.
     At time of writing, there appears to be a political realization that Hamas must be
     included in any Middle East peace talks. Richard Viets, a former US diplomat and
     politician, has stated that Washington has to deal with Hamas. He claimed that the
     siege on Gaza has been unsuccessful and has actually served in strengthening
     Hamas. The former British cabinet minister, Peter Hain, has called on Britain to
     open talks with Hamas. France has also admitted having contacts with Hamas. See
     'Ex-Diplomat Says US Should Engage with Hamas', http://www.middle-east-
     online.com/english/?id=26603; Hain, 'We Must Talk to the Enemy', and Erlanger,
     'France Admits Contacts with Hamas'. Such announcements may be pointing
     towards more pragmatic, diplomatic tactics from all sides.
56. Hutchings, 'Modelling Democracy', 50.
57. Leader. 'Palestine. Talking to Hamas', 36.
58. Cooke, 'Bottom-up Peace-building in the Occupied Territories'.
59. Youngs, *Europe and the Middle East*, 16. See also International Crisis Group,
     Islamism in North Africa I.
60. Cooke, 'Bottom-up Peace-building in the Occupied Territories'.
61. Sadiki, *The Search for Arab Democracy*, 72.
62. Author's interview, Council of the European Union, January 2004.
63. Benhabib, *Democracy and Difference*, 74. For more on such new sites of political
     contestation in Egypt see the contribution by Thomas Demmelhuber in this issue.

Bibliography

Agence France Presse. *EU Lawmakers Vow Not to Yield to Egyptian Pressure*. Strasbourg: European Parliament, 2008.

Amnesty International. EU Office. *EU-Egypt Association Council Meeting. Amnesty International's Key Human Rights Concerns*. Brussels, 13 June 2006.

Baracani, Elena. 'From the EMP to the ENP: New European Pressure for Democratization?'. *Journal of Contemporary European Research* 1 (2005): 54–70.

Benhabib, Seyla, ed. *Democracy and Difference: Contesting the Boundaries of the Political*, Princeton, NJ: Princeton University Press, 1996.

Bennis, Phyllis. 'Democratising the Unborn State: Palestine, the PLO and the Struggle for Democracy'. Chap. 9 in *Democracy and International Relations*. Basingstoke: Macmillan, 2000.

Boix, Charles, and Susan C. Stokes. 'Endogenous Democratization'. *World Politics* 55 (2003): 517–49.

Brittain, Victoria. 'Obituary: Tanya Reinhart'. *The Guardian* (21 March 2007): 40.

Brown, Nathan. *Requiem for Palestinian Reform. Clear Lessons from a Troubled Record.* Washington DC: Carnegie Endowment for International Peace, Carnegie Article no. 81, February 2007.

Commission of the European Communities. *Report on the Implementation of Measures Intended to Promote the Observance of Human Rights and Democratic Principles 1996–99*. Brussels: European Commission, 2000.

Commission of the European Communities. *Strengthening the EU's Relations with the Arab World*. Brussels: Commission of the European Communities, December 2003.

Cooke, Alastair. 'Bottom-up Peace-Building in the Occupied Territories'. *Conflicts Forum* (3 December 2007), http://conflictsforum.org/2007/bottom-up-peacebuilding-in-the-occupied-territories/

Diamond, Larry, Linz Juan, and Seymour Martin, Lipset. *Democracy in Developing Countries* 1–4. Boulder: Lynne Rienner, 1988–1989.

Diez, Thomas, and Michelle Pace. 'Normative Power Europe and Conflict Transformation'. Paper presented at the European Union Studies Association conference, Montreal, Canada, 17–19 May 2007.

Emerson, Michael, *et al. Democratisation in the European Neighbourhood*. Brussels: Centre for European Policy Studies, 2005.

Erlanger, Steven. 'France Admits Contacts With Hamas'. *New York Times* (20 May 2008), http://www.nytimes.com/2008/05/20/world/europe/20france.html?ei=5124&en=5537556d5fe1c77d&ex=1369022400&partner=permalink&exprod=permalink&pagewanted=print

EUobserver. 'EU Trio Takes London By Surprise With Middle East Plan' (17 November 2006), http://euobserver.com/9/22895/?rk=1

Euro-Mediterranean Conference. *Barcelona Declaration*. Barcelona, 1995.

European Communities. *The European Union: Furthering Human Rights and Democracy Across the Globe*. Luxembourg: Office for Official Publications of the European Communities, 2007.

European Parliament. *Resolution of 17 January on the Situation in Egypt. P6_TA(2008)0023*. Strasbourg: European Parliament, 2008.

Ferrero-Waldner, Benita. 'The Middle East in the EU's External Relations'. Conference, *Madrid: Fifteen Years Later* Madrid, 11 January 2007.

Fourth Meeting of the EU-Egypt Association Council. Luxembourg, 28 April 2008, http://www.eu-delegation.org.eg/en/doc/Assoc_Council_EU_Statement_28-4-08_final.doc and http://europa.eu/rapid/pressReleasesAction.do?reference=IP/08/394&format=HTML&aged=0&language=EN&guiLanguage=en

Freedom in the World 2008. Washington and New York: Freedom House, 2008.

Gillespie, Richard, and Richard Youngs, eds. *The European Union and Democracy Promotion: The Case of North Africa*, London: Frank Cass, 2002.

Grugel, Jean. *Democracy without Borders*. London: Routledge, 1999.

Hain, Peter. 'We Must Talk to the Enemy'. *Guardian* (5 June 2008), http://www.guardian.co.uk/commentisfree/2008/jun/05/northernireland.uksecurity/print

Huntington, Samuel P. *The Third Wave. Democratization in the Late Twentieth Century*. Norman: University of Oklahoma Press, 1991.

Hutchings, Kimberly. 'Modelling Democracy'. Chap. 2 in *Democracy and International Relations. Critical Theories/Problematic Practices*. Basingstoke: Macmillan, 2000.

Ibrahim, Saad Eddin. *Egypt, Islam and Democracy*. Cairo: American University in Cairo Press, 1996.

International Crisis Group. *Egypt's Muslim Brothers: Confrontation or Integration*, Middle East/North Africa Report 76, 18 June 2008.

International Crisis Group. *Islamism in North Africa I: The Legacies of History*. Briefing. Brussels: International Crisis Group, April 2004.

International Crisis Group. *Reforming Egypt: In Search of a Strategy*. Brussels and Cairo, 2005, Middle East/North Africa Report.

International Crisis Group. *Ruling Palestine I: Gaza Under Hamas*. Gaza/Jerusalem/Brussels: ICG, 19 March 2008.

Israel Ministry of Foreign Affairs. 'The European Union Upgrades Its Relations with Israel' (16 June 2008), http://www.mfa.gov.il/MFA/

Johansson-Nougés, Elisabeth. 'Civil Society in Euro-Mediterranean Relations: What Success of EU's Normative Promotion?' (2006), Firenze: EUI Working Articles RSCAS 40.

Kelley, Judith. 'New Wine in Old Wineskins: Promoting Political Reforms through the New European Neighbourhood Policy'. *Journal of Common Market Studies* 44 (2006): 29–55.

Kubosova, Lucia. 'EU Moves to Resume Talks With Palestinians'. *EUobserver* (21 March 2007), http://euobserver.com/9/23745/?rk=1

Malmvig, Helle. *State Sovereignty and Intervention. A Discourse Analysis of Interventionary and Non-Interventionary Practices in Kosovo and Algeria*. London: Routledge, 2006.

Manners, Ian J. 'Normative Power Europe: A Contradiction in Terms?'. *Journal of Common Market Studies* 40 (2002): 235–58.

Manners, Ian J. 'Normative Power Europe Reconsidered: Beyond the Crossroads'. Special Issue, *Journal of European Public Policy* 13 (2006): 182–99.

Leader. 'Palestine. Talking to Hamas'. *Guardian* (20 March 2007): 36.

Lipset, Seymour Martin, Seong Kyoung-Ryung, and John C. Torres. 'A Comparative Analysis of the Social Requisites of Democracy'. *International Social Science Journal* 136 (1993): 155–75.

Lucarelli, Sonia, and Ian J. Manners. *Values and Principles in European Union Foreign Policy*, ed. Sonia Lucarelli and Ian, J Manners. London: Routledge, 2006.

McCarthy, Rory. 'Israel and Hamas Agree Ceasefire As Air Strikes Kill Six Palestinian Fighters'. *Guardian* (18 June 2008), http://www.guardian.co.uk/world/2008/jun/18/israelandthepalestinians.egypt

Menon, Anand. *Europe. The State of the Union*. London: Grove Atlantic, 2008.

Meyer, Hartmut, and Henri Vogt, eds. *A Responsible Europe? Ethical Foundations of EU External Affairs*, London: Palgrave, 2006.

Moss, Kenneth B. 'Europe, the Mediterranean and the Middle East'. *Middle East Review of International Affairs* 4(2000), http://meria.idc.ac.il/journal/2000/issue1/jv4n1a5.html

Pace, Michelle. 'The Construction of EU Normative Power'. *Journal of Common Market Studies* 45 (2007): 1039–62.

Pace, Michelle. 'Notions of "Europe". Where does Europe's Southern Margin Lie?'. Chap. 9 in *The Geopolitics of Europe's Identity: Centers, Boundaries, and Margins.* Basingstoke: Palgrave Macmillan, 2008.

Pace, Michelle. *The Politics of Regional Identity. Meddling with the Mediterranean.* London: Routledge, 2006.

Pool, David. 'The Links Between Economic and Political Liberalization'. *Economic and Political Liberalization in the Middle East,* 40–54. London: British Academic Press, 1993.

Pridham, Geoffrey, ed. *Encouraging Democracy: the International Context of Regime Transition in Southern Europe,* Leicester: Leicester University Press, 1991.

Pridham, Geoffrey. *Designing Democracy. EU Enlargement and Regime Change in Post-Communist Europe.* Basingstoke: Palgrave MacMillan, 2005.

Pridham, Geoffrey. *The Dynamics of Democratisation: A Comparative Approach.* London: Continuum International Publishing Group, 2000.

Pridham, Geoffrey, and Tom Gallagher, eds. *Experimenting with Democracy: Regime Change in the Balkans,* London: Routledge, 2000.

Pridham, Geoffrey, and Tatu Vanhanen, eds. *Democratization in Eastern Europe. Domestic and International Perspectives,* London: Routledge, 1994.

Przeworski, Adam, and Fernando Limongi. 'Modernization: Theories and Facts'. *World Politics* 49 (1997): 155–83.

Remmer, Karen L. 'New Theoretical Perspectives on Democratization'. *Comparative Politics* 28 (1995): 103–22.

Rorty, Richard. *Philosophy and Social Hope.* London: Penguin Books, 1999.

Rueschemeyer, Dietrich, Evelyne Huber Stephens, and John D. Stephens. *Capitalist Development and Democracy.* Cambridge: Polity, 1992.

Sadiki, Larbi. *The Search for Arab Democracy. Discourses and Counter-Discourses.* London: Hurst & Company, 2004.

Schimmelfenning, Frank, and Ulrich Sedelmeier, eds. *The Europeanization of Central and Eastern Europe,* Ithaca: Cornell University Press, 2005.

Schmitter, Philippe C. 'The Influence of the International Context upon the Choice of National Institutions and Policies in Neo-Democracies'. *The International Dimensions of Democratization. Europe and the Americas,* 26–54. New York: Oxford University Press, 2001.

Schmitz, Hans Peter. *Transnational Mobilization and Domestic Regime Change. Africa in Comparative Perspective.* Basingstoke: Palgrave Macmillan, 2006.

Smith, Hazel, ed. *Democracy and International Relations,* Basingstoke: Macmillan, 2000.

Stetter, Stephan. 'Democratization Without Democracy? The Assistance of the European Union for Democratization Processes in Palestine'. *Euro-Mediterranean Relations After September 11,* 153–73. London: Frank Cass, 2004.

Tocci, Natalie. 'Does the EU Promote Democracy in Palestine?'. *Democratization in the European Neighbourhood,* 131–52. Brussels: CEPS, 2005.

University of Liverpool. Report on 'the EU and Civil Society Development in North Africa'. Europe in the World Centre, 2002, http://www.liv.ac.uk/ewc/activites/past_activities. htm#2002

Vachudova, Milada Anna. *Europe Undivided. Democracy, Leverage, and Integration After Communism.* Oxford: Oxford University Press, 2005.

Van Houtum, Henk, and Roos Pijpers. 'The European Community as a Gated Community: Between Security and Selective Access'. *EU Enlargement, Region Building and Shifting Borders of Inclusion and Exclusion,* 53–62. Aldershot, Hampshire: Ashgate, 2006.

Whitehead, Lawrence, ed. *The International Dimensions of Democratization. Europe and the Americas*. New York: Oxford University Press, 2001.

Yacoubian, Mona. *Algeria's Struggle for Democracy*. Studies Department Occasional Article 3. New York: Council on Foreign Relations, 1997.

Youngs, Richard. *Europe and the Middle East. In the Shadow of September 11*. London: Lynne Rienner Publishers, 2006.

Youngs, Richard. 'The European Union and Palestine: A New Engagement', O *penDemocracy* (2007), http://www.opendemocracy.net/conflict-middle_east_politics/union_engagement_4485.jsp#

Youngs, Richard. *The European Union and the Promotion of Democracy*. Oxford: Oxford University Press, 2001.

Hamas in transition: the failure of sanctions

Are Hovdenak

International Peace Research Institute, Oslo (PRIO), Norway

This article discusses the nature of the political transformation process that the Islamic Resistance Movement (Hamas) has undergone over the past decade regarding, first, political participation in Palestinian institutions, and second, the issue of negotiations and compromise with Israel. Finally, it explores how the European and international pressure on Hamas for unconditional concessions towards Israel has affected the internal political dynamics of the movement. Based on fieldwork interviews with Hamas leaders in Palestine, Syria, and Lebanon, the article analyses the transition process as perceived on the part of Hamas, and concludes that Hamas was, at a certain point, receptive to external pressure for moderation as it adapted a range of 'moderate' positions in its quest for international recognition. However, when the chain of conciliatory steps undertaken by Hamas failed to ease the international sanctions on the Hamas government, the pressures backfired by weakening the moderate forces in the Hamas leadership and strengthening the radical forces that apparently took the lead when Hamas-affiliated forces took over the Gaza Strip in June 2007. It is argued that the entrance of Hamas into politics represented an opportunity rather than an obstacle for Palestinian democratization, although the opportunity was spoiled by the EU-backed international boycott of the Hamas government.

Introduction

Since Hamas's electoral victory in 2006, Palestinian democratization has become heavily dependent on developments within Hamas, including its attitude to democracy, its policies toward Israel, and its international relations. The starting point of this analysis is the observation that Hamas, an acronym for Harakat al-Muqawamah al-Islamiyah (Islamic Resistance Movement) has undergone a rapid de-radicalization process over a relatively short period of time. After having performed as a classical spoiler throughout most of the Palestinian–Israeli peace process during the 1990s,[1] actively by its military operations against Israeli targets and passively by its boycott of the first Palestinian legislative elections in 1996, Hamas took on a very different role a decade later. Hamas declared, and respected, unilateral ceasefires towards Israel in 2003 and in 2005–2006; it decided to take part in the second elections of the Palestinian Legislative Council (PLC) in 2006, and, following its landslide victory, it took on its parliamentary responsibility by forming a government.

The democratic victory of the Palestinian Islamists took most observers by surprise and represented a major blow to the EU's democratization strategy, which was based on the assumption that the nationalist Fatah party of the Palestine Liberation Organization (PLO) would prevail as the leading political force among the Palestinian people. Among many elements of inconsistency in the EU's policy towards Hamas, the EU had supported Hamas's inclusion in the political process prior to the elections, while it refused to accept the outcome of the people's vote. In contradiction to its declared goal of promoting democratic principles in the EU's European Neighbourhood Policy (ENP) *vis-à-vis* its neighbours, the EU decided to join the rest of the Quartet (the UN, the US, and Russia) in boycotting the Hamas government in order to force it to comply with three demands: recognition of Israel, renunciation of violence, and acceptance of past Israeli–Palestinian agreements.

Although Hamas rejected these demands, it went as far as granting the PLO and the Palestinian Authority (PA) president the mandate to conduct peace negotiations with Israel, accepting the goal of establishing a Palestinian state within the pre-1967 borders of the West Bank and the Gaza Strip, and finally, it agreed to 'respect' previous agreements.[2] These new signs of political moderation, here used in the sense of willingness to accept compromises at the expense of ideological dogmas and maximalist positions, were not easily reconciled with Hamas's long-held, ideological purity, creating internal tensions between radical and moderate factions of the Islamist movement.[3] Rather than engaging in a gradual process of influencing Hamas by rewarding the pragmatic steps that had been taken, the EU decided to stand firm on demanding full compliance with the three principles of the Quartet.

How do the transformation process of Hamas, and the international responses to Hamas's electoral success, feed into the democratization process in the Palestinian arena? In a protracted conflict such as the Israeli–Palestinian one, the issue of democratization cannot be studied independently from the conflict itself. The 'democratic peace' literature suggests a direct, causal link between the presence of democratic structures and peaceful international relations, emphasizing the type of political system as a principal, explanatory variable for the prevalence of peace.[4] However, the causality in the relationship between democratic level and peace has been questioned by William R. Thompson, who argues that the relationship is reciprocal and that the creation of regional 'zones of peace' or 'cooperative niches' usually has 'preceded substantial progress in democratization'.[5] For obvious reasons, the respect for basic human rights – the right to life, liberty and security – which are the pillars of democratic rule, suffer in the absence of peace. This observation deems it necessary to include the context of violent conflict when analysing an ongoing democratization process for a people living under the constraints of military occupation.

In the Palestinian case, the domestic political climate and agenda have been completely dominated by the conflict with Israel. Although the question of democratic structures has been a point of dispute within the Palestinian national movement from time to time throughout its history, that topic has largely been overshadowed by the primary goal of national liberation and self-determination. The guerrilla warfare conducted previously by the PLO and its main component, al-Fatah, and more recently also by Hamas, necessitated a high degree of internal secrecy that clearly suppressed the growth of democratic practice.[6]

Acknowledging the prevalent interrelationship between domestic democratization efforts and external conflict, this article discusses the nature of the political transformation process that Hamas has undergone regarding first, participation in Palestinian national elections, and second, regarding the issue of negotiations and compromise with Israel. Finally, it explores how the massive European and international pressure on Hamas for unconditional concessions towards Israel has affected the internal political dynamics of the movement. The underlying key question is whether the EU's failure to respond positively to the chain of conciliatory steps undertaken by Hamas in effect hampered the transformation process towards political moderation that was set in motion by Hamas's parliamentary participation. In other words: has the confrontational policy of the EU nurtured or quelled the potential for further moderation of Hamas policies?

The following empirical analysis is largely based on interviews conducted by the author with 25 Hamas leaders, including PLC members, Political Bureau members, and local leaders. The interviews were conducted in the Occupied Palestinian Territories (OPT), Syria, and Lebanon during March and August/ September 2007. By focusing on the perceptions of the interviewees as expressed during interviews, the analysis attempts to bring to the forefront the reasoning behind Hamas's decision-making processes, as viewed and explained from within the organization. The sample of interviewees includes different segments of the Hamas leadership, representing different geographical areas, men and women, and 'hard-liners' and 'moderates', but it is not claimed that the sample is representative in any statistical sense. Although the article focuses on the developments in the OPT, representatives of the Hamas leaders in exile are included, due to the central role of the Damascus-based Political Bureau of Hamas.

Gradual steps towards moderation

Hamas was born with the first *intifada*, the Palestinian uprising against Israeli occupation of the West Bank and the Gaza Strip, in 1987. The creation was a result of a radicalization process within its father organization, the Palestinian branch of the Muslim Brotherhood, at a time when the mainstream Palestinian nationalist movement, represented by the PLO and Fatah, was engaged in preparations for diplomacy, negotiations, and compromise based on the idea of a two-state solution. Thus, the radicalization process within the Muslim Brotherhood and Hamas happened simultaneously with the opposite trend, a process of de-radicalization, within the PLO. With the failure of the PLO to secure, through negotiations, Israeli withdrawal from the occupied territories and the establishment of a Palestinian state on the liberated part of the land, the Islamist alternative to the PLO gained credibility and legitimacy among the stateless inhabitants of the West Bank and Gaza Strip, leading to the landslide victory of Hamas's electoral list, under the name 'Change and Reform' in January 2006.[7]

The transformation process in Hamas did not, however, start with its entrance into parliamentary politics in 2006, but can be traced back to the mid-1990s when Hamas started searching for political accommodation within the status quo of Palestinian society.[8] The substantial changes that the movement has undergone since that time can be observed at the ideological as well as at the behavioural level. At the ideological level, the evolution in the movement's main documents is illuminating. The 1988 Hamas Charter identifies the goal of the movement as 'the liberation of Palestine' through the individual duty of *jihad*, leading to the establishment of an Islamic state 'from the river to the sea'.[9] The conflict with Israel is framed largely in religious terms and the land of Palestine is called an Islamic *waqf* (trust), implying that no political leader will ever have authority to relinquish parts of it through peace agreements.[10]

It is noteworthy that the dogmatic and maximalist positions of the charter all disappeared in the Hamas Election Manifesto from autumn 2005. The election programme aimed at limited goals, such as 'resisting occupation' rather than liberating Palestine, and achieving internal 'administrative reform' and 'combating corruption' within PA institutions, rather than imposing Islamic laws.[11]

The moderation evident in Hamas's ideological documents[12] was accompanied by moderation in behavioural policies along three dimensions. First, with regard to domestic political participation, Hamas developed from boycotting the first presidential and legislative elections in 1996 to participating in the legislative elections in 2006. Although Hamas cited contextual rather than principled reasons for its 1996 boycott,[13] its entrance into the institutions of the PA created by the Oslo process was nevertheless a major shift in Hamas's political praxis.

A second dimension of Hamas's de-radicalization process concerns the use of violence. Hamas developed the military tool only gradually, as the main focus during the first uprising, the *intifada* from 1987 to 1991, was mass mobilization in demonstrations and strikes in protest against the Israeli occupation, not the use of firearms.[14] A process of radicalization can be observed from 1992, reaching a first climax with a series of suicide operations against Israeli civilians from 1994 to 1996, and a second peak from 2001 to 2003[15] when Hamas's armed wing, the Izzedin al-Qassam Brigades, took a lead in the militarization of the second *intifada* on the part of the Palestinians. But from 2003, Hamas leaders actively sought to de-escalate the conflict with Israel by declaring, and keeping, unilateral ceasefires.[16]

However, in the domestic arena, the picture was somehow different: while Hamas tried to reduce tension with Israel, conflict intensified internally between

Hamas and Fatah following its election victory in January 2006. Although Hamas in the past had repeatedly asserted that it would 'not cross the red line to civil war',[17] bloody clashes erupted frequently in Gaza during 2006–2007, ending with a five-day battle and the subsequent military takeover of the entire Gaza Strip by Hamas forces in June 2007. In other words, de-radicalization on the Hamas–Israel frontier was accompanied by a radicalization of Hamas's position towards its long-term rival, Fatah.[18]

Finally, a third important dimension is Hamas's attitude to negotiations with Israel. Hamas leaders appear unified behind the tenet that Israel's 'moral legitimacy' as a Jewish state cannot be recognized. However, Hamas leaders have, since the early 1990s, suggested that Hamas would be prepared to accept a *hudna*, an Islamic concept for a long-term truce as an alternative to a full peace agreement.[19] Following Hamas's election victory, Hamas has displayed further flexibility, most notably by accepting the PLO president's mandate to conduct peace negotiations with Israel, as mentioned earlier.[20]

The EU has generally failed to respond to these developments within Hamas in a dynamic way that would facilitate further reconciliatory steps on the part of Hamas. Rather, EU policy towards Hamas has evolved within the context of internal differences between member states on the one hand and the challenge of establishing a policy independent from that of the US on the other.[21] From the late 1990s, European diplomats began to argue that Hamas could not be eliminated by force and should be included in the political process. EU officials engaged actively with Hamas representatives until 2003, when the EU, at the height of the second *intifada*, classified Hamas as a terrorist organization.[22] Following the local elections in 2005, several European governments re-established de facto contacts with elected Hamas officials at the municipal level, but this contact was suspended later the same year. The frequent shifts in European policy and practice towards Hamas left an impression of ambivalence rather than one of a firm strategy for how to implement the EU's stated goals in the visionary democratization schemes within the framework of the 1995 Euro-Mediterranean Partnership (EMP), and the 2003 ENP. In 2004 the PA and the EU approved an Action Plan within the ENP framework that emphasized the goals of 'political dialogue and reform' and 'building the institutions of an independent, democratic and viable Palestinian State'.[23] Several initiatives within these frameworks explicitly call for strengthening engagement with Islamist organizations.[24] The contradiction between declaratory support to integration of Islamists into the political sphere on the one hand and the practice of denying Hamas such a role on the other represents a basic inconsistency in the EU's democracy promotion in the Palestinian case.

Hamas and democracy

During the course of fieldwork interviews conducted for this study, Hamas leaders consistently emphasized that the movement envisions a pluralistic and democratic society within an Islamic framework. A recurring argument in response to Western pressure for democratization was that political pluralism and respecting the choice of the people are not a Western construct, but rather deeply rooted in Islamic tradition, implying that building a Palestinian democratic system is not necessarily a result of political influence from Europe or the USA. Mashhour Abdel Halim, Hamas's leader in the Bourj el-Barajneh Camp in Beirut, referred to the *shura* (assembly) system as described in the Quran to illustrate that the idea of a people's assembly is not foreign to Islam. 'It is crystal clear according to a verse in the Holy Quran that within the system of *shura* Islamic decision makers must respect the view of the majority.'[25] Furthermore, Abdel Halim explained that Hamas belongs to a tradition within the Islamic movement that accepts that there is room for *ijtihad*, that is, interpretation of the Holy Scripture, which is important for Hamas's appearance as a politically flexible movement with high capabilities to adapt to rapidly changing circumstances and conditions.[26] Notably, such a claim of Islamic 'ownership' of democracy mirrors Volpi's discussion in this special issue of a (partial) convergence of Islamist and liberal-democratic political agendas.

In contrast to this harmonious view of Islamic democracy, some secular critics, Palestinian as well as foreign, distrust the sincerity in Islamists' adherence to democratic rules and claim that Hamas would use elections as a vehicle to obtain power and, thereafter, never leave power voluntarily. Ahmad Yousef, the political advisor of Hamas's Prime Minister Ismail Haniyeh, dismissed such allegations as unfounded polemics. The basic problem is, according to Yousef, that 'unfortunately, nobody is prepared to test the Islamists' intentions to see whether they really will get stuck in power by offering them a fair chance to complete their four-year term in power without external interference.'[27] Yousef viewed the international boycott of Hamas as another missed opportunity to let an Islamist party handle the challenge of political power and responsibility.

Hamas members claim to practice democracy internally by applying the Islamic principle of *shura* (consultation) as an important element in its decision-making process. Given the circumstances of occupation and war, which require a certain degree of secrecy and limitation on transparent structures, Hamas actually demonstrates a relatively advanced culture of including the rank and file in policy discussions.

Geographically, the Hamas movement is divided into three geographical sections: Gaza, West Bank, and exile. A fourth branch is the prisoners (currently jailed in Israeli prisons). In addition, there is the military branch, the Izzedin al-Qassam Brigades, which has its own internal structure and leadership. Each section of Hamas is divided into smaller sub-units, down to local neighbourhood committees, led by a political leader with the title of *amir al-manteqa* ('prince of the neighbourhood'). An anonymous *amir al-manteqa* in the Zeitun neighbourhood of Gaza City explained that important policy questions are being discussed at seminars at the local level and that local and regional leaders communicate opinions expressed within their area further up in the organization. The highest decision-making body is the *Majlis al-Shura*, which is an elected assembly, while executive powers rest with *al-Maktab al-Siyasi*, the Political Bureau with some 10–20 members.[28] While members claim that they have a voice in the movement's policy-making process, they also tend to be loyal to the outcome once a decision is taken, as few will publicly voice opposition to official positions. Interestingly, this practice appears to be an Islamic version of the communist doctrine of democratic centralism.[29]

Moreover, the *amir* explained that all PLC candidates on the Change and Reform list were first elected in a three-stage primary election process within Hamas. From each level, five candidates continued to the next level, until the final list was fixed.

Local Hamas leaders in exile confirmed the practice of organizing local conferences from which policy input is conveyed to the leadership. A Hamas leader in the Bourj el-Barajneh Camp in Beirut explained that 'Usually, for the important decisions, the leaders consult all the local leaders.'[30] This practice reflects the traditional, Islamic ideal of rule through consultation and consensus, representing an idealized model for Islamic democracy. Asked about the procedures for registering the opinions expressed at the camp level, he explained that:

> We organize big meetings, for instance here in Bourj, where members can express their views. For some important issues – such as that of participating in elections and about the Prisoners' Document – there have been questionnaires distributed among local leaders, who will base their answers on the views expressed by the members.[31]

The display of such a level of internal democracy among the Palestinian Islamists makes it timely to raise the issue of who are the driving forces for democratization among the Palestinians. Knowing that the main secular rival, Fatah, has, for years, resisted internal demands for reforms that would end the autocratic structures which dominate the backbone of the PLO, it is a remarkable paradox that European funds for democratization still target the secular 'liberals' while bypassing Hamas-affiliated civil society organizations.[32] The pattern is very much like that in Morocco, which Cavatorta elucidates in this volume, with regard to the exclusion of democracy funding for Islamic associations. Consequently, European fear of Islamic influence and the exclusion of Islamists may in reality represent major obstacles to democratic progress.

From boycott to participation

Hamas's decision to boycott the 1996 elections was taken after a prolonged internal debate. A range of Hamas leaders, mostly from inside the OPT, considered a tactic of 'opposition from within' the PA. From his prison cell, the late Sheikh Ahmad Yassin wrote a series of letters arguing that Hamas's participation in professional and municipal elections since the early 1990s had set a precedent for participating in PA elections.[33] In spite of the apparent ambivalence within the organization, Hamas announced in November 1995 that it would boycott any forthcoming elections for the presidency or the legislative council of the PA.[34]

Hamas leaders consistently separate the question of accepting democratic principles from the issue of under which conditions Hamas should accept to run for elections. They reject the interpretation that Hamas's shift from boycotting the 1996 PLC elections to participating in 2006 represented a change in the movement's attitude towards pluralism and democracy. They cite a range of contextual reasons for their decision to boycott the 1996 elections, including opposition to the peace process, the continued Israeli occupation of the Palestinian territories, and the autocratic rule of Yasser Arafat. Mahmoud Zahar, one of the founding members of Hamas, stated:

> We have never been against elections as a principle. We boycotted the 1996 elections because they were held within the framework of the Oslo Agreement, which we were against because it provided nothing to us Palestinians, and because the administration of the PA apparatus was completely in the hands of Yasser Arafat. He cheated and fabricated results in the 1996 elections.[35]

The deputy leader of the Damascus-based Political Bureau, Musa Abu Marzuq, explained that Hamas refused to participate in the first PLC elections 'because we didn't want to provide the Oslo Agreement with any legitimacy at that time' and because Hamas would not give up the right to resisting the occupation.[36]

It is noteworthy, though, that Hamas actually applied a 'light' boycott, which implied refraining from participating, but without trying to have the elections cancelled. Abu Marzuq claimed that Hamas had no intention of spoiling the election process. 'We didn't want to make any obstacles for these elections and we didn't call people to boycott. We simply didn't participate', said Abu Marzuq, who explained this carefully calibrated protest position by a wish on the part of the Hamas leadership to see what the participation of the people would be.

This reasoning was reiterated by Hamas's representative in Lebanon, Osama Hamdan, who said that the policy of boycotting, on the one hand, and refraining from sabotaging the process, on the other, rested on Hamas's positive attitude to the principle of elections. In spite of all its shortcomings, Hamdan viewed the 1996 election as a step in the right direction, as a preparation for building a democratic system. 'If you want to build a political system you have to choose whether you want a dictatorship or a democratic system. Our choice was, from the beginning, the democratic option' said Hamdan.[37]

The leadership also tactically considered the possible negative effects of a boycott on Hamas's public standing. The elections were at the time widely understood as a referendum over the peace process, which had solid backing, according to opinion polls.[38] Musa Abu Marzuq reasoned that 'if we called the electorate to refrain from voting and people still voted, it would be interpreted as if they voted against Hamas and, if people stayed away from the ballots, it would appear as a measure of Hamas's strength.'[39]

The turning point for Hamas's entrance into the political arena came with a series of meetings that were hosted by the Egyptian government between the main Palestinian factions in 2004 and early 2005. The talks were held in an atmosphere of historical change following President Yasser Arafat's death in November 2004, and prior to the announcement of unilateral Israeli withdrawal from the Gaza Strip.[40] The talks in Cairo produced what has been known as the six-point Cairo Declaration of March 2005, which succeeded in having 13 Palestinian factions endorse a common platform, on elections, a ceasefire with Israel, and reforming the PLO. One of the participants, Musa Abu Marzuq, maintained that the agreement was made possible as the newly elected President Mahmoud Abbas realized that any agreement with Israel needed Hamas's acceptance for implementation and that he could not move on the political track without talking to Hamas.[41]

Furthermore, Hamas's successful participation in the municipal elections held in late 2004 and early 2005 boosted the organization's confidence. Hamas won the majority of seats in many of the main cities, both in the West Bank and the Gaza Strip. The participation in local elections was never a contested issue within Hamas, as municipalities were not part of the institutions created by the Oslo peace process.

According to Ghazi Hamad, a former Hamas government spokesman, the local elections showed 'that people were looking for an alternative, due to the corruption and mismanagement among Fatah people. Hamas understood that people wanted them as the alternative'.[42] This massive popularity was also felt as a sort of political obligation that Hamas could hardly shirk: 'It was the people that pressured Hamas to participate, because they wanted Hamas to be represented and they wanted the elections to reflect the true will of the people.'[43]

The entrance of Hamas into municipal elections represented an early opportunity for the EU to reorient its policies and adapt to the reality of Hamas as an important political player. The fact that Hamas, throughout 2005, largely kept its commitment to a unilateral ceasefire towards Israel, presented the EU with another good reason for normalization of relations. However, this opportunity was not taken, although some contact was established for a brief period between EU governments and Hamas members at the municipal level.[44] On the contrary, the EU, along with the US, renewed its ban on contact with Hamas and its classification of Hamas as a terrorist organization in October 2005.[45]

Finally, the context of the *intifada* also played a role in Hamas's desire for entering elections. The uprising broke out following the collapse of the final status negotiations between Israel and the PLO in 2000. In spite of the heavy human losses on the Palestinian side during the *intifada*, the unilateral withdrawal, or 'disengagement' in Israeli terms, of Israeli troops and settlers from the Gaza Strip, which was carried out in mid-2005, was widely celebrated by the Palestinians as a victory of the resistance in general and of Hamas in particular. The lesson that was repeatedly preached by Hamas leaders was that 'what Fatah and the PLO failed to achieve by negotiations, Hamas managed to take by force'.[46]

Although Hamas was apparently militarily weakened by the Israeli assassination campaign against dozens of its top and medium-level leaders, the fact that the movement's leaders suffered no less than its rank and file activists provided the movement with a degree of popular sympathy and political legitimacy that probably outweighed any military losses. By running in the 2006 elections, Hamas showed it was prepared to harvest the political fruits of its military resistance at a time when it was most convenient to downplay the military option anyway.

However, the main political argument applied by Hamas to justify entering the institutions of the PA was the interpretation that the Oslo Agreement and the peace process were 'dead' and, thus, electoral participation no longer implied any commitment to the outcome of the failed peace exploration of the 1990s.[47]

Hamas's view that the Oslo Agreement was no longer a valid reference was supported by the fact that the stipulated five-year interim period expired already in 1999, and that the Israeli prime minister, Ariel Sharon, in 2002 publicly retracted Israel's commitments to the signed agreements with the PLO.[48] The Israeli move facilitated Hamas's claim that the PA institutions were now detached from the Oslo process, paving the way for Hamas's entrance. Furthermore, the apparent conformity in opinion between Hamas and Likud in rejecting the validity of the Oslo Agreement displayed one of many unbalanced positions of the EU and the Quartet. While the Sharon government acted decisively on its anti-Oslo stance by violating or ignoring past Israeli–Palestinian agreements without attracting more than rather mild criticism from Europe, the Hamas government was put under sanctions to alter its view on the same agreements.

Hamas's wish to improve its standing in the international society may also have been a factor supporting democratic participation. 'We decided to participate in the political game to show the world that we are not a terror organization,' said Jamal Iskaik, PLC member in Gaza, hoping that this would 'give the international society a chance to understand our conflict through dialogue.'[49] Iskaik admitted that international pressure did have an impact on Hamas's moderation: 'We have an Arabic saying that what you take by force you have to return by force – meaning that the occupied land can only be returned from Israel by force. But we have come to be more realistic, as we realized that we could not fight all the great powers. So we decided to be more moderate and to participate in elections to gain at least something.' Other Hamas leaders, however, upheld that the relationship with the rest of the Arab and Islamic worlds plays a more significant role in Hamas's geopolitical orientation than that of the West.

In sum, the explanations reviewed above regarding a pressing 'need' or 'obligation' for Hamas to enter politics reflect a growing desire within Hamas for political power, based on pragmatic considerations of its opportunities within that sphere of Palestinian life.

The burden of victory

The process leading up to the 2006 elections constituted just the first phase of the transformation that Hamas was to go through. The second phase was the period following the election victory in January 2006, was even more challenging for the movement. Hamas won 74 out of 132 parliamentary seats and was left with the obligation to form a government.[50] The leadership admitted that they were taken by complete surprise by the victory and that they were not prepared for the scenario of forming a government alone. 'When we decided to participate in elections, we considered two options: either to participate in a national unity government or to be a strong opposition; nobody talked about forming the government,' claimed Osama Hamdan.[51] The express journey from a guerrilla movement to government went apparently faster than the leadership could handle. Ghazi Hamad described an atmosphere of confusion and tension among the members following the election victory:

> Most Hamas members had, until the elections, considered their movement primarily as a military organization fighting the occupation. But when they woke up one morning and found that Hamas had won the majority of the parliament and was to form the government, everything was changed. Just two days earlier, all the members had been against joining the government; they just wanted to be a big opposition in the parliament and monitor the politics of the PA. The leadership tried to accommodate this new situation and to convince its members that it was an obligation to move along this track. But inside Hamas it was not easy to spread a culture of political visions because the mindset was always built on resistance and martyrdom.[52]

Hamas tried to relieve the burden of governmental responsibility by inviting Fatah to join a unity government. But Fatah had no interest in coming to Hamas's rescue, and refused to accept the humiliating position as the minor party in a Hamas-led coalition.[53]

Eventually, Ismail Haniyeh formed the first Hamas government, which, from the first day, faced formidable challenges at all levels: Not only were the movement's cadres inexperienced in parliamentary and governmental work, but at the domestic level it faced a fully uncooperative Fatah, which had a hard time accepting its electoral defeat, showing little interest in helping the Islamists to achieve any success whatsoever. This had dramatic implications for the internal security situation as the Fatah-loyal security forces refused to obey orders from the Hamas Interior Minister, although the Palestinian Basic Law prescribed a coordinating role on internal security to the Interior Ministry.[54] It is a key point in this context that it was the Quartet that initiated a security reform process in the first place as part of the 2003 Road Map peace initiative. The goal at that time was to strip Yasser Arafat of his powers by transferring the control over the security apparatuses from the president to the government.[55] However, with Hamas controlling the government in 2006, the EU in fact supported a reversal of the prescribed security reforms in order to prevent the Hamas government from gaining control over the security sector. This manoeuvre of the EU and the rest of the Quartet clearly exacerbated the tension between the Hamas government, on the one hand, and the security forces loyal to the Fatah opposition and to President Mahmoud Abbas on the other, opening the stage for the bloody strife that was to develop over the following year, eventually leading to the violent takeover of the Gaza Strip by Hamas-controlled forces in June 2007.[56]

On the economic front, the main obstacle for the Hamas government to function normally was the international sanctions that were applied by the US-led Quartet, which suspended all economic aid and diplomatic contact with the Palestinian government. In addition, Israel continued its practice of withholding taxes on goods imported into the Palestinian territories via Israel, which Israel collects on behalf of the Palestinian Authority.[57] The Quartet established alternative channels for its increasing humanitarian aid, which was donated through NGOs, UN organizations as well as through the President's Office, while bypassing the government and the ministries. The boycott had thus a major paralyzing impact on all governmental structures of the PA and it hurt governmental employees, most of whom were Fatah loyalists, whose salaries were not paid for a period.[58] The paralysis of the Palestinian local industry led to a dramatic shift from development assistance to humanitarian assistance, the latter increasing from 16% of all aid in 2005 to 56% by late 2006.[59]

It would be safe to say that the boycott had the unintended effect that people lost the chance to judge Hamas from its record in power. Hamas could, and did, blame all its shortcomings on the external hostile environment.[60] Thus, as an experiment of showing what Hamas could contribute to Palestinian democracy, the output was meagre.

The boycott applied by the EU and the rest of the Quartet left the Hamas leadership with a very concrete dilemma. On the one hand, resisting unified international pressure would apparently lead to political isolation, economic recession, and institutional collapse of PA structures. On the other hand, complying with the Quartet's demands would imply a capitulation on Hamas's most basic ideological doctrines. The movement, which had vested so much political prestige as well as human sacrifice in the struggle to 'save' the Palestinians from what was seen as a disastrous peace process, could obviously not suddenly surrender on its core tenets without risking a serious internal crisis. According to a leading scholar on Hamas, Ali Jarbawi, the leadership of Hamas could probably not have complied with the Quartet's demand of recognizing Israel without causing a full split in the organization.[61]

Consequently, Hamas had to choose between risking the complete disintegration of PA institutions if it rejected the Quartet's demands, and a split within Hamas if it accepted these demands. Seen in this light, the choice of the Islamist leadership to preserve the unity of the movement rather than giving in to the Quartet's ultimatum appears fully rational.

Hamas's approach towards Israel

In spite of the fierce criticism that Hamas voiced against the Quartet's three demands, few Hamas leaders reject them outright on principle. Many Hamas leaders would rather link their opposition to specific Israeli positions or to circumstances that may change in the future. This is another observation of key importance because it implies that Hamas's position is not fixed, but may be revised if and when circumstances allow for it. In the words of Musa Abu Marzuq: 'We are against these demands, but we are willing to talk about them. We asked the Americans to mediate, to make a dialogue, not to boycott the Palestinian people.'[62]

A main objection frequently raised by Hamas leaders is linked to the lack of reciprocity in the Quartet's approach, as the three demands which Hamas was pressured to comply with, were not required from Israel. This point was summed up accurately by Hamas legislator Jamal Saleh from Gaza:

The international community asks us to stop using violence, but Israel doesn't stop [using violence]; it asks us to recognize the Israeli state, but Israel doesn't recognize our right to a state. It asks us to comply with previous agreements, but Israel violates them every day. We would respect it if the Quartet had asked us both to comply with these demands – but they are demanding it from us, the weaker party, only.[63]

The message to the Quartet is clear: if the great powers took a balanced approach and applied the same measures to Israel as to the Palestinian side, Hamas would likely respond with flexibility on a range of topics.

The most difficult point of the Quartet's demands appears to be the one concerning recognition of Israel, which contradicts the most basic tenet in Hamas's view of the state of Israel as a foreign implant on Palestinian soil. Hamas leaders consistently claim that the issue of recognition is not on the table for the time being, while referring to Hamas's official position regarding a *hudna*, a long-term truce between a Palestinian and an Israeli state as a pragmatic alternative. A *hudna* is, according to the spokesman for the Hamas bloc in the PLC, Saleh Bardawil, 'the best and most practical solution for everyone as long as Israel is not ready to recognize our Palestinian state now – and we are not ready to recognize Israel. Then we leave the issue of recognition for the next generation to decide.'[64]

Hamas's restrictive approach to the issue of recognition reflects the fact that the movement is not politically ready for such a dramatic, symbolic step now. However, there may also be tactical assessments underpinning that position. Ahmed Yousef admitted that he considered the issue of recognition to be a valuable asset for the future:

This is one of our cards in our hands, and we are not going to give it for free. So we are not addressing this issue now, until the ending of the occupation, then we can talk about what is going to be the future relation between the Israelis and the Palestinians. I know that if I say I recognize Israel it will not lead to anything in return from Israel ... There are certain factors they [the Quartet] have to address before they push Hamas to recognize Israel.[65]

This tactical assessment is important as it reflects a long-term strategy in which Hamas is positioning itself in preparation for any upcoming negotiations. Far from being contradictory to negotiations, such positions may, in fact, be a component in Hamas's preparations for future negotiations. The EU has failed to appreciate and to act on such crucial political signals representing an opening for creative diplomacy. Instead, the EU has pursued its narrow and short-term focus on the issue of immediate formal recognition of Israel.

Hamas leaders claim to have learned a lesson from what is judged as Yassir Arafat's strategic mistake of offering Israel recognition at the outset of peace negotiations. In the words of Mahmoud Zahar: 'Arafat's and the PLO's recognition of Israel was not reciprocated by an equivalent Israeli recognition of a Palestinian state or national rights. It was a dirty game, and we are not going to repeat it. When in history did any occupied people recognize its occupiers?'[66]

Although such a statement may appear as an expression of militancy, it does not preclude the option of recognition in the future. Rather, it may be interpreted as yet another signal emphasizing that Hamas's flexibility depends on Israeli actions. At this point Hamas is basically advocating respect for international law and the implementation of UN resolutions.

The Quartet's demand of renouncing violence is also dismissed by Hamas as another fundamentally unbalanced demand. In Hamas's reasoning, the use of violence is, even more than the question of recognition, linked to Israeli policies, pointing to Israeli military operations or to the occupation itself as the two main driving forces behind the resistance. Although Hamas in its ideological documents emphasizes armed resistance as the main tool to liberate Palestine, leaving the impression of an offensive strategy behind its warfare, the military ambitions expressed by its leaders appear as much more modest. Hamas officials generally describe military activities of the Izzedin al-Qassam Brigades as defensive by nature and usually initiated as direct responses to specific Israeli military operations. PLC member Mushir al-Masri claimed that all the big waves of violence from the part of the Izzeddin al-Qassam have been set off by Israeli actions:

> Remember that the first Palestinian martyr operations, in 1994, were preceded by the Massacre of Baruch Goldstein in Hebron; the attacks in 1996 came after the Israeli assassination of [Hamas operative] Yahiya Ayyash; and the renewed martyr operations from March 2001 came after hundreds of Palestinians were killed in the preceding six months of the second *intifada*.[67]

Both actions and statements of Hamas in this regard illustrate the extent to which the pressure of the Israeli occupation is keeping Hamas preoccupied on the military front, while at the same time narrowing the political options at hand for the policy-makers in Hamas, including that of pursuing the path of democratization.

Hamas's receptiveness to external pressure

Hamas politicians were partly provoked, partly surprised, and certainly disappointed by the European role in the Palestinian democratization experiment. While most Hamas leaders would easily admit that they had no expectations for a balanced policy on the part of the USA, they did expect the EU to take a different stance. Deputy prime minister in Haniye's first government, Nasr al-Din al-Sha'er, offered this analysis on the difference in American and European perceptions:

> There are two ways of thinking – the American and the European. The American way is dealing with the Palestinian issue without Hamas; they would like to kick Hamas out of the political picture altogether. But I feel that a lot of Europeans prefer to talk with the whole Palestinian people. And they prefer an agreement to be signed by all Palestinian factions, including Hamas. They see that if there is an agreement without Hamas, it will not work.[68]

The widespread frustration within Hamas about the EU's attitude towards the Palestinian election process in 2006 indicates that the policy of sanctions has backfired and weakened the political stature of the EU in Palestinian eyes. 'They defended democracy everywhere, but when democracy brought Hamas to power, they changed their position,' complained ex-refugee minister Atef Adwan, who believed the Palestinian people understood well that the guilty party for the sanctions was the Western world, not Hamas. In addition, Adwan claimed that the boycott was obviously counter-productive: 'The aim of the siege is to weaken Hamas and pressure it to withdraw from its positions. Instead, Hamas hardened their stance on many things,' said Adwan. [69]

The claim that Hamas will not be changed by coercion is illustrated well by the attitude of Izzat al-Rashaq, who said that 'Hamas stood up against this embargo, which did not achieve its goal of changing Hamas'.[70] Apparently, it became a point of prestige for the Political Bureau in Damascus to resist the Western pressure and the sanctions.

One of the more visible effects of the boycott was that it caused increased internal tension between and within Palestinian groups. Hamas became divided over how to respond to the demands. Fatah was also ambivalent about how to deal with the isolation of Hamas. Hamas blamed Fatah for instigating strikes in the Ministry of Education and the Ministry of Health. 'The goal of these strikes was to oust Hamas from the government,' claimed Hamas legislator Muna Mansour.[71]

Eventually, Hamas decided to move closer to international demands. There seemed to be a genuine attitude among Hamas legislators and political leaders that Hamas indeed made some historical decisions by signing, first, the National Conciliation Document of the Prisoners[72] in June 2006, and second, the Mecca Agreement[73] in February 2007.

The Mecca Agreement marked the peak of moderation in the sense of signalling willingness for compromise over its previous positions on the part of Hamas. The leadership expected to be rewarded for its willingness to establish a National

Unity Government (NUG), and for its promise to 'respect' previous Israeli–Palestinian agreements; diplomatic steps which had been taken only with the cost of increased internal tension within the movement. Hamas leaders strongly recommended, almost begged, the Western world to respond: 'Hamas is a flexible movement, responding to international community claims. This should be a good opportunity for the international community to communicate with Hamas,' claimed legislator Mushir al-Masri a day after the inauguration of the NUG.[74]

Although the NUG was welcomed as a positive development by European governments, it failed to have the sanctions lifted.[75] Only non-EU states Norway and Switzerland established diplomatic links with the NUG, a step that was highly appreciated by Hamas. However, according to diplomatic sources, several EU states, including France, were in a process of reassessing their policies and might have recognized the NUG if it had survived longer.[76] Without the materialization of the expected rewards from the compromises reached at Mecca, internal frustration rose within Hamas.

With the sanctions in place, the unity government collapsed within three months amidst a bloody showdown, in which Hamas overran PA security forces and established full control over the Gaza Strip. Hamas claimed that their military offensive was triggered by secret collaboration between Fatah-loyal security forces and the US preparing to crack down on Hamas.[77] The failure of the Quartet to reward the achievement of the NUG and the direct US intervention in internal security affairs seemed to have contributed directly to the chaos and violence that followed in Gaza.

Hamas's military takeover of Gaza marked the end of democratic and constitutional rule in both the Gaza Strip and the West Bank, cementing the political division between Hamas and Fatah with a territorial division of the OPT.

Within the ranks of Hamas, an atmosphere of bitterness spread following the political breakdown, which it saw as a direct outcome of the boycott of the Quartet. In hindsight, Nasr al-Din al-Sha'er claimed that an historical opportunity was lost when the Quartet failed to appreciate those steps taken by Hamas up to the Mecca Agreement:

> There was a big chance for the whole world, for the Palestinians – and every single person in this region – when Hamas offered the opportunity and authority to President Abbas to go and negotiate with Israel and to give him a security network that never happened before, even for [late President] Arafat. But unfortunately, they spoiled this opportunity.[78]

Nasr al-Din, Ahmed Yousef, and Ghazi Hamad were all leaders who had invested much of their personal and political capital in convincing the movement to accept the compromises aimed at securing international recognition. When this strategy of moderation failed, the militant forces took the lead on the ground, while the moderates were sidelined. Ghazi Hamad resigned as Hamas spokesman, while political advisor Ahmed Yousef admitted that his influence was radically reduced:

Yes, my position is weakened. In internal discussions, people tell me that 'we followed you for a year and a half, but you failed; we trusted your assurances that the Europeans would change their mind once Hamas forms the unity government and accepts the previous agreements or renounce terrorism.' But nothing changed. This weakened my argument, and I am no longer a credible source for any political change.[79]

Illustrative of the apparent fragmentation between moderates and militants in Hamas is the fact that all political leaders interviewed for this study consistently claimed that the military takeover of the Gaza Strip was neither planned nor approved by the top political leadership. This indicates a serious weakening of the whole political leadership in a movement that generally has been considered very disciplined.

One underlying message that can be read out of all these frustrations cited above is increased resentment against the West and against Europe more specifically. This resentment may well lead to the opposite result than the declared goal of compliance with Western wishes. Several Hamas leaders expressed the fear that pressure on Hamas would not result in bolstering Fatah and President Abbas, but rather, more militant forces than Hamas. In the words of Izzat al-Rashaq: 'the Americans have to know that if they don't deal with Hamas today they will have to face Al Qaeda in the future. If you neglect our rights and the West continues to boycott Hamas, I am afraid this ideology will grow in the region.'[80] Nasr el-Din al-Sha'er feared, furthermore, that even Hamas itself would move its policies in that direction as a consequence of Western pressure: 'I'm afraid that Hamas itself in Gaza – if the whole world makes a lot of pressure – might choose a policy that seems close to that of al-Qaeda, even though they are not really al-Qaeda. But the pressure makes the political person very weak and the militant person very powerful.'[81]

Paradoxically, the European strategy aiming at supporting liberal democrats apparently became a liability for those voices in Hamas who had tried their best to push the political line in a moderate direction.

Conclusion

The apparent inconsistency between the EU's rhetoric and its actual policies in regard to democracy promotion is, as correctly interpreted by Hamas politicians, a display of European double standards. The counter-productive consequences of this misguided strategy are not limited to the obvious regress in the process of democratization, institution-building, and economic development within the PA structures. Even more serious is the devastating impact this policy has inflicted on internal Palestinian politics, as it has weakened political moderates within Hamas and strengthened the more militant factions of the movement, and also fuelled the intra-Palestinian strife between Hamas and Fatah that led to the division of the West Bank and the Gaza Strip into two separate political units, a situation that will paralyze any diplomatic efforts toward renewed final status negotiations. Finally, the EU has seriously discredited itself in the eyes of not only Hamas supporters, but also among larger segments of the Palestinian public by its misguided policies. The failure of the EU to honour a democratic election in the Arab world seems also to have backfired in the sense that the EU's democracy promotion agenda itself has lost much of its credibility and legitimacy, as Pace elucidates more extensively in this volume.

The outcome of the EU's policies appears thus as detrimental to the EU's own interests. If the EU is 'a realist actor in normative clothes' as Seeberg assumes in the article on Lebanon in this special issue, it has clearly failed to protect its own interests by its campaign to exclude Palestinian Islamists from political power.

At the heart of the EU's democratization failure lies the strategy of demanding that Hamas abandons its militancy towards Israel as a precondition for accepting Hamas as a legitimate actor in Palestinian parliamentary politics. However, the three conditions that the US-led Quartet applied went far beyond a demand for non-violent behaviour and adherence to democratic principles and had dubious relevance for Hamas's right to fulfill its governmental responsibilities after having received the confidence of the Palestinian electorate. In addition, the demands appeared as clearly biased in the sense that Israel was not required to comply correspondingly.

The interviews with Hamas leaders presented in this study document that Hamas presents pragmatic positions on key issues both in the domestic field as well as with regard to Palestinian–Israeli negotiations. The EU's strategy of forcing Hamas to accept an ultimatum rather than to encourage gradual steps in the right direction has clearly not succeeded in nurturing the apparent potential for further moderation and compromise on the part of Hamas. The main Palestinian Islamist party has demonstrated that it should not be seen as an obstacle to democratization. To the contrary, any successful democratization as well as peacemaking in Palestine depends on the contribution from Hamas as a key political player. The EU's refusal to accept such a role for Hamas has contributed largely to the failure of the EU's democratization agenda.

Notes

1. Malka, 'Forcing Choices', 42.
2. Milton-Edwards, 'Hamas: Victory with Ballots and Bullets'.
3. Amayreh, 'Hamas and al-Qaida'.
4. Ray, *Democracy and International Conflict*.
5. Thompson, 'Democracy and Peace', 142.
6. For the organizational development of the PLO and Fatah, see Sayigh, *Armed Struggle and the Search for State*.
7. Abu-Amr, 'Hamas: from Opposition to Rule', 169; Tamimi, *Hamas. Unwritten Chapters*, 220.
8. Roy, *Failing Peace*, 294.
9. For English translation of the Hamas Charter, see Appendix 2 in Hroub, *Hamas. Political Thought and Practice*, 267–91.

10. However, the militant language of the Charter, which had little space for political visions, was already, from the first years, contradicted by pragmatic signals by top leaders. For instance, the idea of entering a *hudna*, a long-term ceasefire, with Israel as an interim solution was brought up by several top Hamas leaders from the early 1990s. See Tamimi, *Hamas. Unwritten Chapters*, 158.

11. For English translation of the Hamas Election Manifesto, see Appendix VI in Tamimi, *Hamas. Unwritten Chapters*, 274–94.

12. See Hroub, 'A "New Hamas" through its New Documents'.

13. Butenschøn and Vollan, *Interim Democracy*, 52–3.

14. Andoni, 'A Comparative Study', 212.

15. Website of Israeli Foreign Ministry, http://www.mfa.gov.il/MFA.

16. Tamimi, *Hamas. Unwritten Chapters*, 204, 212.

17. Hroub, *Hamas. Political Thought and Practice*, 56.

18. The tension between Hamas and Fatah loyalists was further exacerbated by the reasserted role of traditional clan allegiances. See International Crisis Group, *Inside Gaza*.

19. Tamimi, *Hamas. Unwritten Chapters*, 158.

20. Milton-Edwards and Crooke, 'Elusive Ingredient', 45.

21. FRIDE, 'Europe and Palestinian Democracy'.

22. International Crisis Group, *Enter Hamas*, 22.

23. See discussion on the content of the EMP and the ENP by Pace in the preceding article in this issue. The 'EU/Palestinian Action Plan' is available at http://ec.europa.eu/world/enp/pdf/action_plans/pa_enp_ap_final_en.pdf

24. Emerson and Youngs, *Political Islam and European Foreign Policy*, 5.

25. Mashhour Abdel Halim (Hamas leader, Bourj el-Barajneh Camp, Beirut), interview by the author, Beirut, September 2007.

26. See Pace, 'A "Modern" Islamist Democracy?'.

27. Ahmed Yousef (political advisor of Hamas Prime Minister Ismail Haniyeh), interview by the author, Gaza, August 2007.

28. Due to the need of privacy/secrecy, the exact number of members of the Political Bureau is not known. For more on the organizational structure of Hamas, see Mishal and Sela, *The Palestinian Hamas*.

29. Inspiration from Leninist organizational structures has influenced several, modern Islamist organizations, for instance Hizballah in Lebanon. See Abu Khalil, 'Ideology and Practice of Hizballah', 390–403.

30. Mashhour Abdel Halim, interview by the author.

31. Ibid.

32. Author's interview with Islamic civil society organizations, Gaza, March 2008.

33. Milton-Edwards, *Islamic Politics in Palestine*, 163.

34. Ibid., 165.

35. Mahmoud Zahar (Foreign Minister in Hamas's first government), interview by the author, Gaza, March 2007. However, the international observer delegation to the 1996 elections concluded that 'the elections can reasonably be regarded as an accurate expression of the will of the voters on polling day'. Appendix in Butenschøn and Vollan, *Interim Democracy*, 128.

36. Musa Abu Marzuq (deputy leader of Hamas Political Bureau), interview by the author, Damascus, August 2007.

37. Osama Hamdan (Hamas representative in Lebanon and member of Hamas Political Bureau), interview by the author, Beirut, September 2007.

38. Seventy-eight per cent of the Palestinians in the OPT supported the peace process according to a poll in December 1995. See the collection of polls on Palestinian attitudes to the peace process in: Jerusalem Media and Communications Center, *Palestinian Public Opinion*, 19.

39. Musa Abu Marzuq, interview by the author.
40. The death of Arafat represented, in the words of Osama Hamdan, 'a new chapter and a new era in Palestinian politics'. Author's interview, Beirut, September 2007.
41. Musa Abu Marzuq, interview by the author.
42. Ghazi Hamad (ex-spokesman of the Hamas government), interview by the author, Gaza, August 2007.
43. Mashhour Abdel Halim, interview by the author.
44. International Crisis Group, *Enter Hamas*, 28.
45. Ibid., 23.
46. Ghazi Hamad, interview by the author.
47. Izzat al-Rashaq (member of Hamas Political Bureau), interview by the author, Damascus, March 2007.
48. In an interview with the Israeli newspaper *Ma'ariv* on 6 September 2002, Sharon declared that 'Oslo doesn't exist any more, Camp David doesn't exist, neither does Taba ... We will not return to these places'. BBC, 'Sharon Calls for New Palestinian Security'.
49. Jamal Iskaik (Hamas legislator), interview by the author, Gaza, August 2007.
50. Final election results released by the Central Elections Commission-Palestine. Available at http://www.elections.ps/template.aspx?id=291.
51. Osama Hamdan, interview by the author.
52. Ghazi Hamad, interview by the author.
53. International Crisis Group, *Palestinians, Israel and the Quartet*, 9.
54. See the Palestinian Basic Law of 2003, http://muqtafi.birzeit.edu/mainleg/14138.htm
55. Hovdenak, 'Middle East', 505.
56. International Crisis Group, *After Gaza*, 7–9.
57. Sayigh, 'Inducing a Failed State in Palestine', 17–9.
58. Tocci, 'The International Dimension'.
59. Edanger, 'Aid to Palestinians'.
60. See Brown, 'The Peace Process Has No Clothes'.
61. Ali Jarbawi (Professor at Bir Zeit University), interview by the author, March 2007.
62. Musa Abu Marzuq, interview by the author.
63. Jamal Saleh (Hamas legislator), interview by the author, Gaza, March 2007.
64. Saleh Bardawil (Hamas legislator and spokesman for the Hamas block in the PLC), interview by the author, Gaza, March 2007.
65. Ahmed Yousef, interview by the author.
66. Mahmoud Zahar, interview by the author.
67. Mushir al-Masri (Hamas legislator), interview by the author, Gaza, March 2007.
68. Nasr al-Din al-Sha'er (deputy prime minister and education minister in Hamas's first government), interview by the author, Nablus, August 2007.
69. Atef Adwan (minister of refugee affairs in Hamas's first government), interview by the author, Gaza, March 2007.
70. Izzat al-Rashaq, interview by the author.
71. Muna Mansour (Hamas legislator), interview by the author, Nablus, March 2007.
72. For English translation of the National Conciliation Document, see: http://www.jmcc.org/documents/prisoners2.htm
73. For English translation of the Mecca Agreement, see: http://www.jmcc.org/new/07/feb/meccaagree.htm
74. Mushir al-Masri, interview by the author.
75. See International Crisis Group, *After Gaza*,
76. Author's interview with a Norwegian diplomat in the Middle East, September 2007.

77. On the collaboration between PA security forces and the US against Hamas, see Rose, 'The Gaza Bombshell'.
78. Nasr al-Din al-Sha'er, interview by the author.
79. Ahmed Yousef, interview by the author.
80. Izzat al-Rashaq, interview by the author.
81. Nasr al-Din al-Sha'er, interview by the author.

Bibliography

Abu-Amr, Ziad. 'Hamas: From Opposition to Rule'. *Where Now for Palestine? The Demise for the Two-State Solution'*, ed. Hilal Jamil, 167–87. London and New York: Zed Books, 2007.
Abu Khalil, As'ad. 'Ideology and Practice of Hizballah in Lebanon: Islamization of Leninist Organizational Principles'. *Middle Eastern Studies* 27 (1991): 390–403.
Amayreh, Khalid. *Hamas and al-Qaida. The Prospects for Radicalization in the Palestinian Occupied Territories*. A Conflicts Forum Monograph. Beirut-London-Washington: Conflicts Forum, 2007.
Andoni, Ghassan. 'A Comparative Study of Intifada 1987 and Intifada 2000'. *The New Intifada. Resisting Israel's Apartheid*, ed. Carey Roane, 209–18. London: Verso, 2001.
BBC. 'Sharon Calls for New Palestinian Security' (8 September 2002), http://news.bbc.co.uk/2/hi/middle_east/2243763.stm
Brown, Nathan J. 'The Peace Process Has No Clothes. The Decay of the Palestinian Authority and the International Response'. Carnegie Endowment Paper. Washington, DC: Carnegie Endowment for International Peace, 2007, http://www.carnegieendowment.org/files/BrownCommentaryjune072.pdf
Butenschøn, Nils, and Kåre Vollan. *Interim Democracy: Report on the Palestinian Elections, January 1996*. Human Rights Report No.7. Oslo: Center for Human Rights, 1996.
Edanger, Steven. 'Aid to Palestinians Rise Despite Embargo'. *New York Times* (23 March 2007).
Emerson, Michael, and Richard Youngs. *Political Islam and European Foreign Policy. Perspectives from Muslim Democrats of the Mediterranean*. Brussels: Centre for European Policy Studies, 2007.
FRIDE. 'Europe and Palestinian Democracy'. FRIDE Democracy Backgrounders. Madrid: FRIDE, 2006, http://www.fride.org/eng/File/ViewLinkFile.aspx?FileId=926
Hovdenak, Are. 'Middle East: More Need for Traffic Police than Road Maps'. *Security Dialogue* 34 (2003): 503–10.
Hroub, Khaled. *Hamas. Political Thought and Practice*. Washington DC: Institute for Palestine Studies, 2002.
Hroub, Khaled. 'A "New Hamas" Through its New Documents'. *Journal of Palestine Studies* 35, no. 4 (2006): 6–27.
International Crisis Group. *After Gaza*, Middle East Report No.68. Brussels: ICG, 2 August 2007.
International Crisis Group. *Enter Hamas: The Challenges of Political Integration*, Middle East Report No.49. Brussels: ICG, 18 January 2006.
International Crisis Group. *Inside Gaza: The Challenge of Clans and Families*, Middle East Report No.71. Brussels: ICG, 20 December 2007.
International Crisis Group. *Palestinians, Israel and the Quartet: Pulling Back from the Brink*, Middle East Report No.54. Brussels: ICG, 13 June 2006.
Jerusalem Media and Communications Center. *Palestinian Public Opinion since the Peace Process*. Jerusalem: JMCC, 1998.

Malka, Haim. 'Forcing Choices: Testing the Transformation of Hamas'. *The Washington Quarterly* 28 (2005): 37–54.

Milton-Edwards, Beverley. 'Hamas: Victory with Ballots and Bullets'. *Global Change, Peace & Security* 19 (2007): 273–91.

Milton-Edwards, Beverley. *Islamic Politics in Palestine*. London and New York: I.B. Tauris, 1999.

Milton-Edwards, Beverley, and Alistair Crooke. 'Elusive Ingredient: Hamas and the Peace Process'. *Journal of Palestine Studies* 33 (2004): 39–52.

Mishal, Shaul, and Avraham Sela. *The Palestinian Hamas. Vision, Violence, and Coexistence*. New York: Columbia University Press, 2006.

Pace, Michelle. 'A "Modern" Islamist Democracy? Perceptions of Democratisation in Palestine: The Case of Hamas'. Paper presented at The University of Birmingham's Department of Theology and Religion, 18 March 2008.

Ray, James Lee. *Democracy and International Conflict: An Evaluation of the Democratic Peace Proposition*. Columbia: University of South Carolina Press, 1998.

Rose, David. 'The Gaza Bombshell'. *Vanity Fair* (April 2008), http://www.vanityfair.com/politics/features/2008/04/gaza200804?printable=true&currentPage=all

Roy, Sara. *Failing Peace. Gaza and the Palestinian-Israeli Conflict*. London: Pluto Press, 2008.

Sayigh, Yezid. *Armed Struggle and the Search for State: The Palestinian National Movement, 1949–1993*. Oxford: Oxford University Press, 1999.

Sayigh, Yezid. 'Inducing a Failed State in Palestine'. *Survival* 49 (2007): 7–39.

Tamimi, Azzam. *Hamas. Unwritten Chapters*. London: Hurst & Company, 2007.

Thompson, William R. 'Democracy and Peace: Putting the Cart before the Horse?'. *International Organization* 50 (1996): 141–74.

Tocci, Nathalie. 'The International Dimension: Western Policies towards Hamas and Hezbollah'. In *Domestic Change and Conflict in the Mediterranean: The Cases of Hamas and Hezbollah*. EuroMeSCO Paper 65. Lisboa: EuroMeSCO, January 2008, http://www.euromesco.net/index.php?option=com_content&task=view&id=690&Itemid=48&lang=en

The EU as a realist actor in normative clothes: EU democracy promotion in Lebanon and the European Neighbourhood Policy

Peter Seeberg

Centre for Contemporary Middle East Studies, University of Southern Denmark, Campusvej 55, 5230 Odense M, Denmark

The article takes recent research on the difficulties for the EU in successfully promoting democracy in the Middle East and North Africa (MENA) region as its point of departure, with a specific focus on the European Neighbourhood Policy EU-Lebanon Action Plan. It is shown that, in spite of the fact that Lebanon does not present the same authoritarian institutions and character as most of the other countries in the region, the EU seems to have difficulties dealing with the political realities of Lebanon. This has to do with its consociational system and the existence of political elites in Lebanon, who see avoiding another breakdown of the political system as the decisive political issue. In addition, the existence of a 'dual power' situation, where two sources of authority are competing for power and legitimacy, constructs a Lebanese reality which the EU chooses to address by neglecting its own normative, democracy promotion ambitions. The article concludes that the vagueness and inconsistency of EU policies in Lebanon cannot only be explained by tactical considerations, but also imply that the EU pursues a realist agenda: in other words it is a realist actor dressed in normative clothes.

Introduction

The academic debate on EU commitment to democracy promotion in the Mediterranean has more or less established that the goals of the European Union have been only inconsistently, or even reluctantly, pursued. It has been claimed that the Barcelona process as a foreign policy strategy and democracy promotion instrument has been, at best, disappointing.[1] The European Neighbourhood Policy (ENP) can be seen as a reflection of a more expansive power projection ambition and as a corrective to the Euro-Mediterranean Partnership (EMP), the ENP reconfiguring rather than replacing the EMP.[2] The article discusses how Lebanon as a case-study provides important insights into the working of the EU and its democracy promotion attempts.

The ENP EU–Lebanon Action Plan was adopted by the European Union on 17 October 2006 and by Lebanon on 12 January 2007,[3] stating that 'The European Neighbourhood Policy offers through its Action Plan a strategic tool for the EU to accompany Lebanon in its reform process.'[4] The Action Plan takes its point of departure in the enlargement of the European Union of May 2004, claiming that the EU and Lebanon 'are now closer together than before and, as near neighbours, will reinforce their political and economic interdependence'.[5] The ENP Action Plan is the latest in a number of agreements and documents reflecting the development in EU–Lebanon relations, and it forms an important part of the EU's democracy promotion attempts in Lebanon.

The timing of the document was to some degree coincidental. It was the result of a historical process, which took place over a long time, but was intensified in recent years in connection with the development of the ENP policy. Hence, it is the development of the ENP, more than the recent political turmoil in Lebanon, which explains the timing of concluding and issuing the agreement.

This article discusses the conditions concerning democracy promotion that the EU is facing in Lebanon and analyses the political, economic, and security agendas which the EU is pursuing. The first, theoretical, part focuses on theories of authoritarian persistence and political elites in the Middle East and the role of the Hezbollah as an actor in Lebanese society, analysing the organization as a political party and a strong social movement, which is both integrated in the political system and, in some ways, stands above or outside the system.

The second part of the article examines the EU–Lebanon Action Plan, seen as an expression of EU democracy promotion efforts. This part examines how the EU, as a realist actor, attempts to exert influence on the political realities in Lebanon, with a special focus on the ENP programmes. The article concludes by discussing EU political agendas and democracy promotion ambitions in Lebanon.

The Lebanese elites and the 'dual power' of Lebanon

The literature on European Union external policy-making in the Middle East and North Africa often emphasizes the inability of the EU to successfully promote democracy in the region. Different scholars point to different reasons as to why the EU seems to be unsuccessful, with some arguing that the inability of the EU is due to institutional shortcomings, while others postulate that the current policies in place are specifically designed to fail due to the realist needs and interests of the European Union itself.[6] However, some scholars argue quite convincingly that the genuine attempts of the EU to promote democracy are thwarted by the targeted regimes.

So far, only a limited number of analyses of the actual Action Plans and their implementation in the Middle Eastern states have been carried out.[7] The case of Lebanon is an interesting one to examine because the country does not present the same authoritarian institutions and character as other Arab countries in the region. Thus, in principle, it should be easier in many ways for the European

Union to implement its strategy more successfully, as the Lebanese polity might be more receptive to it.

In recent years, European foreign policy rhetoric has emphasized an EU commitment to strengthening relations with Islamist organizations in the Mediterranean,[8] and it is shown by Rees and Aldrich that the EU, compared to the US, conceptualizes radical Islam in less absolute terms.[9] Nonetheless, the EU has been reluctant to approach the Islamists, as shown in this special issue by, for example, Demmelhuber (Egypt), Cavatorta (Morocco), and Powel (Tunisia), and this is also the case in Lebanon. So far, as noted by Youngs, the EU has chosen only low-level contact with, for instance, Hezbollah:

> European states opposed the US push for a blanket proscription of Hezbollah, recognizing the latter to be the fastest growing political organization in Lebanon ... A number of European embassies commenced low-level dialogue with Hezbollah, with the aim of backing the group's political arm against the militia wing.[10]

At higher levels, as shown later, the normative ambitions of the EU, expressed in the EU–Lebanon ENP Action Plan, are gradually hidden behind a discretionary language, which indirectly points to a downgrading of EU democracy promotion ambitions. This reveals a certain pragmatism on the part of the EU, which has realized that the positive conditionality of the ENP (see the Introduction of this special issue) would imply a higher degree of relative reform willingness than is realistic for Arab states, *in casu* Lebanon. Lebanon made a transition from wartime anarchy to stability around the turn of the century. Since then, the Lebanese consociational democracy has experienced a regression back to a state of anarchy – especially after the 2006 war between Israel and Hezbollah.

The article posits that the main reason why the EU's democracy promotion has not been successful in Lebanon is a result of a combination of two conditions, which function as obstacles for the EU democracy promotion attempts. Firstly, the Lebanese political elites have experienced considerable difficulty in implementing the 1989 Ta'if Agreement, which ended the Civil War.[11] Secondly, the Lebanese political reality is characterized by a 'dual power' situation, with the alliance around Prime Minister Fouad Siniora on one side and with Hezbollah leading the opposition on the other.

It is the contention of this article that these complex political conditions result in the EU indulging in both tactical and strategic deliberations. The dual power situation influences the EU, which for tactical reasons maintains a low profile, imagining that by contributing to the current status quo a strengthening of Hezbollah might be avoided. In both the short and the long term, the complex and unstable post-Ta'if setup in Lebanon creates difficult conditions for the EU in pursuing its strategic interests in creating a stable neighbourhood. The article aims to show that this could be achieved by toning down the conditionality embedded in the ENP, or omitting it altogether, thereby accepting a dilution of its democracy promotion commitments.

The Lebanese exceptionality and its elites

As a political system, Lebanon is a special case in the Middle East. The political system, in spite of its shortcomings in connection with the above-mentioned sectarian imbalances, is less autocratic than that of most other Arab states. The Lebanese population can vote for parties, which are free to decide their party programmes without censorship or constraint. Still, Lebanon contributes to the 'resistance' to democratization processes in the Arab world, as discussed by Waterbury,[12] for instance, especially because of the unjust distribution of seats in the National Assembly and the obvious lack of a well functioning political system.

In order to analyse these aspects of Lebanese society, Raymond Hinnebusch's analysis of authoritarian persistence in the Middle East is relevant.[13] Hinnebusch points to authoritarianism as the modal form of governance in the region and explains the reasons for the limited democratization through 'hostile structural conditions that include limited modernization, an unsolved national problem and particular class configurations'.[14] Hinnebusch mentions that the long-lasting, yet imperfect political system of Lebanon has been the most democratic of any Arab country. He points to the sectarian fragmentation and the bourgeoisie, which 'in alliance with the traditional notability (zuama)'[15] is dominating and has reached a cross-sectarian power sharing pact. Theories of political elites are, therefore, relevant for analysing the Lebanese exceptionality.

Volker Perthes' concept of a politically relevant elite (PRE), by which is meant a stratum of people 'in a given country who wield political influence and power in that they make strategic decisions or participate in decision-making on a national level',[16] can be utilized in explaining how the working of the Lebanese political system is maintained. The Lebanese PRE seems to be unified around the threat of another breakdown and an attempt to make the Ta'if agreement work. From time to time they make small adjustments in the regime, for instance, by changing electoral practices, but without making amendments as to the fundamentals of the consociational political system.[17]

According to Rola el-Husseini, the post-Ta'if elites can be described as five groups who have been able to reposition themselves through elections or appointment. The groups consist, in el-Husseini's analysis, of former warlords, religious rebels (including Hezbollah), Syria's clients, the entrepreneurs (among them Rafiq Hariri), and military personnel. It is part of the theory that these groups are struggling to uphold their own political power and, at the same time, are manoeuvring to gain influence for their own group; but a main characteristic is persistence and stability in order to maintain the dominance of the 'consensually unified' elites:

> The confessional representation model creates a political system that is not viable in the long run, as demonstrated in 1975. The current system still contains the seeds of its own destruction. A change of the system would doubtlessly lead to a change in elites; therefore the members of the PRE do not seem to open such a scenario.[18]

This does not mean, however, that the elite groups do not internally oppose each other. In Lebanese political reality, there is a permanent struggle between the different groups in order to gain influence at the expense of the others.

Hezbollah and the 'dual power' of Lebanon

The most efficient and dynamic actor in this respect is Hezbollah, which, as an actor in Lebanese society, is both integrated within the political system and in some ways stands above or outside the system.[19] The Hezbollah is a strong or even dominant actor, competing with the official government for political hegemony, thereby constructing a 'dual power' situation in Lebanon: a situation where two sources of authority are competing for power and legitimacy. Hezbollah is a well-organized movement. As well as being a huge social movement and having one of the most potent militias in the Middle East, it is represented in the National Assembly and sets up political alliances and electoral pacts with most of the other parties.

Hezbollah, as a highly important institution in Lebanese society, is adding dimensions to the political culture of the country in ways which hardly can be compared to other countries in the Middle East. Even though, as shown by the other case studies in this special issue, there are other strong, Islamic movements in the Arab world, be they illegal, tolerated or co-opted, no other Islamic group has the same dominant position *vis-à-vis* an Arab state as Hezbollah in Lebanon.[20]

While the core members of the PRE in Lebanon are the president, the cabinet members, and the parliament, Hezbollah MPs and their allies can, according to el-Husseini, be placed in the third circle of the PRE. El-Husseini emphasizes that the number of Hezbollah members of parliament demonstrates the party's importance, and claims that charisma is perhaps Hezbollah's key form of political legitimacy. In addition to that, her analysis shows that someone like the secretary of Hezbollah, Hassan Nasrallah, belongs to the PRE, 'moving between the third and second circles of influence, depending of the issue at hand'.[21] The question is, however, if this is realistic. If concepts of dual power and dual legitimacy are applied to the analysis, it can be claimed that the Hezbollah and its leaders occupy positions in the elite circles of Lebanon that are much closer to the decisive core.

The weak Lebanese state is dependent on a sectarian balance which creates constant conflict, threatening to send the sorely tried nation back to civil war or at least to temporary political chaos. Added to the 'consensually unified' elites, the concept of 'dual power' can be applied to the Lebanese reality, allowing the Lebanese situation to be compared with, for instance, the situation in Iran right after the revolution of 1977–1978, where Ayatollah Khomeini for some time sought an alliance with Mehdi Bazarghan.[22] Masoud Kamali describes this process as follows:

Bazarghan's provisional government was a liberal government, not a clerical one. In part, Khomeini chose liberals to head the government to show his democratic intentions and to legitimize his leadership for the whole people as well as to gain support from the West and to isolate the Shah and his supporters. In the final phase of the Revolution, the clergy isolated liberals and removed Bazarghan's government.[23]

But whereas in Iran the revolutionary, Islamic leader Khomeini chose to legitimize his leadership for tactical reasons by letting the 'Revolutionary Council' propose Bazarghan as prime minister of the 'Provisional Revolutionary Government', in Lebanon the 'dual power' situation finds expression through a legitimate, yet weak government and a strong, self-appointed power centre in the shape of Hezbollah.[24] The traditional historical context that is mentioned in relation to the phrase of 'dual power' is that of the revolution in Russia in 1917, where Lenin coined the phrase to describe the situation after the February Revolution in which two powers, the Soviets and the official state apparatus of the Provisional Government, coexisted with each other and competed for legitimacy.

Beside the 'dual power' theme, there is a more subtle duality connected to the Hezbollah movement that can be called a 'dual legitimacy' or 'dual identity'.[25] The Hezbollah is, in one way, just another Lebanese political actor, a political party pursuing power by being represented in Parliament, and because of its efficient political work (and extensive social activities among poor Shi'ites in Lebanon), a popular and legitimate political entity in the country. However, Hezbollah is also a religious movement drawing on a Khomeini-inspired version of Shi'ism,[26] which is expressed in the rhetoric of the Hezbollah leaders Nasrallah and Mohammad Hussein Fadlallah in speeches, on the internet, and via Al Manar, the satellite TV station.

These activities are being carried out with a multitude of references to the Quran and the ideals of Shi'ism, thus giving the movement a religiously founded legitimacy, especially among its supporters in the poor areas of the larger Lebanese cities. This 'dual identity' as an actor within the system, and a religious symbol or icon above and outside the political and social reality of Lebanon, gives Hezbollah a special status or superiority compared to other actors in Lebanon. Its status as 'the resistance', made possible by its strong military organization, means that Hezbollah is able to act on its own and even challenge the strongest military power in the Middle East, Israel. The autonomous organization will hardly, or at least not in the near future, voluntarily lay down its weapons and in the short term it is unlikely that Hezbollah will come to terms with a situation where the official Lebanese army possesses a monopoly on the 'legitimate use of violence', as termed by Max Weber.[27]

Hezbollah is in many ways the phenomenon around which regional interests revolve. The organization's strong position is a result of its power as a player on the Lebanese scene. The EU has major difficulties dealing with political Islam and Hezbollah as a strong and significant organization; added to this, the EU has difficulties clarifying its position in relation to the regional political challenges. The regional role of Iran, which has grown stronger in recent times, is because the alliance between Hezbollah and Iran (and this also applies, to some degree, to Syria) acts as another barrier for the EU in pursuing democracy promotion in Lebanon. The EU seeks to avoid any potential strengthening of Hezbollah and therefore the ambitions of the EU in Lebanon establish a conflict of interests between the EU and Iran (and Syria), making it more complicated for the EU to pursue both its foreign policy interests and its normative agendas in the Middle East.

EU attempts at democracy promotion in Lebanon have to take into account the demographically unjust representation in the National Assembly of the Shi'ite population.[28] This theme in Lebanese politics has been accentuated since the war in July–August 2006: the subsequent political strengthening of Hezbollah motivated the Shi'ite movement to intensify its fight for political influence, thereby revitalizing the struggle for a fairer distribution of seats in the Lebanese parliament. This is reinforced by the foreign policy of Iran, which is rhetorically supportive of Hezbollah, claiming that the political leaders of Lebanon ought to make changes to the confessional system to make it conform more with demographic realities.

An example of this was the influential Ayatollah Ahmad Khatami, who during a Friday prayer in Teheran in September 2006, praised Hezbollah for its confrontation with the current Lebanese government and said, 'Shi'ites, Sunnis, and Christians should have a share in the cabinet in proportion to their weight. The call of Lebanese Hezbollah is logical and stems from within the Lebanese nation.'[29] The Iranian Shi'ite leadership is trying to increase its influence in the Arab region, taking Lebanon 'hostage' to serve Iran's foreign policy interests and thereby presenting yet another version of the narrative of what Vali Nasr called the 'Shia revival'.[30]

The complexity of the situation in Lebanon is accentuated by a rarely seen alliance between Hezbollah and the Maronite Christian Free Patriotic Movement (FPM) led by Michel Aoun, seemingly establishing a new division within Lebanese society, this time to some degree along social lines. At the regional level, the Hezbollah and its allies are supported by Iran and Syria against the Lebanese political establishment around Fouad Siniora, who is supported in the Middle Eastern context by Egypt, Jordan, and Saudi-Arabia.

Lebanese exceptionality is what the EU has to take into consideration when deciding on its foreign policy towards Lebanon. The combination of, firstly, a 'consensually unified' PRE in Lebanon, which sees maintaining its own power and avoiding another breakdown of the political system as the decisive political issues, and, secondly, the important differences between the two sides of the system of 'dual power', constructs a Lebanese reality which the EU chooses to address by neglecting its democracy promotion ambitions. This can be explained by political pragmatism and/or tactical considerations on behalf of the EU: the EU considers that affecting the complex power sharing of the consociational Lebanese elites is beyond its potential sphere of influence. The EU reluctance to strengthen relations with Islamist organizations in the Mediterranean puts pressure on the EU in Lebanon, in the sense that it has to position itself in relation to the complexities of the 'dual power' situation there.

The EU, Lebanon and the ENP Action Plan

When the EU launched the ENP, Lebanon became one of the 16 countries with which agreements were concluded. The implementation documents of the ENP are founded in a number of earlier agreements and documents developing the ENP in relation to Lebanon: first of all the *Country Report* of March 2005;[31] then, a *Country Strategy Paper* for 2007–2013 (following the paper covering 2000–2006); and the *National Indicative Programme* for 2007–2010. These are the central documents behind the EU–Lebanon Action Plan.

The Action Plan is a political document laying out strategic objectives of cooperation between Lebanon and the EU, covering a timeframe of five years. It is said in the Introduction that:

> The Action Plan will be taken forward in the context of our common commitment to achieving a comprehensive, just and lasting peace in the Middle East, acknowledging the important objective of restoring Lebanon's full sovereignty and territorial integrity, in accordance with International Law and relevant United Nations Resolutions. It is also in this context that a solution to the Palestinian refugee issue in Lebanon will be found.[32]

Noteworthy is the mention of the EU's ambition to contribute to bringing Lebanon's sovereignty and integrity into accordance with international law. The question of Palestinian refugees in Lebanon is also mentioned, indirectly with reference to UN Resolution 194, and is thereby included in the EU democracy promotion ambitions. It is difficult to avoid the impression that the EU states are realizing that the possibilities of solving Lebanon's fundamental problems are limited. It is even more explicitly expressed in the section, 'Political dialogue and reform', which states that the EU's ambition is simply to 'Establish a political dialogue between the European Parliament and the Lebanese Parliament'.[33]

Democracy promotion and the Neighbourhood Policy Action Plan

In the political dialogue and reform-section of the Action Plan, it is mentioned that key priorities, beside the political dialogue, are to:

> Work together to promote the shared values of democracy and the rule of law including good governance and transparent, stable and effective institutions ... [and] [S]trengthen measures against corruption through the effective implementation of a national anti-corruption strategy, including the institutional framework and the enforcement capacity and public awareness and advocacy.[34]

The first sentence about promoting the shared values of democracy and the rule of law is couched in an ideal and non-binding narrative and is typical of the expressions in the Action Plan dealing with the issue of democracy. This constitutes a difficulty in analysing the democratic ambitions of the EU concerning Lebanon. It is, of course, scarcely meaningful without more precise descriptions of the intentions of the EU, to speak of shared values between the democratic, welfare states of the EU and the imperfect democracy of unregulated, liberalist, and socially uneven Lebanon.

The ambition to promote democracy remains a postulate. The passage about corruption underlines one of the main obstacles in Lebanese society to the establishment of a well-functioning political culture. It is a well-known fact that a culture of corruption, which was created by the 1975–1990 Civil War and has never been eliminated, is widespread in Lebanon, as documented by Gambill.[35] For obvious reasons, it is not possible to document the exact extent of illegalities, but under any circumstances it will be difficult to cure this curse of Lebanon. Because of its prevalence in Lebanese political reality, the phenomenon of corruption is a challenge for the EU's democracy promotion ambitions.

Demography and democracy

The relations between sectarian demography and limited democracy in Lebanon constitute significant obstacles to democratic progress. The EU has in many ways difficulties in dealing with the sectarian and ethnic-religious conflicts in the country. The recent political turmoil in Lebanon is partly due to long-term structural conditions and unresolved problems from the Ta'if-accords of 1989, and partly due to recent discrepancies in Lebanese politics, reinforced by the war between Israel and Hezbollah in the summer of 2006. Furthermore, it has to do with the highly problematic conditions of the Lebanese economy, characterized by trade deficit, public debt, and lack of foreign investments.[36]

The capture of two Israeli soldiers and the killing of three others on 12 July 2006 in what the Hezbollah codenamed 'Operation Truthful Promise' created an opportunity for the Israelis to launch an attack on southern Lebanon. It was obvious that Israel was not merely reacting to Hezbollah's raid.[37] As discussed by Richard Norton, it was claimed after the war, particularly by Arab media, that Hezbollah emerged as the winner of the conflict.[38]

However, Lebanese reality was more complex than that. According to Shibley Telhami, 40% of the Lebanese population, when asked to describe their attitudes to Hezbollah after the war, said that they viewed the organization more positively, but 30% viewed the organization more negatively.[39] The important point, though, was that: 'Pluralities of over 40 per cent among Sunnis, Christians and Druze expressed more negative views, while an overwhelming majority of Shiites expressed positive views'.[40]

So once again, the significant ethnic-religious contradictions and conflicts in Lebanon came to the fore and, in the months after the war, the political tensions of Lebanon were aggravated.[41] One of the ways for Hezbollah to increase its influence is via alliances in the Lebanese Parliament. During the summer of 2006, there were meetings between Hezbollah and Michel Aoun, the leader of the Christian Free Patriotic Movement (FPM), and it appears that the FPM promised its new partner that it would support some of the political goals of Hezbollah.

One of the viewpoints that Aoun supported was 'one-man-one-vote',[42] a perspective which, according to ethnic-religious demographics, would result in bringing the Lebanese Shi'ites much more than the 27 seats in Parliament given to them by the Ta'if Agreement. The important issue here is not the political manoeuvres, which most of all served internal political purposes, but the fact that an interesting new constellation came into being, which seemed to be able to gather considerable groups of the Lebanese population behind its leaders.[43]

The groups supporting FPM and Hezbollah were recruited from the lower segments of Lebanese society: first and foremost from the huge population of relatively poor Shi'ites living in the southern part of Beirut and the southern parts of Lebanon, but also from groups within the Christian segments which had been marginalized from the labour market by immigrant workers from Syria, Egypt or Asia. They were attracted by aggressive anti-Israeli rhetoric and heavy criticism directed towards the Siniora government, which was accused of being passive in its social policies and incapable of providing the ordinary citizen with the necessities of life.

The Ta'if Agreement described Lebanon as an Arab country.[44] This would, at first, appear to be a triumph for Arab nationalism and the forces in Lebanon which found their ideological strength in this. Research by Theodor Hanf shows that the Lebanese, in spite of the heavy losses throughout the civil war, seemed to stick to their nationality.[45] Based on opinion polls taken during the civil war, Hanf claimed that most Lebanese wanted to live in peaceful coexistence within the framework of one country. As early as 1993, Hanf pointed out that apparently, and despite the violent conflicts, the civil war had given rise to a process where Lebanon was becoming a nation.[46]

The support for political parties, the state, and the nation has been a key theme in Lebanese politics since the end of the civil war. Nonetheless there is little doubt that the national consensus is fragile and only to some degree shared by the large Shi'ite minority. Hanf's results were confirmed by Telhami, who carried out a survey in November 2006 which concluded that:

> One of the remarkable findings in this poll, and potentially the most promising for the Lebanese people, is that – despite the polarizing effect of the war with Israel, and the contentious political environment that emerged afterwards – Lebanese of all sects retain strong identification with the Lebanese state.[47]

The question, though, is how far this identification goes. Can it transcend a deep feeling among the poor Lebanese in southern Beirut of being let down by a government whose main concern is to stay in power supported by the US and the West, as is often claimed by Hezbollah leader Nasrallah in his anti-Siniora rhetoric?

In the Action Plan, the political dimension of the strategy is expressed by saying that the government should: '[P]romote the establishment of a comprehensive strategy for reform of the system of political representation and the election framework ... taking into account the recommendations set out in the final report of the EU Election Observation Mission'.[48] This is the closest that the Action Plan comes to pointing out the unjust distribution of seats between the main ethnic-religious groups in the Lebanese Parliament. The EU Election Observation Mission referred to is extremely cautious in its recommendations, claiming simply that: 'It is widely recognized in Lebanon that the system of political representation and the election framework need to be overhauled ... For a diverse society as the Lebanese it is crucial to have as many different views as possible represented in Parliament.'[49]

The remarks are symptomatic in the sense that, in a diplomatic fashion, they point to deficiencies in the Lebanese political system. By using these ambiguous and non-binding passages, the obvious injustices which need to be reformed in the Lebanese parliamentary system are hidden. The EU may not be able to influence the complex process of bringing the sectarian proportions in the parliament into line with the distribution of the religious groups in the population. However, not committing itself to anything more than pointing to the fact that it is 'widely recognized' that the system needs overhauling, is a noticeable lack of ambition.

Cooperation on foreign and security policy

It is one of the overall ambitions of the ENP to enhance stability and security at EU borders and in proximate geographical areas. Lebanon constitutes a part of this ambition, and within this important and at the same time highly complex issue lies the intention of the EU to strengthen political dialogue and co-operation on Common Foreign and Security Policy matters by developing 'an enhanced political dialogue and regular exchange of information on Common Foreign and Security Policy (CFSP) and European Security and Defence Policy (ESDP) matters'.[50]

It is not obvious in which ways it will be possible to develop foreign policy cooperation, as there are only very few examples of such cooperation. What these passages are emphasizing is that the EU wants Lebanon to take part in building a security environment in the Mediterranean area by developing cooperation within this area between the two partners.

As I have demonstrated elsewhere, European security is very much a focus of European foreign policy.[51] An important aspect of this is the internal security of Europe itself and, in this respect, Lebanon is relevant, because of EU fears that Lebanon and its Palestinian refugee camps are breeding grounds for radical groups known to operate in Europe.[52] This might explain why the Action Plan section covering the issue of terrorism is more explicit when compared to other sections (see below), implying that the EU is focusing on its own security rather than democracy promotion in Lebanon.

Cooperation on preventing and combating terrorism

According to the Action Plan, an important issue in relation to preventing and combating terrorism is the question of the role of the UN. The measures aimed at strengthening EU–Lebanon co-operation in the fight against and prevention of terrorism include both 'Ensure respect of human rights in the fight against terrorism based on the recommendations of the relevant UN bodies' and 'Cooperate to reinforce the role of the UN in the multilateral fight against terrorism, including through implementation of all relevant United Nations Security Council Resolutions and through signature, ratification and full implementation of all relevant UN Conventions.'[53] All relevant UNSC Resolutions include Resolution 1559, initiated by France and the US, the aim of which is to disarm Hezbollah and expel Syria from Lebanon.

A striking phenomenon in this context is related to the question of the different ways in which Hezbollah is perceived in Lebanon and in the EU. In Lebanon, Hezbollah, or 'the resistance', is a mass movement that possesses seats in the Parliament and is regarded by its supporters as the sole successful challenger of Israel in its many wars since 1948. Hezbollah is on the US list of terror organizations, but not on the EU terrorist list, even though Hezbollah in European public discourse is often perceived as a terrorist movement.

It might, therefore, prove somewhat controversial in the Lebanese context that the Action Plan has been agreed upon by the Lebanese government, the government of Siniora. The Action Plan is ambiguous regarding the terror issue and, as far as Hezbollah is concerned, not in accordance with Lebanese realities. The different underlying interpretations of the future role of Hezbollah might inhibit progress as regards the EU playing a role in promoting democracy in Lebanon as long as the EU is reluctant to approach this in a Lebanese context highly important Shi'ite organization. Progress is furthermore prevented as long as the official Lebanon more or less finds itself in a permanent state of political crisis, in which the Hezbollah is playing a crucial role.

In addition to previous mention in this article of low-level contacts between European embassies to Lebanon and Hezbollah (in the section entitled 'The Lebanese Elites and the 'Dual Power' of Lebanon'), there have been only sporadic contacts between EU officials and members of the Hezbollah. In connection with the presidential election process in Lebanon in 2007 and 2008, members of the European Parliament's Foreign Affairs Committee visited Lebanon to urge the Lebanese to find a solution to the president issue. During those visits, they met representatives from the majority and the opposition.

Regional and international issues

Some sections of the ENP documents contain elements pointing to a more regionalist approach, and the EU–Lebanon Action Plan is no exception. The subtitle of the section concerning regional and international issues is to 'strengthen dialogue and cooperation on regional and international issues, conflict prevention and crisis management and common security threats in accordance with national law', which shows that the broader EU foreign policy interests in the region are explicitly present in the bilateral setup of the EU–Lebanon Action Plan. Some of the issues agreed upon are dependent on developments within processes where no guarantee of progress can be presumed. Examples of this can be seen in relation to the Middle East Peace Process (MEPP), within which the EU and Lebanon will further develop co-operation 'with the ultimate objective of reaching a just, comprehensive and durable peace in accordance with the relevant UN resolutions', and even more explicit within Mediterranean cooperation: 'Promote the objective of reaching, once conditions are favourable, a Euro-Mediterranean Peace and Stability Charter.'[54]

The regional dimension of internal conflicts in Lebanon is not only a question of political influence. Another important aspect concerns the traditional role of Lebanon as the financial centre of the eastern Mediterranean and, to some degree, of the Middle East. This role is dependent on external investments and support as well as an economic policy of the Lebanese government that contributes to solving the long-standing problems of foreign debt and low growth rates. The relation between France and Lebanon, which for years was maintained by a personal friendship between Jacques Chirac and Rafiq Hariri, is challenged by political instability in Lebanon and the more dominant role of the opposition.

French interests in the Levant date back to the situation in the Middle East between the two World Wars, where French suzerainty created the confessional system in Lebanon based on the census of 1932. French dominance has since then been very much reduced, but France still plays an important role in discussing the fate of Lebanon in international fora, such as the UN, and in promoting Lebanon's economic interests. Before the Paris III meetings in January 2007, entitled 'Recovery, Reconstruction and Reform, International Conference for Support to Lebanon', the French President Jacques Chirac had already announced that France would support Lebanon with a loan of €500 m.[55] It was important for Chirac to show the international media that France, Lebanon's traditional ally, had not forgotten it. It was not only a question of economic support; by giving Chirac a political reputation for providing important funding for westernized Beirut, it was also an attempt to relaunch France as an important player in the Levant.

José Manuel Barroso, President of the European Commission, promised to provide assistance of €400 m and Condoleezza Rice, US Secretary of State, promised on behalf of the US, to support rebuilding projects in Lebanon with US$770 m. All in all, the Paris meeting ended with gathering a sum of US$4.3 billion, an impressive amount, but still far from what was needed for the reconstruction efforts. The war of 2006, furthermore, had the effect that foreign investors became more reluctant to get involved in joint projects in Lebanon. Support from abroad was important for a government that was under heavy pressure from the fraught domestic political situation, but it was not necessarily a positive outcome for the government to receive financial support from western states, although support from France was less problematic than support from the US. Indeed, Hezbollah did try to exploit the situation in its rhetoric towards the Siniora government,[56] prioritizing their interests as an opposition force rather than – in this case – the economic interests of Lebanon.

The resemblance between the ENP documents and the regionalist perspective of the Barcelona process has to do with the fact that the Action Plan is dealing with issues that go beyond the national level – an example being the MEPP. However it is also important to note that the vague character and more discretionary language of several sections of the EU–Lebanon Action Plan entails, that the difference between the bilateralist approach of the ENP and the regionalist approach of the Barcelona process gradually disappears.[57] There is no operational language on democratic conditionality; no benchmarking or schedule for progress in the Action Plan.

Conclusion: EU democracy promotion and the ENP

Very little is said in the EU–Lebanon Action Plan about the foreign policy challenges concerning the influence of other Middle Eastern states in Lebanon, i.e. the regional dimensions. The role of Iran and its influence on the status and power of Hezbollah are only indirectly touched upon, even though, as shown, this is relevant to the EU's chances of influencing the Lebanese polity. These issues are mentioned in the background material, the *Country Report* and indirectly in the Country Strategy Paper and the National Indicative Programme. The international dimensions, including the role of the US, are also touched upon in the background analyses, whereas in the implementation documents, the regional and international dimensions, by and large, are absent.

Foreign policy dimensions are explicit in the Action Plan as far as the economic aspects are concerned, this being in accordance with the EU's practice of donating generously to reconstruction efforts. Thus, adopting the Action Plan has not contributed to changing the image of the EU in Lebanon. There is a strange vagueness about the heterogeneous or even diffuse focus on issues in the document. Therefore, it can be questioned if the EU is actually interested in investing its foreign policy resources in promoting democracy in Lebanon.

The reconstruction of Lebanon after the Civil War looked for a long time, despite setbacks and all kinds of obstacles, to be moving in a positive direction. But in the period after the assassination of Rafik Hariri in February 2005, the situation deteriorated as a result of the many subsequent assassinations, the war of July–August 2006, and the political crisis of 2007–2008. In this complex political situation, the EU and Lebanon adopted the ENP Action Plan in 2006–2007. The Action Plan covers a wide range of important issues in Lebanon, but it is in many ways a defensive plan. Analysis of the plan shows an absence of operational language concerning democratic conditionality and leads to the conclusion that the EU, in contrast to its democracy promotion agenda, is pursuing a pragmatic, realist agenda. The EU does not attempt to confront deficiencies in the Lebanese political system, and by using ambiguous and non-binding passages, hides its neglect of its democracy promotion ambitions.

As discussed, it is difficult to avoid the impression that some of the important questions dealt with in the Action Plan are not in reality considered solvable, but will have to be dealt with in connection with processes which are not necessarily interconnected or even affected, even if a closer cooperation between the EU and Lebanon was developed. The MEPP or the French agenda promoting a Mediterranean Union in the summer of 2008 can be mentioned as examples.[58] It is, furthermore, shown that the EU, through its ENP Action Plan is focusing on its own security, particularly within the section of the plan that covers preventing and combating terrorism.

There is a discrepancy between the way the Hezbollah is perceived in the EU and in Lebanon. The EU cannot in the long term exclude important parties in Lebanon in its attempts to promote democracy. Considering the role of Hezbollah in Lebanon, the movement will have to be part of future progress in EU–Lebanese political dialogue.

As pointed out in the section entitled 'The Lebanese elites and the "dual power" of Lebanon', the EU is facing a dilemma in Lebanon, one which relates to the consociational democratic system, the 'dual power' situation, and the composition of the elites in Lebanon. Pursuing its democracy promotion agenda, the EU might contribute to a strengthening of Hezbollah, especially if the democratic deficiencies of the Ta'if Agreement are addressed and altered. Members of the Lebanese elites know that a change of the system would lead to political changes affecting their power, and hence they do not want to open a scenario of this kind.

The 'dual power' situation in Lebanon is an obstacle for the EU in the sense that the EU has difficulties dealing with an entity like Hezbollah and its 'dual identity': sharing political power with other actors in Lebanon, maintaining a status as '*the* resistance', and at the same time pursuing short- and long-term political Islam agendas. The 'foreign policy relations' of the Hezbollah with Iran and Syria add to these difficulties, and are another reason why the EU has half-heartedly supported the political establishment behind the Siniora government, in a Lebanon with all its unsolved sectarian, social, and political conflicts. The EU policy on Lebanon is launched in the Action Plan as a normative enterprise. However, the EU is also in Lebanon managing its conflicts of interest with other regional players in the region, acting as a realist actor in normative clothes.

Notes

1. Del Sarto and Schumacher, 'From EMP to ENP'; Bicchi, 'Our Size Fits All'; Pace, *The Politics of Regional Identity;* Dannreuther, 'Recasting the Barcelona Process'.
2. Dannreuther, 'Recasting the Barcelona Process', 46.
3. The negotiations with Lebanon on an EU–Lebanon Action Plan were concluded in May 2006, just before the start of the July–August hostilities.
4. Dannreuther, 'Recasting the Barcelona Process'.

5. European Commission, *European Neighbourhood Policy EU–Lebanon Action Plan*.
6. This is discussed in Bicchi, *European Foreign Policy Making*. See also Seeberg, 'European Security and the "Clash of Civilisations"'.
7. See for instance Jones and Emerson, 'European Neighbourhood Policy in the Mashreq Countries'; Herman, 'An Action Plan or a Plan for Action?'; Del Sarto, 'Wording and Meaning(s)'.
8. Emerson and Youngs, 'Political Islam and the European Neighbourhood Policy', 5.
9. Rees and Aldrich, 'Contending Cultures of Counterterrorism'.
10. Youngs, *Europe and the Middle East*. For an introduction to Hezbollah, see the section 'Hezbollah and the 'Dual Power' of Lebanon' in this article.
11. El-Husseini, 'Lebanon: Building Political Dynasties'.
12. See Waterbury, 'Democracy Without Democrats?'.
13. Hinnebusch, 'Authoritarian Persistence, Democratization Theory and the Middle East'.
14. Ibid., 391.
15. Ibid., 389.
16. Perthes adds, in defining the politically relevant elites, that they 'contribute to defining political norms and values, and directly influence political discourse on strategic issues'. See Perthes, 'Politics and Elite Change in the Arab World', 5.
17. El-Husseini, 'Lebanon: Building Political Dynasties', 241.
18. Ibid., 261.
19. For an introduction to the emergence of Hezbollah in Lebanon, see Norton, *Hezbollah. A Short History*.
20. Jones, *Negotiating Change. The New Politics of the Middle East*, 9.
21. Ibid., 247.
22. Kamali, *Revolutionary Iran. Civil Society and State in the Modernization Process*.
23. Ibid., 203. See also Schirazi, *The Constitution of Iran*.
24. See Skovgaard-Petersen, 'Democratization and the New Arab Media', 97.
25. In developing this concept of a 'dual power' in Lebanon I was inspired by Becker, 'The Struggle for Power in Lebanon and the Middle East', http://www.globalresearch.ca/index.php?context=viewArticle&code=BEC20061210&articleId=4117. See also the paper by political analyst Kammourieh, 'Hezbollah's "Dual Legitimacy": Origins, Evolutions and Vulnerabilities', http://artsci.wustl.edu/~ppri/StuConf07Papers/kammourieh.doc
26. See Byman, *Deadly Connections. States that Sponsor Terrorism*, 93.
27. Weber, *The Theory of Social and Economic Organization*, 154.
28. See Norton, 'The Role of Hezbollah'. See also Norton, *Hezbollah. A Short History*.
29. Reported by Arabicnews.com, 12 September 2006, http://www.arabicnews.com
30. See Nasr, *The Shia Revival. How Conflicts within Islam Will Shape the Future*. See also Nasr, 'When the Shiites Rise'. Note the comment by Faour, 'Counting Shiites'.
31. Commission of the European Communities, *Commission Staff Working Paper. Annex to: 'European Neighbourhood Policy'. Country Report. Lebanon*, http://ec.europa.eu/world/enp/pdf/country/lebanon_country_report_2005_en.pdf
32. Commission of the European Communities, 'European Neighbourhood Policy–EU-Lebanon Action Plan'.
33. Ibid., 4.
34. Ibid.
35. Gambill, 'Syria after Lebanon: Hooked on Lebanon'.
36. The central problems of the Lebanese economy are well documented in the Lebanese section of *The Middle East and North Africa 2008*.
37. Evidence in Israel in the aftermath of the war has, according to Telhami, shown that Israel for years worried about the build-up of strike capability by Hezbollah and that,

38. Norton, 'The Role of Hezbollah', 485.
therefore, Israel had for long time been preparing contingency plans to attack these capabilities. See Telhami, 'Lebanese Identity and Israeli Security', 21.
39. Telhami, 'Lebanese Identity and Israeli Security', 23.
40. Ibid.
41. For a thorough description of the consociational democracy of Lebanon, see Ziadeh, *Sectarianism and Intercommunal Nation-Building in Lebanon*.
42. In his campaigning before and during the elections in May–June 2005, Michel Aoun called for the abolition of 'political feudalism and the religious system that dates back to the 19th century'. *Jordan Times*, 12 May 2005.
43. For a description of the alliance, see Seeberg, 'Fragmented Loyalties. Nation and Democracy in Lebanon'.
44. El-Solh, *Lebanon and Arabism*.
45. Hanf, *Coexistence in Wartime Lebanon* and 'The Sceptical Nation.'
46. Hanf, *Coexistence in Wartime Lebanon*. For an analysis with focus on the contradictions within the Shi'ite population, see Norton, *Amal and the Shi'a*.
47. Telhami, 'Lebanese Identity and Israeli Security', 26.
48. Ibid., 5.
49. European Commission. *European Union Election Observatory Mission. Parliamentary Elections. Lebanon 2005. Final Report.* http://ec.europa.eu/external_relations/human_rights/eu_election_ass_observ/lebanon/final_report.pdf
50. Commission of the European Communities: European Neighbourhood Policy, *EU-Lebanon Action Plan*, 7.
51. Seeberg, *EU and the Mediterranean*.
52. See El-Khoury, 'Lebanese Palestinian Dialoque Aids Refugee Prospects', http://www.euromesco.net/images/a_elkhoury.pdf
53. Ibid., 8.
54. Ibid.
55. 'Impact Of Paris III'.
56. See Quilty, 'Winter of Lebanon's Discontent', 7, http://www.merip.org/mero/mero012607.html
57. This perspective on the ENP is also developed in Youngs, *Europe and the Middle East*, 111ff. The impression that the issue of conditionality within the framework of the ENP is not sustained by precise benchmarking is supported by interviews by the author with senior EU officials in April/May 2006, Brussels.
58. See Aliboni et al., 'Putting the Mediterranean Union in Perspective'.

Bibliography

Aliboni, Roberto, *et al*. 'Putting the Mediterranean Union in Perspective'. *EuroMeSCo Paper* 68 (2008): 1–33.
Bicchi, Federica. *European Foreign Policy Making Toward the Mediterranean*. New York, Basingstoke: Palgrave Macmillan, 2007.
Bicchi, Federica. 'Our Size Fits All: Normative Power Europe and the Mediterranean'. *Journal of European Public Policy* 13 (2006): 286–303.
Byman, Daniel. *Deadly Connections. States that Sponsor Terrorism*. Cambridge: Cambridge University Press, 2005.
Commission of the European Communities. 'European Neighbourhood Policy EU–Lebanon Action Plan'. Brussels: European Commission, 2007.
Dannreuther, Roland. 'Recasting the Barcelona Process: Europe and the Middle East'. *EU and the Mediterranean. Foreign Policy and Security*, ed. Peter Seeberg, 38–58. Odense: University Press of Southern Denmark, 2007.

Del, Sarto, and A. Rafaella. 'Wording and Meaning(s): EU–Israeli Political Cooperation according to the ENP Action Plan'. *Mediterranean Politics* 12 (2007): 59–75.

Del, Sarto, A. Rafaella, and Tobias Schumacher. 'From EMP to ENP: What's at Stake with the European Neighbourhood Policy towards the Southern Mediterranean?'. *European Foreign Affairs Review* 10 (2005): 17–38.

El-Husseini, Rola. 'Lebanon: Building Political Dynasties'. *Arab Elites. Negotiating the Politics of Change*, ed. Volker Perthes, 239–66. London: Lynne Rienner Publishers, 2004.

El-Solh, Raghid. *Lebanon and Arabism. National Identity and State Formation*. London: I.B. Tauris, 2004.

Emerson, Michael, and Richard Youngs. 'Political Islam and the European Neighbourhood Policy'. *Political Islam and European Foreign Policy. Perspectives From Muslim Democrats of the Mediterranean*, ed. Michael Emerson and Richard Youngs. Brussels: Centre for European Policy Studies, 2007.

European Commission. 'European Neighbourhood Policy EU–Lebanon Action Plan'. Brussels: European Commission, 2007.

Faour, Muhammad A. 'Counting Shiites'. *Foreign Affairs* 86 (2007).

Gambill, Gary. 'Syria after Lebanon: Hooked on Lebanon'. *Middle East Quarterly* 12 (2005): 35–42.

Hanf, Theodor. *Coexistence in Wartime Lebanon. Decline of a State and Rise of a Nation*. Oxford: Oxford University Press, 1993.

Hanf, Theodor. 'The Sceptical Nation. Opinions and Attitudes Twelve Years after the End of the War'. *Lebanon in Limbo. Postwar Society and State in an Uncertain Regional Environment*, ed. Hanf Theodor and Salam Nawaf. Baden-Baden: Nomos Verlagsgesellschaft, 2003.

Herman, Lior. 'An Action Plan or a Plan for Action? Israel and the European Neighbourhood Policy'. *Mediterranean Politics* 11 (2006): 371–94.

Hinnebusch, Raymond. 'Authoritarian Persistence, Democratization Theory and the Middle East: An Overview and Critique'. *Democratization* 13 (2006): 373–95.

'Impact Of Paris III'. *Middle East Monitor (East Med)* 16 (2006).

Jones, Jeremy. *Negotiating Change. The New Politics of the Middle East*. London & New York: I.B. Tauris, 2007.

Jones, Stephen, and Michael Emerson. 'European Neighbourhood Policy in the Mashreq Countries. Enhanced Prospects for Reform'. *CEPS Working Document* 229 (2005): 1–27.

Kamali, Masoud. *Revolutionary Iran. Civil Society and State in the Modernization Process*. Aldershot: Ashgate, 1998.

Nasr, Vali. 'The Shia Revival. How Conflicts within Islam will Shape the Future'. New York: Norton, 2006.

Nasr, Vali. 'When the Shiites Rise'. *Foreign Affairs* 85 (2006): 58–74.

Norton, Augustus Richard. *Amal and the Shi'a. Struggle for the Soul of Lebanon*. Austin: University of Texas Press, 1987.

Norton, Augustus Richard. *Hezbollah. A Short History*. Princeton: Princeton University Press, 2007.

Norton, Augustus Richard. 'The Role of Hezbollah in Lebanese Domestic Politics'. *The International Spectator* 42 (2007): 475–91.

Pace, Michelle. *The Politics of Regional Identity. Meddling with the Mediterranean*. Abingdon: Routledge, 2006.

Perthes, Volker. 'Politics and Elite Change in the Arab World'. *Arab Elites. Negotiating the Politics of Change*, ed. Volker Perthes, 1–34. London: Lynne Rienner Publishers, 2004.

Rees, Wyn, and Richard J. Aldrich. 'Contending Cultures of Counterterrorism: Transatlantic Divergence or Convergence'. *International Affairs* 81 (2005): 905–23.

Schirazi, Ashgar. *The Constitution of Iran. Politics and the State in the Islamic Republic.* London: I.B. Tauris, 1998.

Seeberg, Peter. *EU and the Mediterranean. Foreign Policy and Security.* Odense: University Press of Southern Denmark, 2007.

Seeberg, Peter. 'European Security and the "Clash of Civilisations" Divergence in the Policies of France, Germany and the UK towards the Mediterranean'. In *Clash or Cooperation of Civilizations? Overlapping Integration and Identities*, ed. Zank Wolfgang. London: Ashgate, 2008.

Seeberg, Peter. 'Fragmented Loyalties. Nation and Democracy in Lebanon after the Cedar Revolution'. *Working Paper Series, Centre for Contemporary Middle East Studies. University of Southern Denmark* 8 (2007).

Skovgaard-Petersen, Jakob. 'Democratization and the New Arab Media'. *Democratization and Development. New Political Strategies for the Middle East*, ed. Jung Dietrich. New York: Palgrave, 2006.

Telhami, Shibley. 'Lebanese Identity and Israeli Security in the Shadows of the 2006 War'. *Current History* 106 (2007).

The Middle East and North Africa 2008. London: Routledge, 2007.

Waterbury, John. 'Democracy Without Democrats? The Potential for Political Liberalization in the Middle East'. *Democracy Without Democrats. The Renewal of Politics in the Muslim World*, ed. Salame Ghassan. London: I.B. Tauris, 1994.

Weber, Max. *The Theory of Social and Economic Organization.* New York: The Free Press, 1964.

Youngs, Richard. *Europe and the Middle East. In the shadow of September 11.* London: Lynne Rienner Publishers, 2006.

Ziadeh, Hanna. *Sectarianism and Intercommunal Nation-Building in Lebanon.* London: Hurst & Co, 2006.

Constraints on the promotion of the rule of law in Egypt: insights from the 2005 judges' revolt

Sarah Wolff*

Department of International Relations, London School of Economics and Political Science, London, WC2 2AE, UK

During the 2005 elections in Egypt, newspapers around the world widely reported on the 'judges' revolt'. The judiciary, supported by civil society, confronted the executive by denouncing the fraudulent results of the constitutional referendum, as well as 2005 presidential and legislative elections. The 'judges' revolt' was a test case for external promoters of the rule of law in Egypt. Following a detailed analysis of the events of 2005 in Egypt and the case of the judges' revolt, this article aims to understand the reasons for the EU's difficulties in promoting rule of law in Egypt. This article reveals that the EU's action in the field of rule of law promotion in Egypt was constrained by two categories of factors: 'exogenous factors' related to the external promoters of rule of law (the EU, the US) and then 'endogenous factors' related to the domestic context. At an exogenous level, it is possible to distinguish three main factors interacting with rule of law promotion. Firstly, the EU's intergovernmental nature as a foreign policy actor weakens its position as a rule of law promoter. Secondly, ongoing negotiations over the ENP Action Plan (Egyptian–EU relationship) at the time of the revolt, coupled with a third factor (Egyptian–US relationship), have compelled the EU to opt for an integrated approach towards promoting rule of law in Egypt. Then, at an endogenous level, the instrumentalization by the Egyptian regime of external aid funding in the field of human rights and democratization complicates the EU's activities in the country, compelling the EU to look for strategies that bypass domestic constraints.

Introduction

Not only is the concept of the rule of law central to the European Union's (EU) common values, along with the principles of liberty, democracy, respect for human rights, and fundamental freedoms,[1] but it is also at the heart of the EU's

---

*The views expressed here are solely those of the author and do not reflect those of the European Commission.

external relations. Originally implemented within the context of its development policy,[2] rule of law promotion has become a foreign policy instrument that drives EU diplomacy and Common and Foreign Security Policy (CFSP).[3] More importantly, rule of law is one of the Copenhagen criteria[4] and, therefore, is used as one of the EU's political conditionality instruments towards countries aspiring to become members of the EU, as well as towards neighbouring countries. Lately, it has also become a buzzword in EU foreign policy discourse, which maintains that if the rule of law is implemented in a country, then everything is possible, from reform to democratization: 'like a product sold on late-night television, the rule of law is touted as able to accomplish everything from improving human rights to enabling economic growth to helping to win the war on terror'.[5]

But what does the term rule of law actually cover? Although the EU frequently resorts to the concept in its policy documents, there is little consensus on its significance and, hence, on the ways to promote it abroad. As Rachel Kleinfeld Belton observes, there are two ways to interpret rule of law. The first emphasizes 'the *ends* that the rule of law is intended to serve within society (such as upholding law and order, or providing predictable and efficient judgments)', whereas the second insists upon the *means*, namely the 'institutional attributes believed necessary to actuate the rule of law (such as comprehensive laws, well-functioning courts, and trained law enforcement agencies)'.[6]

Diplomats and lawyers have retained the latter definition. The problem, however, is that the *means* approach ignores the quality of rule of law and the adequacy of a functioning legal system with democratic principles. Rule of law should be:

> more than just forcing governments to respect their legal obligations. The rule of law implies that law and legal considerations become part of the political process itself, shaping and constraining political decision-making. . . . An effective rule of law must also be legitimate and thus responsible to democratic concerns.[7]

Applied to the context of the Mediterranean region, the *means* approach seems inadequate for responding to the recent phenomenon of liberal authoritarianisms. After 10 years of Euro-Mediterranean Partnership (EMP), the Middle East and North African region (MENA) has not moved towards any substantial democratic reforms. While European discourse acknowledges the modernization and the openness of some regimes, such as those in Morocco and Jordan, the majority of the Arab world is far from presenting the conditions for a democratic transition. Rather, autocratic regimes have been able to adjust themselves to globalization through minor economic reforms, which have enabled them to tie the loyalties of the emerging class of entrepreneurs. These cosmetic changes have led to the appearance of different varieties of autocratisms[8] and Mediterranean autocracies have successfully adapted to their particular environments.[9]

EU member states and the United States are not totally independent of this development, since their policies have, traditionally, indirectly favoured the stability of authoritarian elites, notably in the 1960s, when the rise of pan-Arabism[10] was perceived as a threat. Today, this trend persists, pan-Arabism having been replaced by Islamism, and acts as a structural constraint on the current relationship between the EU and its Mediterranean neighbours.

The *means* approach of democracy promotion still very much characterizes the situation in Egypt. Since 2005, Egypt's autocratic regime has been challenged by different sections of society, such as labour forces, human rights activists, and the Muslim Brotherhood. The judges' revolt is one of the most striking instances of such a challenge and constituted a test of the EU's rule of law promotion programmes, given that an independent judiciary constitutes one of the pillars of a democratic transition. Based on the case study of the judges' revolt, this article reveals that several factors constrained EU rule of law promotion in Egypt. These factors can be classified into two types: 'exogenous factors' related to the external promoters of rule of law (the EU, the US) and 'endogenous factors' related to the domestic context. At an exogenous level, it is possible to distinguish three main factors interacting with rule of law promotion. Firstly, the EU's intergovernmental nature as a foreign policy actor tends to weaken its position as a rule of law promoter. Secondly, ongoing negotiations over the ENP Action Plan at the time of the revolt (the Egyptian–EU relationship), coupled with a third factor (the Egyptian–US relationship), have compelled the EU to opt for an integrated approach of promoting rule of law in Egypt, which includes gender reform, justice reform, socio-economic rights, etc. Then, at an endogenous level, the instrumentalization by the Egyptian regime of external aid funding in the field of human rights and democratization complicates the EU's activities in the country, compelling the EU to look for strategies to bypass domestic constraints.

The judges' revolt or the 'integrated dissidents': a permanent feature of Egyptian politics

Before turning to the 2005 judges' revolt per se, a brief historical overview of the tense relationship between the Egyptian judiciary and the executive is necessary. Despite the opening of a window of opportunity for foreign promoters of rule of law, the EU ran into difficulties in providing the judges and other reform activists with any significant support, even at the mere discursive level.

Egyptian judges, duly depicted as 'integrated dissidents' of the regime by Holger Albrecht, have experienced an abiding conflict with the executive since the second world war. Tensions were exacerbated in the context of the 2005 presidential and parliamentary elections, which gave the judges an opportunity to contest the legality of the elections. As Albrecht notes, 'a telling assessment of the Egyptian judicial system is that we have independent judges but no independent judiciary'.[11]

The 'judges' massacre' of 1969 constituted a crucial turning point in this unremitting conflict. Following the Judges' Club[12] request to strengthen the independence of the judiciary, President Gamal Abdel Nasser issued several presidential decrees, which led to the subordination of the judiciary to the executive. New institutions were established, such as the Supreme Court, whose members are appointed for three years directly by the president, as well as a Supreme Council of Judicial Organization, headed by the president, which controls the appointment of magistrates.[13] Furthermore, hundreds of judges were forbidden to exercise their functions: hence the expression the 'massacre of the judges'.

Under the leadership of Anwar El Sadat and in the early years of Hosni Mubarak's presidency during the 1980s, administrations striving for some legitimacy granted certain social benefits to the judges, who then became a favoured class in Egyptian society.[14] This is in line with the tradition of the Egyptian executive to accommodate the opposition by allowing for their promotion when needed:

> the regime permits, or even promotes, the emergence of opposition while, at the same time, co-optative and clientelist arrangements serve as the primary control mechanisms. Political opposition in Egypt, thus, serves functions entirely different from those in liberal democracies where opposition comprises an alternative to the incumbents in a competitive contest for political power.[15]

The writing of a new Constitution in 1971, as well as the reform of the 1972 law,[16] empowering the Supreme Council of Judicial Organization to nominate and promote magistrates, entrusted the judiciary with some autonomy. The judges resumed their role of guarantors of the rule of law and allowed, through their jurisprudence, political parties from the opposition to be legalized.[17] Several judgements of the State Security Courts denounced the torture of Islamist activists, accused of political violence following the assassination of Sadat in 1981.[18] Since then, through a prolific jurisprudence, the Supreme Constitutional Court was able to guarantee the right to establish syndicates on a democratic basis, the right to form political parties, the right of a person not to join a political party, and the right to criticize public officials and public servants.[19]

This brief historical overview brings into focus the tense relationship between the executive and the judiciary in Egypt and the ensuing deficiencies in the rule of law. Since the implementation of the State of Emergency law by Mubarak in 1981, the situation has worsened. This legal exceptionalism allows the government to perform regular, arbitrary detention and to torture 'suspects' who are considered a 'threat' to national security and public order. Fair trials are virtually non-existent, seriously endangering the rule of law in the country.[20] Exploiting the opportunity of the war in Iraq and the global context of the fight against terrorism, the Egypt's People's Assembly renewed the law of emergency on 30 April 2006 until the future adoption of an anti-terrorist law. This was denounced by non-governmental organizations (NGOs) activists, who believed that this would lead to a normalization of the emergency law and the introduction of these exceptional and transitory measures into ordinary law.[21]

This tension between the executive and the judiciary takes place within the wider context of a securitization process. The Egyptian state has indeed evolved from a time in the 1960s when it was willing to provide security (economic, social, etc.) to its citizens, through the movement of pan-Arabism inspired by socialism, to a situation where the state has become a security provider for an autocratic regime rather than for its citizens.[22] It also denotes a permanent concern of the Egyptian regime to legitimize its stance against the presence of an Islamist threat, since the government has not been able to provide socio-economic security to its citizens, as the latest labour strikes, in September 2007, in the textile industry demonstrated.[23] Instead, the Egyptian government has developed a securitization discourse whereby it has turned some entities (such as the Muslim Brothers) into a threat. This securitization has led the Egyptian regime to justify exceptional measures that suspend normal rules of the political game, as theorized by the Copenhagen school.[24] Officially, the state of emergency law is used in the fight against terrorism. In reality, though, it enables the government to tackle 'domestic' problems, such as the Bedouins in the Sinai and the Muslim Brotherhood, and to muzzle political opposition. An example of the excessive and dangerous character of legal exceptionalism occurred in the aftermath of the terrorist attacks of Taba in October 2003, when 38 persons were killed and 135 injured. Following these events, the Egyptian police arrested more than 5,000 women and men in the cities of El Arish and El Sheikh-Zwaid. The Fédération Internationale des Droits de l'Homme (FIDH) reported systematic torture; some of those arrested died while in custody, and many were hospitalized. Those unlawfully detained remained in custody without any judicial process.[25]

The 2005 elections and the judges' revolt: is 'enough' enough?

Against the backdrop of unrelenting breaches of the rule of law while under pressure from the US government, President Mubarak announced his intention to hold the first, multiparty elections in 2005, a landmark decision in 24 years of his presidency.[26] Even though the move hinted at reform, the Mubarak regime sought some guarantees. Although other parties were able to propose presidential candidates for 2005, the criteria adopted for the elections 'were so stringent that no party other than the NDP [National Democratic Party] would be able to meet them in the next election, to be held in 2011 or earlier (should Mubarak not finish his current term)'.[27]

Undoubtedly, one of the main concerns of Mubarak and the NDP was to prevent the Muslim Brotherhood, which is still a prohibited organization, to run in future elections. Mubarak was re-elected with 88% of the votes on 7 September 2005. Those results must be treated with caution since, according to a report of the House of Commons, out of the 32 million voters registered, only seven million went to the polls.[28] The closest runner-up was Ayman Nour, the leader of Al Ghad Party (The Tomorrow Party), who would later be imprisoned for forgery of signatures to create his party, with 'officially' 7.3% of the votes. Later in 2005, during the parliamentary elections, the Muslim Brotherhood, whose candidates were obliged to stand as independents in Egypt's first multiparty elections, won 88 seats out of a total of 454, almost 20% of the seats, an unprecedented phenomenon in the Egyptian context, turning the Muslim Brothers into the biggest opposition group to Mubarak's NDP, and hence normalizing the Brotherhood into Egyptian political life.[29] The electoral year was punctuated by fraud, as reported by NGO activists. Accordingly, ballot boxes were emptied out in the Nile, voters did not have voter cards, and the indelible ink to mark voters' fingers was not indelible.[30]

Parallel to the elections, some judges voiced a desire to supervise the entire electoral process and took the opportunity of the presidential campaign to request full independence from the executive. For the 2005 presidential elections, a new electoral commission, composed of magistrates (50%) and other public figures close to the government, was established to supervise the ballot. Although part of the judiciary agreed to such an institutional novelty, some judges pointed to the fact that 'their integrity [was] being used to lend credibility to a process over which they have only a limited control'.[31]

In the light of unsatisfactory responses to their requests and with the proof of alleged fraud in their hands, the judges, led by two vice presidents of the Court of Cassation, Mahmoud Mekki and Hisham Bastawisi, publicly denounced the vote-rigging,[32] prompting the mobilization of a huge civil society movement. The regime put in place its repressive mechanisms: 'protestors were physically attacked by the Egyptian police during the demonstrations in support of the judges and the Interior Ministry announced that all such demonstrations would be deemed illegal'.[33] The protests by Egyptian civil society created a pretext for the authorities to arrest 254 members of the Muslim Brothers as well as activists from Kifaya, a high-profile protest group whose name means 'Enough'.[34] The two judges were ordered to appear in front of a disciplinary panel on 27 April 2006 for criticizing the fraud. According to an Amnesty International (AI) report, 'Mahmoud Mekki was cleared and Hisham Bastawisi was reprimanded and denied his upcoming promotion'.[35] They benefited from an impressive and popular mobilization by civil society, ranging from trade unions to opposition parties. On March 2007, Article 88 of the Egyptian Constitution was amended by a referendum and removed the overseeing of the elections from the judiciary to an electoral commission, hence 'effectively squelch[ing] efforts at more open and fair elections'.[36]

To summarize, this section has stressed the fundamental role played by the judges in the emergence of a fragile rule of law in Egypt. Despite intimidation, different courts have attempted to remain independent and have provided an important set of law cases, enabling the creation of some niches of rule of law under an authoritarian regime. The 2005 elections constituted another episode in the long-running conflict between the executive and the judiciary. This time, however, the judges were not isolated dissidents and were supported by a heterogeneous, civil society movement headed by Kifaya and the Muslim Brothers, who claimed to have had 'enough' of the current regime.[37] This reformist dynamism from various political activists illustrates that Egypt possesses the fundamental domestic ingredients to move towards some democratic reforms. It is, therefore,

S. Wolff

legitimate to question the EU's reaction to such political dynamics, given the importance of rule of law and democracy promotion in its official discourse.[38]

Exogenous constraints on EU rule of law promotion in Egypt

Democracy and rule of law promotion have usually been at the heart of the EU's strategy in the Arab world. Proclaimed as objectives of the CFSP which shall 'develop and consolidate democracy and the rule of law, and respect for human rights and fundamental freedoms',[39] these values have at their disposal instruments ranging from positive and negative conditionality to democracy aid, as well as political dialogue and election observation.[40]

In political science discourse, the opening of 'policy windows' refers to moments when opportunities to launch or re-launch some policy initiatives arise. Policy windows usually open for only a short period and it is argued that 'if the participants cannot or do not take advantage of these opportunities, they must bide their time until the next opportunity comes along'.[41] Hence, one could have foreseen from the Egyptian judges' revolt and from the events of 2005 the opening of a policy window for European diplomats to exert an influence over the course of reforms. Since then, demonstrations in the streets of Cairo have continued: angry textile workers and hungry Egyptian citizens have manifested their discontent with the current regime, which is not able to provide them with employment and food.[42] This window of opportunity for external democracy and rule of law promoters, such as the EU and its member states, was nonetheless difficult to exploit due to various factors. Firstly, the prevalence of intergovernmental modes of governance made it difficult for the European Commission (EC) delegation to take initiatives on its own. Secondly, difficult negotiations over the ENP Action plan complicated the opening of a window of opportunity. Thirdly, geostrategic considerations regarding the Egyptian–US relationship as well as Egypt's own geostrategic position have to be taken into account. The following three sub-sections will explore these structural factors in greater depth.

EU's institutional structure constraints

To begin with, let us examine the problems posed by the intergovernmental nature of the EU as a foreign policy promoter. The revolt of the judges has shown that the position of EC delegations was weakened by the structural deficiencies of the CFSP. In general, the EC's delegations suffer from the fact that they represent 'embassies without a state',[43] conducting 'diplomacy without a flag',[44] but even more from the fact that the EU does not possess a traditional foreign policy. Despite its evolution since the entry into force of the Treaty of Maastricht in 1993, the EU's foreign policy is still mainly the product of national foreign policies of member states, which sometimes utilize the EU level to promote their own domestic interests. For outsiders it is difficult to identify where their interlocutors belong, in the EC delegation or in the different national embassies in the country. Troikas and coordination meetings with other European embassies are regularly held, sometimes also with other international donors in order to ensure coherence, and these therefore oscillate between 'autonomy' and 'integrated action' within the group of European diplomats.[45] Since the 2000 reform of EC external aid, many competences have been devolved to EC delegations in terms of identifying, formulating, and implementing external aid. But this autonomy is counterbalanced by the fact that the main function of the EC delegation is, 'to co-ordinate, energize and develop what is predominantly a system of intergovernmental co-operation'.[46] In that sense, when important crises occur in a country, such as the revolt of the judges in Egypt in 2005, the delegation could only rely on its coordinating power to ensure at least a minimum of cohesion between the member states in responding to the situation.

In spite of these institutional constraints, and in the wake of the mobilization of the Egyptian population, the EC delegation in Cairo issued a statement in which it denounced the repressive mechanisms of the Egyptian authorities. Drafted under the leadership of the head of the EC delegation,[47] this statement unambiguously pointed out the overreaction of the Egyptian police forces and their breaches of rule of law:

> The scale of the police operation and the harsh manner in which these demonstrations have been policed appear as disproportionate. The European Union expresses its concern that many persons taking part in these demonstrations have been arrested and are being held in custody. The European Union is particularly concerned that, according to lawyers of the detainees, a number of those held have been arrested under the provisions of the Emergency Law, for instance without an arrest warrant which is a procedure only authorised under the State of Emergency.[48]

The EU also reiterated its concern that the state of emergency was actually being used to muzzle civil society activists, lawyers, and magistrates, when this law should only be applied for the purposes of countering terrorists and urged 'the Egyptian authorities to limit the application of the law on the state of emergency to cases of terrorism and to end the state of emergency as soon as possible'.[49] An EU official confirmed that, when enquiring about the incident, the Egyptian authorities legitimated their action by affirming that terrorist activists were hiding amongst the crowd.[50]

With respect to the judges' revolt and the mobilization of the population, the EU presidency commented that it was 'tak[ing] note of the judicial supervision of the election and the efforts by civil society groups to observe it. The EU attaches great importance to the role played by civil society groups in the preparation and observation of elections and stands ready to support their efforts'.[51]

The EU–Egyptian ENP Action Plan

A second structural factor of importance was that, in their statements, the EC delegation and the EU presidency had to take into account the fact that at the time of the judges' revolt the EU had just finalized the EU–Egypt association agreement and was painfully negotiating the European Neighbourhood Policy (ENP) Action Plan with Egypt. Those negotiations proved to be more difficult than was initially anticipated by the European Commission. In 2005 the ENP Action Plan, although agreed upon at the EU level, had still not been approved by the Egyptian side. The main point of contention focused, firstly, on the reference to weapons of mass destruction and, secondly, on the reference to a sub-committee for individual cases of human rights. According to an Egyptian diplomat, this situation was the result of a strategic mistake made by the EU with regards to Israel, when the latter refused to establish a human rights subcommittee or an ENP subcommittee on political issues: 'This gave ample reasons to the Arab countries to resist as well'.[52] The final compromise was to give the EU–Egyptian sub-committee the title of 'Human Rights and Democratization: International and Regional Affairs'.

This peculiar situation explains the moderate stance of the EC delegation and of EU member states towards the 'judges' revolt'. The integrated approach and the difficult negotiations over the ENP Action Plan, and in particular on the question of human rights, required some caution from European diplomats in broaching this issue. The ENP Action Plan went through a long process of negotiation, involving high-level actors to solve the crisis over the human rights clause. The cost for the European side of damaging those negotiations would have been probably too high, especially knowing that the ENP Action Plan endorsed an integrated approach towards democratization and human rights by setting up a human rights sub-committee.

The US factor

Thirdly, the EU–Egypt relationship has never been an easy one, given the crucial relationship that Egypt has maintained with the US since the signing of the Camp David Accords in 1978. The Egyptian–US relationship is an important structural factor in the EU's foreign policy towards Egypt. Given its hegemonic position, the US was able to take a different stance towards Egypt. According to a spokes-person at the US State Department, the Nour case revealed 'both a miscarriage of justice by international standards and a setback for the democratic aspirations of the Egyptian people'.[53] Reportedly, the US–Egyptian Free Trade Agreement negotiations were stalled in January 2006, despite the mediating role played by Mubarak at the beginning of 2005 in the Middle East process, which led to the meeting at Sharm el Sheikh. Notwithstanding these criticisms, the Bush adminis-tration, through Congress, substantially increased US annual spending on democ-racy assistance in Egypt from $5 million to $50 million, a strong signal to a 'crucial strategic' partner for the US.[54] It appears that behind US criticism about the lack of political and economic reform in Egypt lay a desire in Washington to signal its disagreement on a series of regional issues, such as the reluctance of Egypt to back the US agenda at the International Atomic Energy Agency and in the UN

Security Council, or to send troops to Iraq: it was a way for the US to build a discourse around democratic conditionality.[55]

This special relationship with the US renders EU leverage quite limited in the Egyptian context. In addition, benefiting from a geostrategic position with the Suez Canal, important gas reserves and its role in the mediation of the Middle East Peace Process, Egypt is an important regional player, which undermines the effectiveness of EU conditionality. The head of the EC delegation himself recognized that Egypt was not in a hurry to engage with the Association Agreement, which took more than seven years to negotiate and two more years to ratify; he also recognized that, despite the fact that the EU and its member states provide more than 36% of total official development aid,[56] there are 'limits to what [the EU] can do'.[57]

At the same time, Egypt is an important trade partner for the EU and has also been the main beneficiary of Mesure d'Accompagnement (MEDA)[58] aid under the Barcelona process, receiving about €1 billion since 1995. The signature of the ENP–Egypt Action plan was accompanied by an aid package of €558 m for the period 2007–2010, mainly directed towards education (€120 m), health (€120 m), support for the institutions and the economic sector (€220 m), and €10 million for governance and human rights (with €10 million explicitly for the Ministry of Justice, €13million for decentralization and €17 m for human rights). In addition to this budget, Egypt is also eligible for the thematic programmes and instruments, including the European Instrument for Democracy and Human Rights (EIDHR).

The EU as a promoter of rule of law in Egypt was, therefore, constrained by the structural deficiencies of CFSP, but also by the difficult negotiations within the ENP Action Plan over the issue of human rights. Also, the position of Egypt as a strategic partner for the US, recipient of its second-largest military aid budget, significantly limits the EU's impact. Further to these considerations of external promoters of rule of law, it is also necessary to look at the domestic situation. The following analysis suggests that national sensitivities can indeed be an additional hurdle.

Endogenous constraints on EU rule of law promotion in Egypt

The EU is considered by some opposition groups as 'a potential partner in the process of democratizing the Egyptian political scene, mainly through the strengthening of civil society autonomy in the face of governmental pressure'.[59] The EU is indeed an important provider of funds worldwide for many of those organizations which depend upon foreign financing resources. In the 2007 reform of EC external cooperation instruments, the EU established the EIDHR[60] for the purpose of supporting local organizations worldwide, although this has certain shortcomings. The next section looks at how, on the Egyptian domestic scene, the instrumentalization of human rights and democratization issues by the current regime to contest the interference of foreign rule of law promoters in domestic affairs adds another layer of complexity to the EU's rule of law promotion.

In response to the Broader Middle East and North Africa (BMENA) initiative by the Bush administration and launched in 2004 in Rabat with the meeting 'Forum for the Future', and following the European Commission's activism led by External Relations Commissioner Chris Patten during his mandate (1999–2004), there have been many projects designed to encourage political reforms in the post-9/11 world. The European Commission elaborated a new instrument called the 'European Initiative for Democracy and Human Rights (EIDHR) Micro Projects',[61] which aimed at supporting 'small-scale human rights and democratization activities carried out by grassroots NGOs'.[62] The micro projects, which were designed in the context of decentralized reform of EU aid, empowered EC delegations by assigning them the responsibility of launching local calls for proposals, selecting projects, drafting contracts, and taking care of the subsequent payments. The key priority identified for the 2002–2004 period worldwide was 'Democracy, Governance and the Rule of Law'. In that context, rule of law projects had the objective of strengthening the effectiveness of the judiciary and the legal sector; raising the awareness of legal rights in civil society; improving access to formal dispute resolution mechanisms; and improving the operation of quasi-judicial bodies, such as national human rights institutions and ombudspersons.[63] Under the EIDHR and MEDA, the EU has promoted rule of law through the modernization of jurisdictions and the training of law enforcement staff.

An example of the EU's tendency to approach democratization in a technical way is the difficulty and occasional counter-productiveness that results from its dealings with the law enforcement agencies of authoritarian governments. Rather than stressing the 'involvement in illicit commercial activities and the "black" or "parallel" economy or crony relationships between senior officers and state managers and their families', the EU prefers, in its rule of law promotion activities, to invest in the training of law enforcement agencies, 'including the instruction in the law and human rights'.[64] However, there is little evidence that these programmes have fundamentally altered 'the nature and purpose of security sector activity, let alone affected the autocratic structure of political power in any meaningful way'.[65]

Also, the overall aid devoted to the EIDHR in the MENA countries has been the smallest share of the total budget of EC cooperation in the region. According to Youngs, while the MENA countries received 12% of the 2001–2004 funds, the African Caribbean and Pacific (ACP) countries and Latin America have respectively received 29% and 23%. Hence, if democratization in the MENA region after 9/11 has been a declared objective of EU policy, in reality the amount devoted to it, compared to the whole EU budget, remained very limited.[66] Paradoxically enough, the Asian continent receives 14% of EIDHR funds while the EU is constantly putting forward the importance of democratization as a source of stability at its borders.

Those weaknesses might be explained *inter alia* by the complex domestic settings which constrain EU action in Egypt. In that sense, the Egyptian regime is well known for utilizing the issue of human rights in order to find new sources of legitimacy. As explained by Abdelrahman, in the 1950s and the 1960s, the Egyptian regime built its legitimacy on the project of (pan)-Arab nationalism, which was used as 'a tool for state-building and for establishing [its] hegemony'; however, the waning primacy of such theories, combined with globalization, incrementally obliged the regime to look into new sources of nationalism, *inter alia*, the denial of human rights abuses formulated by foreign powers.[67] Indeed:

> Since the appearance in the mid-1980s of human rights activists and organisations calling for the recognition of the universality of human rights, which invariably challenges the hegemony of the nation-state and the fiction of the homogeneity of the nation, they have been fiercely resisted by the Egyptian government. The government campaign against them intensified as their numbers grew and their efforts to expose the government's blatant violations of human rights increased – violations which the government persistently denied.[68]

Systematically, human rights activists have been accused of being the Trojan horses of the post-colonialist, Western powers, and any financial aid or political declarations on human rights breaches have been taken as an intrusion into domestic affairs. This view is also shared by many of Egypt's intellectuals, notably the old pan-Arabist and leftist groups, which see foreign aid/intervention as a way to dominate Egypt and its citizens, and all such efforts, therefore, 'undermine people's sense of nationalism from within'.[69] In this context, it is perhaps not surprising that the EU has continued to follow a means approach in its rule of law, democratization, and human rights activities.

The year 2005 marked a turning point for rule of law and democratization promotion in Egypt. The US influence over the course of the 2005 presidential and parliamentarian elections, combined with the prospect of political transition with a possible succession by Gamal Mubarak,[70] led the Egyptian regime to change, if only cosmetically, its discourse on human rights. Initiatives were taken to demonstrate the regime's willingness to carry out political reforms in order to 'sell [Gamal's] image as a young reformer who is remodelling the ruling National Democratic Party (NDP), a few props are required to impress the public'.[71]

This reform, as well as the 2005 elections and the demonstrations surrounding them, have led the EU to be increasingly active in supporting the Egyptian judiciary, notably through the EIDHR, despite difficult domestic conditions. In December 2005, a campaign aimed at 'promoting Egyptian women judges and their empowerment' was launched with a budget of €93,000. In 2005, projects to report on the elections were launched: 'Watch, Monitor and Evaluate Egyptian Parliamentary Elections to Enhance Democratization' (€83,339) and 'Training for Journalists to cover Elections and to Write Fair and Unbiased Press Reports' (€71,422). But it was only after the elections of 2005 that some programmes to ensure fairer elections were put in place with an 'Election Observers Programme' launched in December 2006 (€75,279) together with the 'Egyptian Democratic

Status Watch' (€100,000).[72] Support was also provided through the regional programme 'EuroMed Justice', which brought together prosecutors and judges to exchange best practices and experiences.

This increase in funding for supporting the judiciary in Egypt also stems from the growing externalization of justice and home affairs (JHA) issues on the Euro-Mediterranean agenda, whereby, as argued by, for example, Pace in this special issue, security and stability have become the key objectives, as corroborated by the ENP Action Plans, which all contain important sections on JHA. Rule of law is not only understood at the implementation level, but is also presented as a correlate to democracy promotion. Hence, under the chapter 'Political Dialogue and Reform', 'Democracy and Rule of Law' comes first in the list of priorities, drafted by the European Commission on a 'one-size-fits all' model,[73] and is separated from human rights and fundamental freedoms. An analysis of the ENP Action Plans of Egypt, Jordan, Lebanon, Morocco, the Palestinian Authority, and Tunisia reveal that the rule of law encompasses the following priorities for the EU. First is the strengthening of the judiciary's independence and impartiality. The EU is concerned with the administrative capacity and the effectiveness of judiciaries. Second, a recurring theme is the need for public sector reforms in order to enforce legislation as well as encouraging countries like Morocco to embark upon a decentralization process and strengthen local authorities. The reform of electoral laws as well as the fight against corruption by national law enforcement agencies are key concerns for the promotion of democracy and rule of law. In the case of Egypt, the Action Plan adopted in March 2006 points to the need to improve the administrative capacity of the judiciary and insists upon prison reform.[74]

The external dimension of JHA, together with the European Neighbourhood and Partnership Instrument (ENPI) and MEDA/JHA programmes, represent alternative ways for the EU to finance rule of law programmes by offering Mediterranean law enforcement agencies the opportunity to take part, for instance, in Euromed Justice, Euromed Police, and Euromed Migration programmes. This trend can lead to increased socialization between judges in the Mediterranean, and for that purpose it is necessary not only to exchange best practices and know-how in the field of security, but also with regard to human rights and democratization.[75]

Furthermore, on 17 January 2008, a European Parliament resolution on the situation of human rights in Egypt[76] insisted upon:

> the importance of ensuring and strengthening the independence of the judiciary by amending or repealing all legal provisions that infringe or do not sufficiently guarantee its independence; stresses the need for respect for and protection of the freedoms of association and expression for judges, in accordance with Articles 8 and 9 of the UN Basic Principles on the Independence of the Judiciary

The Egyptian government was very critical of this resolution. The resolution *inter alia* denounced the recurrent arrests of human rights activists, encouraged the

Egyptian government to lift the state of emergency, and called for the immediate release of Ayman Nour. In response, the Egyptian government and parliament denounced the resolution as 'a flagrant interference in Egypt's domestic affairs' that would 'harm the historic relationship between Egypt and Europe'.[77]

Conclusion: constraints on the EU's rule of law promotion in Egypt and in the Mediterranean

The analysis of the 2005 momentum for reform in Egypt and the judges' revolt points to the exogenous and endogenous factors that have affected the EU's rule of law promotion policy. While not disregarding the specificities of Egyptian foreign policy and domestic factors, it appears that rule of law promotion is primarily constrained by structural contradictions within the EU. Amongst these exogenous factors, there is, firstly, the EU's intergovernmental nature as a foreign policy actor, which in this case has weakened the EU's position as a rule of law promoter. Secondly, ongoing negotiations over the ENP Action plan at the time of the revolt, coupled with, thirdly, the Egyptian–US relationship, compelled the EU to opt for an integrated approach towards rule of law promotion in Egypt. The Egyptian domestic situation also constrains what the EU can do in this domain. The instrumentalization by the Egyptian regime of external aid funding in the field of human rights and democratization complicates the EU's activities in the country, and obliges the EU to look for alternative strategies to bypass domestic constraints. A recent development is also the externalization of 'justice and home affairs' (JHA) to the Mediterranean region via increased regional and bilateral funding for the inclusion of JHA elements into the Mediterranean region. Some of those programmes include support for the reform of the judiciary, as is the case in Algeria and Tunisia, with programmes launched in 2004 (respectively €15 million and €22 million).

The main risk for the EU in externalizing JHA to its Mediterranean partners is that there is a lack of judicial review of this *acquis*. Because the Mediterranean partners do not have independent judiciaries and police forces which respect human rights, it is of the utmost importance that EMP institutions, if willing to pursue Euro-Mediterranean cooperation in the field of JHA, also put in place the necessary institutions to ensure that fundamental freedoms and the rule of law are respected. It is therefore argued that the EU must accompany JHA cooperation with a strengthening of the institutional capacities of the judiciaries in terms of financial and human resources, a process which is not only about mere training and cooperation programmes, but should also foster socialization amongst Euro-Mediterranean actors. Institutional twinning programmes make available EU expertise in certain policy sectors to third countries and are thus a way for the EU to export some of its norms by influencing the administrations of third countries, as was experienced on a large scale during the preparations for EU enlargement towards Central and East European countries. Alternatively, policy networks of law enforcement agencies[78] could be established, which would engage in a genuine reflection on how it is best to pursue the promotion of the rule of law within the Euro-Mediterranean space, and ensure that rule of law is not only a *means*, but also an *end* in itself. This way it is expected that rule of law becomes an objective of foreign policy per se and not only an instrument to secure EU's internal security.[79]

Notes

1. European Union, Consolidated Version of Treaty on the European Union. *Official Journal of the European Communities*, C 325/5 (2002), Article 6.
2. European Union, Consolidated Version of the Treaty Establishing the European Communities, *Official Journal of the European Communities*, C 325/33 (2002), Article 177(2) and 181a(1).
3. Along the five main objectives of CFSP is the objective 'to develop and consolidate democracy and the rule of law, and respect for human rights and fundamental freedoms'. Ibid., Article 11.
4. The Copenhagen criteria are as follows. Political: stability of institutions guaranteeing democracy, the rule of law, human rights, and respect for and protection of minorities; economic: existence of a functioning market economy and the capacity to cope with competitive pressure and market forces within the Union; acceptance of the Community *acquis*: ability to take on the obligations of membership, including adherence to the aims of political, economic, and monetary union. Presidency of the European Union, *Conclusions of the European Council in Copenhagen* (1993) SN 180/1/93 REV 1.
5. Belton, 'Competing Definitions of the Rule of Law'.
6. Ibid. Emphasis added.
7. Alter, *Establishing the Supremacy of European Law*, 208
8. Aliboni and Guazzone, 'Democracy in the Arab Countries'.
9. Hinnebusch, 'Prospects for Democratisation in the Middle East'.
10. Hinnebusch, 'Explaining International Politics in the Middle East'.
11. Albrecht, 'How Can Opposition Support Authoritarianism?'.
12. The Judges' Club is the professional association of Egyptian judges.
13. These institutions still exist nowadays. Brown, *The Rule of Law in the Arab World*, 91.
14. Brown and Nasr, *Egypt's Judges Step Forward*, 2.
15. Albrecht, 'How Can Opposition Support Authoritarianism?', 379.
16. The reform of the 1972 law took place in 1984. Brown, *Arab Judicial Structures A Study Presented to the United Nations Development Program*, Washington: POGAR-UNDP, 2001, http://www.pogar.org/publications/judiciary/nbrown/
17. Brown and Nasr, *Egypt's Judges Step Forward*, 97.
18. Ibid., 99.
19. Hill, 'The Supreme Constitutional Court of Egypt'.
20. Wolff, 'The Externalisation of Justice'.
21. Confidential interview conducted by the author with a lawyer in Cairo, Egypt, 4 September 2006.
22. Zuhur, *Egypt: Security, Political and Islamist Challenges*.
23. Barah, 'Egypte: Une Révolution Prolétaire?'
24. Van Munster, 'Review Essay. Security on a Shoestring'; Balzacq, 'The Policy Tools of Securitization', 75.
25. FIDH, 'La Fidh Dénonce Les Excès', www.fidh.org/spip.php?article2112

The European Union's Democratization Agenda   115

26. This evolution implied a revision of Article 76 of the Egyptian Constitution. Prior to this amendment, the People's Assembly would vote to nominate a sole presidential candidate by a two-thirds majority. The name of the candidate was put to the Egyptian electorate in a referendum. Hence commentators would refer to a plebiscite. See International Crisis Group, *Reforming Egypt: In Search of a Strategy*, 38.

27. Dunne, *Time to Pursue Democracy in Egypt*, 3.

28. It is also important to bear in mind that Egypt has 77.5 million inhabitants.

29. Winstone, *Democracy and the Middle East*, 16.

30. Confidential interview conducted by the author with a lawyer in Egypt, Cairo, 4 September 2006. This contrasts with the more moderate report from the Carnegie Endowment, which considers that, while the 2005 parliamentary elections were flawed, 'they were more competitive and transparent than any Egypt had held since the 1952 revolution for two reasons: the active supervision of judges and monitoring by thousands of trained civilian observers'. Dunne, *Time to Pursue Democracy in Egypt*, 5. See also 'Fraud claims mar Egyptian presidential poll', *The Guardian*, 2005, (7 September 2005) and Human Right Watch 'Egypt: election offer public debate'.

31. Brown and Nasr, *Egypt's Judges Step Forward*, 4.

32. 'La Révolte des Juges Égyptiens', *Le Monde*, 4 May 2006.

33. Winstone, *Democracy and the Middle East*, 16.

34. Ibid.

35. Amnesty International (EU office), 'Eu-Egypt Association Council Meeting', 3.

36. Zuhur, *Egypt: Security, Political and Islamist Challenges*, 102.

37. On the heterogeneity of those movements, notably Kifaya, see the article by Demmelhuber in this issue.

38. On the importance of democracy and rule of promotion in the EU's discourse and policy documents, see Börzel and Risse, *One Size Fits All!*

39. Article 11 of the Treaty of the European Union, http://eur-lex.europa.eu/fr/treaties/index.htm

40. Smith, *The Role of Democracy Assistance*, 37.

41. Kingdon, *Agendas, Alternatives and Public Policies*, 166.

42. Barah, 'Egypte: Une Révolution Prolétaire?'.

43. Bruter, 'Diplomacy without a State'.

44. Dimier and McGeever. 'Diplomats without a Flag'.

45. Bruter, 'Diplomacy without a State'.

46. Ibid.

47. Confidential interview conducted by the author with an official from the EC Delegation in Cairo, August 2006.

48. EU Presidency, 'Declaration by the Presidency', http://www.britainusa.com/sections/articles_show_nt1.asp?d=0&i=60058&L1=0&L2=0&a=38613&pv=1

49. Ibid.

50. Confidential interview conducted by the author, Cairo, 31 August 2006.

51. EU Presidency, 'Declaration by the Presidency'.

52. Confidential interview conducted by the author, Egyptian Ministry of Foreign Affairs, Cairo, 13 September 2006.

53. Winstone, *Democracy and the Middle East*.

54. Dunne, 'Time to Pursue Democracy in Egypt'.

55. Wahish, 'Trading Diplomacy'.

56. European Commission and OECD, *EU Donor Atlas 2006. Volume 1* (Brussels: Development Strategies, 2006), http://ec.europa.eu/development/body/publications/docs/eu_donor_atlas_2006.pdf

57. El-Kersh and Nkrumah. 'Limits to What We Can Do'.

58. MEDA was established with Council Regulation (EC) No 1488/96 of 23 July 1996.

59.   Bayoum, 'Egyptian Views of the EU', 331–47.
60.   Following the expiry of Council Regulations No 975/1999 (developing countries) and 976/1999 (other third countries), the legal basis for EIDHR was replaced by the financing instrument for the promotion of democracy and human rights worldwide on 1 January 2007.
61.   Since the 2007 reform of EC external aid it has been called the European Instrument for Democracy and Human Rights, and has a single legal basis (EC Regulation 1889/2006 of 20 December 2006). Before 2007, it is correctly referred to as the European Initiative for Democracy and Human Rights, whereas after, one needs to refer to the European Instrument for Democracy and Human Rights.
62.   European Commission, 'European Initiative for Democracy and Human', 14.
63.   European Commission, 9.
64.   Sayigh, 'US and European Support to Democratic Reform', 52.
65.   Ibid.
66.   Youngs, 'The European Union', 64.
67.   Abdelrahman, 'The Nationalisation of the Human Rights Debate', 300.
68.   Ibid., 288.
69.   Ibid., 293.
70.   See Demmelhuber in this volume.
71.   Abdelrahman 'The Nationalisation of the Human Rights Debate'.
72.   See http://ec.europa.eu/europeaid/where/worldwide/eidhr/documents/updated_report_by_location_en.pdf
73.   The other priorities are human rights and fundamental freedoms, security sector reform, cooperation on foreign and security policy, regional and international issues, and conflict prevention and crisis management.
74.   EU-Egypt Association Council, *EU–Egypt Action Plan*.
75.   Since there has not yet been any evaluation of the programme, it is difficult to assess quantitatively its results.
76.   European Parliament, *Resolution of 17 January on the Situation in Egypt. P6_Ta(2008)0023* (Strasbourg: European Parliament, 2008).
77.   Agence France Presse, 'EU Lawmakers Vow Not to Yield to Egyptian Pressure', 17 January 2008.
78.   Regarding policy networks in the field of JHA please refer to the detailed analysis of Lavenex and Wichmann. 'The External Governance of Internal Security'.
79.   The ideas developed in the conclusion have also been expanded in Wolff, 'The Externalisation of Justice'.

Bibliography

Abdelrahman, Maha. 'The Nationalisation of the Human Rights Debate in Egypt'. *Nations and Nationalism* 13 (2007): 285–300.
Albrecht, H. 'How Can Opposition Support Authoritarianism? Lessons from Egypt'. *Democratization* 12 (2005): 378–97.
Aliboni, Roberto, and Laura Guazzone. 'Democracy in the Arab Countries and the West'. *Mediterranean Politics* 9 (2004): 82–93.
Alter, Karen. *Establishing the Supremacy of European Law. The Making of an International Rule of Law in Europe.* Oxford: Oxford University Press, 2001.
Balzacq, Thierry. 'The Policy Tools of Securitization: Information Exchange, EU Foreign and Interior Policies'. *Journal of Common Market Studies* 46 (2008): 75–100.
Barah, Mikaïl. 'Egypte: Une Révolution Prolétaire?'. Paris: IRIS, 2007.
Bayoum, Soha. 'Egyptian Views of the EU: Pragmatic, Paternalistic and Partnership Concerns'. *European Foreign Affairs Review* 12 (2007): 331–47.

Belton, Rachel Kleinfield. 'Competing Definitions of the Rule of Law, Implications for Practitioners'. Carnegie Papers, Rule of Law Series 55(2005).

Börzel, Tanja A., and Thomas Risse. *One Size Fits All! EU Policies for the Promotion of Democracy, Human Rights and the Rule of Law*. Center for Development, Democracy, and the Rule of Law, Stanford University, http://iis-db.stanford.edu/pubs/20747/Risse-Borzel-stanford_final.pdf

Brown, Nathan J. *The Rule of Law in the Arab World*. Cambridge: Cambridge University Press, 1997.

Brown, Nathan J., and Hesham Nasr. *Egypt's Judges Step Forward. The Judicial Election Boycott and Egyptian Reform*. Washington: Carnegie, Policy Outlook Democracy and the Rule of Law, 2005.

Bruter, Michael. 'Diplomacy without a State: The External Delegations of the European Commission'. *Journal of European Public Policy* 6 (1999): 183–205.

Dimier, Véronique, and Mike McGeever. 'Diplomats without a Flag: The Institutionalization of the Delegations of the Commission in African, Caribbean and Pacific Countries'. *Journal of Common Market Studies* 44 (2006): 483–505.

Dunne, Michelle. 'Time to Pursue Democracy in Egypt'. Washington: Policy Outlook, Middle East Program, Carnegie Endowment for International Peace, 2007.

El-Kersh, Assem, and Gamal Nkrumah. 'Limits to What We Can Do'. *Al-Ahram Weekly* 891, 3–9 April 2008.

EU-Egypt Association Council. EU-Egypt Action Plan (2006), http://ec.europa.eu/world/enp/pdf/action_plans/egypt_enp_ap_final_en.pdf.

European Commission. 'European Initiative for Democracy and Human Rights Programming Document 2002–2004'. 14. Brussels: Commission Staff Working Document, 2001.

Hill, Enid. 'The Supreme Constitutional Court of Egypt on Freedom of Expression and of Association'. Paper presented at The Third Mediterranean Development Forum, Cairo, Egypt, 2000.

Hinnebusch, Raymond. 'Explaining International Politics in the Middle East: The Struggle of Regional Identity and Systemic Structure'. *Analyzing Middle East Foreign Policies and the Relationship with Europe*, ed. Gerd Nonneman, 243–56. New York: Routledge, 2005.

Hinnebusch, Raymond. 'Prospects for Democratisation in the Middle East'. *Democratisation in the Middle East. Dilemmas and Perspectives*, ed. Birgitte Rahbek, 31–40. Aarhus: Aarhus University Press, 2005.

International Crisis Group. *Reforming Egypt: In Search of a Strategy*. Middle East/North Africa Report. Brussels and Cairo, 2005.

Kingdon, John W. *Agendas, Alternatives and Public Policies*. Washington: Longman, 2003.

Lavenex, Sandra, and Nicole Wichmann. 'The External Governance of Internal Security'. *Journal of European Integration* (2009), forthcoming.

Sayigh, Yezid. 'US and European Support to Democratic Reform: The Intentions and Practices as Seen from the Middle East'. *Democratization in the Middle East. Dilemmas and Perspectives*, ed. B. Rahbek, 41–57. Aarhus: Aarhus University Press, 2005.

Smith, Karen. *The Role of Democracy Assistance in Future EU External Relations*. Paper presented at European Conference 'Enhancing the European Profile in Democracy Assistance', The Netherlands, 2004.

Van Munster, Rens. 'Review Essay. Security on a Shoestring: A Hitchhiker's Guide to Critical Schools of Security in Europe'. *Cooperation and Conflict: Journal of the Nordic International Studies Association* 42 (2007): 253–43.

Youngs, Richard. 'The European Union'. *Survey of European Democracy Promotion Policies 2000–2006*, ed. Kristina Kausch, David Mathieson, Irene Menendez, and Richard Youngs, 51–80. Madrid: FRIDE, 2006.

Wahish, Niveen. 'Trading Diplomacy'. *Al-Ahram Weekly* 26 January–1 February (2006).

Winstone, Ruth. *Democracy and the Middle East: Egypt, the Palestinian Territories and Saudi Arabia*. London: International Affairs and Defence Section, House of Commons Library, 2006.

Wolff, Sarah. 'The Externalisation of Justice and Home Affairs to the Southern Neighbours: The EU's Dilemmas in the Fight against Terrorism'. Paper presented at EuroMeSCo Annual Conference 2006, 'Paths to Democracy and Inclusion within Diversity', Working Group on 'The Linkage Between Justice and Terrorism in the Euro-Mediterranean Area', Istanbul, 2006.

Zuhur, Sherifa. 'Egypt: Security, Political and Islamist Challenges'. Washington: Strategic Studies Institute, 2007.

Egypt's moment of reform and its reform actors: the variety–capability gap

Thomas Demmelhuber

Department of Political Science, University of Erlangen-Nuremberg, Erlangen, Germany

Since July 2004, Egypt has undertaken a comprehensive economic reform agenda, put forward by 'newly' emerging political and economic elites with different sources of legitimization than their predecessors. Economic reforms are accompanied by a limited package of political reforms. Following an actor-oriented approach to the analysis of Egypt's reform process, reform actors are defined by a striking dilemma: Reform actors on behalf of the regime show a comprehensive capability in designing the reform agenda ('capability') but only half-hearted efforts to seek public support for their reform package ('variety'). Reform actors from the opposition do have sufficient public support but lack the instruments to alter the reform agenda. This 'variety–capability gap' results from the specifics of an authoritarian regime that only allows a limited degree of public dissent and participation (controlled pluralism). The degree of regime interference and repression regarding oppositional reform actors provides a clear indicator of their potential to acquire the capability not only to articulate their views but also to act on them. Finally, the categorization of Egyptian reform actors suggests rethinking the choice of partners for the European Union's democracy promotion in the Southern Mediterranean, which aims to foster peace, stability, and prosperity in the region.

Introduction

Since the president's second son, Gamal Mubarak, became politically active in 2002 political debate in Egypt has been shaped by two main issues. The first contentious issue centres on the question of who will be the heir of aging President Hosni Mubarak after his sixth and probably last term in office. Despite denying any plans for a father-son succession, Gamal is widely expected to continue the rule of the Mubarak family. Closely connected to his increasing role in Egyptian politics is the second controversial subject, which focuses on a comprehensive economic and, to a lesser degree, political reform agenda. The latter has, since 2004, been initiated in particular by young, pragmatic politicians with economic backgrounds. The reform process has not solely arisen from external pressure; it must, rather, be seen as an attempt by the newly composed ruling elite to respond to changing domestic and international settings, in terms of politics, economics, and society. In empirical analysis of Egypt's moment of reform and its defining actors, the meaning of the term 'reform' helps determine the precondition for who qualifies as a reform actor. Based on this classification, we shall evaluate the capability of reform actors to alter the agenda of Egypt's reform process. Different capabilities and varying public backing of reform actors support the notion of a 'variety–capability gap' that implies a lack of capability despite progress in public support (variety) and vice versa. 'Capability' comprises the impact of one reform actor in the design of the reform process, whereas 'variety' implies the public support in absolute numbers.[1] The latter categorization is of importance for the European Union's (EU) uni-, bi-, and multilateral policies towards Egypt aimed at fostering peace, stability, and prosperity, and at promoting democracy as their core objectives. In order to follow such an ambitious agenda, the EU needs the right partners for effective policy implementation.

Egypt's 'moment of reform' and its 'agents of change'

While focusing on Egypt's 'moment of reform' and its protagonists, two basic determinants have to be kept in mind. The word 'reform' refers to a planned ordering, modification, improvement, and rearrangement of the current state of affairs.[2] Genuine interest in reform is based on the idea that a current situation is no longer acceptable. This broad and not specifically results-oriented definition opens up a range of policy opportunities and a number of differing perceptions of what reforms should encompass, who might benefit from such reforms, and which objective they seek to achieve. Any other attempt to specify the term 'reform' in a more content-oriented fashion regarding the rule of law, human rights, and democracy would make a comparative analysis of Egypt's reform actors futile, as there would be serious doubts whether there are any reform actors in the country at all. The vivid discussions in the early 1990s on democratic change, in which each country that witnessed a gradual opening of the political scene was mistakenly seen as a 'one-way street' to democracy, have finally come to an end. As Frédéric Volpi stresses in his contribution to this special issue, there is an emerging consensus that there has, so far, been no democratic transformation and not even any democratizing reform process in the Middle East and North Africa (MENA) region. Authoritarianism has adapted to new political and socio-economic challenges.[3] It has shown little sign of receding and should, therefore, be seen as a matter of fact rather than as a transitional stage.

The public backing of reform actors does not say anything about their capability to alter the reform agenda. To be successful, reform actors who are seeking an end to the status quo need the spaces of public debate in order to reach and mobilize the people. As Cavatorta (in this special issue) points out, there is a need to implement an institutional framework and, more importantly, through it to provide legitimacy for reforms.[4] These preconditions are challenged by the regime and its associated elites, who try to stick to the pre-existing power structures, preserve the status quo and, thus, try to prevent any potential adversary from acquiring the capability to mobilize the masses and to alter the political agenda. In this way, the level of regime interference and repression can be considered as an indicator of the potential capability of oppositional reform actors not only to articulate their views, but also to act on them. Analysing Egyptian reform dynamics since the early 1990s and in particular since 2004 (when there was a cabinet reshuffle), we can identify roughly seven categories of reform actors in Egypt, based on the understanding of 'reform', 'capability', and 'variety', as presented above. These categories are not 'closed communities'. Particularly among opposition groups, there is a peculiar intersection between two or more categories. In the following model, the seven-fold composition of Egypt's reform actors starts with the 'Gamal group' (the group around the president's son) as the actor with the most comprehensive capability for designing the reform agenda. Afterwards, the analysis focuses on the Muslim Brotherhood (MB), syndicates and professional associations, secular opposition parties, Kifaya, weblogs, and non-governmental organizations (NGOs) as the most relevant reform actors besides those within the regime.

The 'Gamal group': market liberalization vs. competition

A common denominator across the Arab world is a crucial shift in the elite structure. The 'old guard' officials – most of them have a military record – are now approaching their 70s. This faction is being challenged and gradually sidelined by a western-educated and pragmatic younger generation, whose legitimacy is based more on their ability to be connected to satisfactory economic growth rates and their standing as businessmen than on military merits or army rank (until Mubarak's presidency, the military has been the prime source of legitimacy of the political elite). The 27-year rule of the Mubarak family with Hosni Mubarak at the head is likely to continue after his sixth and probably last term in office. After the depressing performance of the National Democratic Party (NDP) in the parliamentary elections of 2000,[5] President Mubarak paved the way for an outstanding career for his second son, Gamal. The son of Hosni and Suzanne Mubarak, a graduate from the American University in Cairo (AUC), Gamal left Egypt in the late 1980s to work in London at the Bank of America and finally returned to Egypt in 1998.[6] He has been climbing the ranks of the party hierarchy, leading the highly influential Policy Secretariat since 2002, and is now widely seen as the informal party leader of the ruling NDP (he has been its Deputy General Secretary since 2006).

The current stage of the political and economic reform process in Egypt – formally initiated with the new cabinet in July 2004 under Prime Minister Ahmed

Nazif[7] – is closely connected with the increasing role of Gamal Mubarak in Egyptian politics. Nazif, a 52-year-old computer scientist, a graduate of McGill University in Canada and former Minister of Communication and Information Technology, has the reputation of being an effective bureaucrat without corruption scandals overshadowing him; this may qualify him to lead the country through one of its most important reform phases, in particular since his predecessors completely failed to lead the country through Egypt's economic depression of 1997– 2003. The appointment of the 'technocrats' was seen as a move to give impetus to domestic initiatives following the weak economic performance of previous governments.[8] The new cabinet was composed of young politicians with a professional business background. All of them were associates of Gamal Mubarak; nine of the new ministers were also members of Gamal's Policy Secretariat.[9] Leading businessmen gained influence through their membership of the Policy Secretariat, such as member of parliament Ahmed Ezz, a business tycoon and close associate of Gamal Mubarak. Young and 'reform-minded' businessmen entered parliament and came on the scene through the media, think tanks, and business chambers. They were even able to establish ties with the military – formerly known as the 'king-maker' of Egypt.[10]

The overlapping of business and politics is considered to be of essential interest for the analysis of Egypt's reform process. Gamal Mubarak is the 'political integration figure' for a continuing status quo in a changing domestic and international environment. The guided reform process preserves the privileges of the closely associated business elites that qualify to be called 'oligarchs'. In their view, economic reforms are wanted, privatization is in their interest, even a market economy is welcome, but competition of market forces should be avoided for the sake of their business interests.[11] The 'Gamal group' is the leading force within the NDP in this staged reform process and in the making of government policy more generally. It is becoming increasingly influential within the regime, leading to a battle of the 'old guard' vs. the 'Gamal group', with the 'old guard' officials fiercely clinging to their rank. The modernization of the party structures aims at building new power structures, new sources of legitimization and, in the end, at preserving the continuing rule of the Mubarak family. Unlike his father, Gamal Mubarak and his associates have no military background and clearly need other sources of legitimization particularly within the diverse segments of the ruling elite. An economic opening sets the frame in this 'win-win-situation' for both the ruling elite and broad segments of the business elite, since an improvement in macroeconomic indicators acts as the new source of legitimacy (albeit among a very small and selective group of the populace). Political and economic reforms are aimed at setting the stage for controlled competition in the economy and controlled pluralism in politics. Pluralism serves as an important element of legitimization but only to a predefined extent, unlike the context of secular-liberal democracies, in which pluralism is the mirror and the basis of competing political, economic, and social forces in decision-making.

Democratic rhetoric is an important tool: it provides a serious show of commitment about embarking on a democratic reform process for the sake of legitimization both inside Egypt and outside for international partners. Rhetoric about democratic reform provides functional legitimacy. In 2005, international observers hailed the coming of the 'Cairo spring' (referring to the events in Prague, former Czechoslovakia, in the late 1960s). It was a clear misperception: all we have been witnessing is an ongoing, major power shift from the 'old guard' to young actors, plus a major shift in sources of legitimization on the Egyptian stage; or what some referred to as the 'theater of democratization',[12] that started the process for these two shifts (young generation and new sources of legitimization) with the 'Gamal group' being the most dominant actor. This comprehensive actor capability (leadership in the draft of the reform agenda) stands in sharp contrast to a missing link in society and limited public support: the attempt to present Gamal as the trustworthy and reform-minded new leader has not been successful so far.[13] Indeed, Gamal is widely considered as the next stage in the seemingly never-ending history of Egypt's authoritarianism. In contrast to the 'Gamal group', opposition actors do have something which the group around Gamal lacks. In the words of a young member of the formally outlawed Muslim Brotherhood in an interview with the author: 'We have the people behind us and we have hope.'[14]

The Muslim Brotherhood: 'Islam is the solution'

If we consider regime repression as one indicator of actor capability, or at least of the potential to acquire it and to use it later on, the Muslim Brotherhood (MB) is the main oppositional force in Egypt, the main advocate of reform, and the one with the greatest potential to mobilize the masses and to alter the agenda through its diverse channels, in particular through its mandates in parliament and its diverse networks in society. In early 2007, *al-Akhbar* (The News), an independent pro-opposition newspaper from Lebanon, focused on the Brotherhood's role during the fierce debate on the Egyptian constitutional amendments of March 2007: 'The Muslim Brotherhood in Egypt announced that it will continue to confront the constitutional amendments despite the security strikes against it last week which resulted in the detention of dozens of the leaders of the Brotherhood.' The Brotherhood's Political Bureau official, al-Aryan, further emphasized 'that the Brotherhood does not fear the security crackdown.' Moreover he stressed: 'We will continue to fight the constitutional amendments and we will urge the whole people to oppose them. ... We will only use peaceful means.'[15] The latest regime offensive mentioned in this quotation was partly the result of a 10 December 2006 march at al-Azhar University in Cairo by masked, black-clothed university students who were Brotherhood members.[16] The Guidance Bureau of the Muslim Brotherhood quickly denied any prior knowledge of the event and soon denounced it as inappropriate. Nonetheless, the event turned out to be a public relations disaster for the Brotherhood as a whole. The regime quickly used it as a pretext to accuse the Brotherhood of operating a militia that endangered

Egyptian national security. In other words, the incident was an opportunity for repressive state action against the Brotherhood, although the reason for applying an iron fist seemed to be the Brotherhood's increasing capability to alter the reform agenda, either directly or indirectly, with comprehensive political networks and within society as a whole.

Founded in 1928 by Hassan al-Banna, the Muslim Brotherhood had the status of a political party from 1939 until the revolution of the 'Free Officers' in 1952. Even in those early days, the movement was under certain pressures arising from, on the one hand, its organizational concept and, on the other, its objective to be both a religious organization/social movement and an actor with a clear political agenda. After a short alliance with Nasser and his associates, the Brotherhood was held responsible for an assassination attempt on Nasser in 1954. The movement was prohibited shortly afterwards. Despite being formally outlawed, the Brotherhood remained deeply rooted in Egyptian society as a broad, religious, charitable socio-economic and socio-political movement.[17] There have been regular regime attempts to crack down on the Brotherhood's structures, but the Brotherhood has been able, for its part, to enlarge its support base in society through social and charity work, in particular since the 'infitah-period' of the 1970s under President Anwar Sadat. The 'infitah-policy' implied a gradual opening of the economy for private entrepreneurs and a successive retreat of the state from social services (established under Nasser's welfare state), which the Brotherhood successfully filled with its own charity network. Over the years, the Brotherhood gained the status of the only real opposition, not co-opted by the regime (despite regular rumours), with massive popular backing. Its unexpected success in the 2005 parliamentary elections, despite the fact that the Brotherhood did not field candidates in all of the 222 constituencies (MB candidates ran as independent candidates),[18] paved the way for the MB to continue its increasing role as a moral, ethical, and political guardian in both government and society (in particular in regard to the preservation of Islamic values and ethics). With the latter strategy, the MB was able to present itself as the only tangible alternative to the status quo.[19] However, there is still no direct MB influence on the reform agenda, which is mainly drafted by the NDP's leading circles, the 'Gamal group', and the government. Yet the regime is indeed aware of the support the Brotherhood enjoys and is increasingly cautious concerning cultural, religious, and moral issues (such as the banning of books deemed offensive to Islam). The regime has lost its supremacy on such topics.[20] The forceful debate and public outcry after critical remarks on the use of the veil by Minister of Culture, Faruk Hosni, in November 2006, is a case in point, showing circumstantial evidence of the Brotherhood's capability of 'agenda setting'.[21]

The growing impact of the Muslim Brotherhood in Egypt is closely connected to several developments within the last decade. First, the Brotherhood's success builds on a general decline in religious-oriented extremism in Egypt. The regime was able to crack down on terrorist organizations that were responsible for numerous attacks on government officials and tourists in the 1990s. Leading imprisoned figures of al-Jihad and al-Jamaat al-Islamiyya have distanced themselves from violence, denounced it as a political instrument, and are currently being released one by one. Second, the Brotherhood has committed itself (both in rhetoric and in practice) to the basic rules of political participation and reform. Both are integral elements of its political agenda, which tries to show competence to take part in political decision-making, opportunities to cooperate with secular opposition actors (even with the leftists, as is the case with Hamas in Palestine),[22] and a will to ease fears among secular segments of the public. One might call these MB moves a pragmatic and ideological 'metamorphosis' in recognizing pluralism as the basic functional element of a political system.[23] Third, Brotherhood members have shown their management skills, which are known not to be corrupt, by taking over many boards of various syndicates since the late 1980s and social community services from the state. Despite the constitutional amendments of spring 2007, which finally thwarted any future attempt to establish a political party based on religion, and despite recent regime crackdowns, the Brotherhood promises to remain a decisive political actor in Egypt in the coming years. It is the oppositional actor with the most comprehensive public support.[24]

Syndicates and associations: 'the moment of the judges'

For over a decade, the main professional syndicates in Egypt (each official job title has its own syndicate)[25] have been inactive. Elections in the Medical and Engineers' Syndicate, one of the largest, have not taken place. The Engineers' Syndicate is under judicial sequestration; it has been actively suspended since 1995 because of alleged financial corruption after Brotherhood affiliates won absolute majority in its board elections in 1987. There are currently 12 professional syndicates with boards whose time in office has ended and no elections have since been held to form new boards. According to Law 100 (1993), a governmental, judicial committee is entrusted with supervising elections. In compliance with the law, the committee is responsible for informing the syndicates that they need to make preparations to hold elections.[26] This judicial committee has regularly failed to send the necessary notifications. Attempts by the government to impose some form of guardianship on professional syndicates must be considered as responsible for the delay in holding elections and, thus, responsible for the marginalization of the syndicates' role.[27] The reason for the regime's repressive approach is a degree of fear that the boards might all be taken over by Brotherhood affiliates, after their strong performance in the 1980s and early 1990s when the Brotherhood (as mentioned above) won the boards' elections in five of the country's most prestigious professional syndicates.[28] Given the restricted political arena, syndicates soon acted as proxy fora for political debate.

With regard to the Judges' Club (an informal syndicate, founded in 1939, comprising about 8,000 judges) and its role during the widely cited 'judges' revolt' in 2005 (see Wolff's contribution to this special issue), the situation is different. According to prominent lawyer and non-governmental organization (NGO) activist Nasser Amin, 'Egypt's political system witnesses free and independent judges (at least within the civil judiciary) but not an independent judiciary.'[29] Egypt's judges can be described as reform actors no matter what primary objective they are aiming at (above all, in terms of independence of the judiciary). Hisham el-Bastawasi, one of the most outspoken reform-oriented judges, has been quoted as saying: 'The public trusts neither the government nor the opposition on freedoms and rights.'[30] Reformist judges have put forward two agendas. First, they have tried to enhance the independence of the judiciary. Second, they have tried to assure free elections by taking their electoral supervisory role seriously. The passing of Egypt's Judicial Authority Law in June 2006, which governs the judiciary's activities, responsibilities, and its relationship with the government, falls short of the original demands and expectations of the Judges' Club.[31] Despite some modifications (for example, separate budget for the judiciary from 2008), Egypt's judiciary remains 'under the thumb' of the executive. Finally, judges are far from being a monolithic entity: Egypt's judiciary is very diverse, and includes, alongside the reformists, more regime-loyal administrative, military, and state-of-emergency judiciary. Nonetheless, the role that regime-critical judges played in 2005 and their steady calls for reform in terms of implementing citizenship's rights as laid down in the constitution. Based on their widely recognized credibility, judges have shown their ability to mobilize people, in particular in 2005 and 2006 during their struggle for more independence and a more sincere role in the supervision of the national ballot. They also have some constitutional and legal leverage to alter the political agenda (in particular the Supreme Constitutional Court, SCC).[32] In contrast to the regular failure of secular opposition parties not only to articulate their agenda but also to act on it through their mandates in parliament, the judiciary sometimes even acts as a proxy for opposition parties.

Secular opposition: 'Abide by the rules or be jailed'

According to Mona Makram Ebeid, NGO activist, former Member of Parliament (al-Wafd), and close associate of jailed former presidential candidate Ayman Nour, Egypt has a political system where parties without followers exist for people without parties.[33] Hardly any connection between politics and society is provided by the 22 licensed opposition parties (as of mid-2008). The judiciary and the MB have replaced opposition parties in many of the tasks opposition parties should undertake to enhance democratization, political participation, and representation. Following the understanding of 'opposition' in political science, opposition parties symbolize a legitimate alternative to the government within the institutional framework of a country.[34] The case of Egypt shows that secular opposition parties (no matter whether al-Wafd, al-Tagammu', the Nasserists or others) do not represent an alternative to the government. They are an integral part of it, a source of its legitimization, and are far from being considered relevant competitors.[35] The continuing struggle between the regime and the religious opposition has squeezed the legal and secular opposition parties out. The landmark SCC ruling from 8 July 2000, which forced the government to place elections under full judicial supervision, is a case in point.[36] The secular opposition's struggle for the same objective in parliament yielded no such result.[37]

The performance of Egyptian opposition parties during the last three decades was rather weak. On the one hand, this was because of the restrictions put upon them by the Political Parties Law[38] and, on the other hand, it was due to a lack of genuine political participation. They concentrated on spending their energy on internal power struggles rather than on trying to reach out and gain popular support. Egyptian opposition parties may be considered as co-opted elements of the authoritarian system. Arising from the strict regulations for the work of the political opposition, they paralyzed themselves through internal power struggles, a lack of national platforms,[39] and a shortage of internal democratic elements.[40] There have been attempts to break out of this system, for instance, the example of the breakaway faction from al-Wafd around the imprisoned Ayman Nour.[41] This charismatic lawyer and former Member of Parliament founded the al-Ghad (Tomorrow) party in 2004, questioned fundamental elements of the ruling elite, and challenged incumbent President Mubarak in the first-ever multi-candidate presidential elections of September 2005. He finished second with 8% of the votes. Shortly afterwards, a defamation campaign, launched by regime-loyal media, gained momentum, Nour lost his 'safe' electoral district Bab al-Sharqiyya in the parliamentary elections of December 2005 and just a few days later, he was sentenced to five years in prison on charges of forgery during the licensing process of the al-Ghad party.[42]

Despite the legitimate role of secular opposition parties in the political arena, they cannot embark on any process beyond verbal actions and demands due to a lack of resources and will to mobilize a large number of supporters. Co-opted or muzzled by the regime through a wide network of strict regulations, they are simply not seen as filling such a role. If there are serious attempts to break out of the controlled political stage, the regime is ready to paralyze them. The failure of secular opposition parties may explain why new socio-political movements, such as Kifaya, at least try to fill the political void by breaking former taboos and embarking on a more active process beyond rhetorical actions.

Kifaya: 'When enough is not enough!'

Kifaya (Enough)[43] can be located between the two defining poles of political debate in Egypt (regime vs. MB). In September 2004, after eight months of vigorous internal discussions among a selected number of politicians, civil society activists, and intellectuals (in particular, George Ishaak, Abu al-Ula Mady, and Abdel Wahab al-Messiri), Kifaya went public with a common declaration and the manifesto 'the cure of the ongoing American occupation and Zionist devastation is political reform'.[44] It was Kifaya that broke former taboos: it crossed former 'red lines' by demonstrating in downtown Cairo and other Egyptian cities, by demanding the end of the pharaoh's ruling (referring to Egyptian history with its long, autocratic leadership periods), by saying 'no' to any plan to set the stage for the succession of Gamal Mubarak, and by demanding substantial political reforms. Thanks to an international impetus for democratic change in East Europe as well as in the Middle East region during 2004 and 2005 (for example, the 'Orange Revolution' in the Ukraine, the 'Cedar Revolution' in Lebanon, and attempts by Western leaders to put the call for democratic reform high on the global and regional agenda), Kifaya quickly gained the status of a new, strong, and decisive movement for democratic change in Egypt. Even civil society veteran and academic Saad Eddin Ibrahim supported the assertion that there was a causal link between 'Ukraine's Orange Revolution' and Kifaya.[45] The subsequent development of the latter fell short of prior hopes.[46]

The heterogeneity of the movement, comprising Nasserists, liberals, communists, and moderate Islamists (in particular from the unlicensed al-Wasat party), led to a diffuse and 'artificial programme',[47] largely focusing on a 'No agenda' with an anti-American and anti-Zionist leaning, in particular until January 2007, when under the tenure of general coordinator George Ishaak.[48] There is a consensus among Kifaya supporters that President Mubarak should step down and that Egypt should not become a so-called hereditary republic, referring here to the prospective future role of Mubarak's son. The rest is up for debate within Kifaya. Change is wanted, but there are as many blueprints for change as there are individuals in this heterogeneous movement. The movement's vivid appearance in downtown Cairo and other smaller cities of the Nile delta in 2005, the boycott of the national referendum on the first constitutional amendment in May 2005, and the attempt to gain an indirect, political mandate by embarking on an electoral alliance (United National Front for Change, UNFC) of 11 secular parties and movements in the parliamentary elections, were followed by a declining public presence, decreasing numbers in demonstrations, and a rather apolitical stance in 2006.[49] One reason may be that Kifaya's agenda does not differ much from that of the Muslim Brotherhood, being in part the result of the strong voice of moderate Islamists in the movement. One may add that the electoral success of the Muslim Brotherhood has channelled popular opposition. The lack of influence on broad segments of society, perhaps including the wrong, agitating 'voice', the heterogeneity of its members, the existence of sub-groups within Kifaya depending on age and profession, and as a consequence the lack of a coherent programmatic output, have made it clear that Kifaya is only a minor reform actor with a limited capability to alter the reform agenda. Heterogeneity might be an asset, but, in the case of Kifaya, the sole commitment to a 'No agenda' is not enough to elaborate a distinct, political programme. Based again on the assumption that the level of regime interference can be considered as an indicator of the capability of oppositional reform actors not only to articulate their views but also to act on them, this leads us to a rather pessimistic categorization where 'Kifaya' may not be 'enough' any more.[50] At the time of writing (mid-2008), the regime's interference is still low compared to its repressive activities *vis-à-vis* the Brotherhood. Based on comprehensive field work from 2005 until

2008, there is enough circumstantial evidence to claim that the regime lets Kifaya get on with its activities not because it is so alarmed by the striking 'new' rhetoric of Kifaya but rather, because it considers it as an unthreatening adversary.

Weblogs: a new challenge

Since 2004 and following substantial attempts by governments in the region to improve internet accessibility, there has been a peculiar trend among young people, from all political spectrums, to put forward their thoughts on almost any topic through weblogs (online fora) and through the internet as a whole. Regime-critical 'bloggers' are playing an increasing role in public debate; for example, they are often the first ones to publicize events or incidents that the state-run media do not focus on. Indeed, they have 'opened a window of free speech'.[51] They provide fora to publish photographs or video clips of violence and even torture by security services or the police. The regime has detected the long-term potential of these activists. In particular, there was a massive crackdown on bloggers in 2006, for instance, the imprisonment of the well-known Alexandrian blogger, Abdel Karim, in November. Eventually, he was sentenced to four years imprisonment on charges of blasphemy and insulting the president in a five-minute court session in Alexandria on 22 February 2007.[52] Online activism is indeed a potential force, but so far still falls short of being considered as a 'prominent weapon for social change'.[53] The access rate of the Egyptian population to the internet is still low (latest figures still show a connectivity of only 15–20%) and the illiteracy rate is still at a high level (30–40% of the populace). This thwarts the weblogs' potential to mobilize a large number of people. Apart from that, it would be a misperception to consider weblogs and their protagonists as a monolithic group. The politically motivated blogger community covers the whole programmatic and political spectrum (such as regime loyalists, Nasserists, liberals, leftists, and Islamists) and, therefore, lacks a distinct, organizational capacity. Despite their new impact in public debate, bloggers should rather be seen as proxy actors of other reform actors depending on their political affiliation (such as leftists, regime loyalists or MB affiliates).

Non-governmental organizations (NGOs): the multiple dilemma

Egyptian civil society, under the precondition of an inclusive non-secular understanding (including religious-motivated actors), is diverse and large. There is enough reason to claim that it is the largest (in absolute numbers) and most diverse in the Arab world.[54] Civil society consists of actors with various backgrounds and objectives, such as syndicates, unions, social movements, and NGOs. An inclusive understanding of the term 'civil society' comprises religious groups, keeping in mind their social, cultural, and community work, which is aimed at the social development of society as a whole. Regarding the field of NGOs, there are currently (as of February 2008) about 21,500 NGOs in Egypt with diverse backgrounds, covering women's rights, environmental work, sustainable development, human rights, protection of the child, and many other fields. One may distinguish four types of NGOs: religious-motivated, classic welfare, professional, and state-sponsored. Following figures from the Cairo-based Egyptian NGO Support Center, only a few (about one-tenth) of these NGOs have the resources and capability to kick-start efforts to implement their agendas. Just a few of them focus on democratic reform or human rights. This is especially true for rural areas in Upper Egypt, in contrast to the more 'open' environment in Cairo or Alexandria.[55] All NGOs face stiff state regulations as formulated in Law 84 (2002), with many difficulties in implementing their agendas. The day-to-day interference of the Ministry of Social Solidarity is ubiquitous if an NGO focuses on 'sensitive' issues, such as human rights and democratic reform.[56] On the one hand, the regime needs civil society actors in order to make sure that the 'social role' the state cannot afford any more (welfare and charity) is implemented by proxies, but, on the other hand, the regime is certainly aware of the possible dynamics of civil society groups and their steady calls for reform. The regime is also afraid of NGOs being targeted by external actors with foreign money to embark on an anti-regime agenda.[57] In the final analysis, compared to the other actors that have been discussed, most of the time it is the bureaucracy and the legal interference of the regime, based on a complex legal setting (and not the iron fist), that makes the work of NGOs difficult. The NGO sector in Egypt is vibrant and has the potential to be a reform actor, but, compared to other actors, it has the least potential for actor capability. In particular, NGOs focusing on reform, human rights, and development are strictly controlled by the regime, lack wide-spread public support, and are countered by indirectly state-sponsored and, thus, regime-loyal NGOs. Last but not least, the heterogeneity of Egypt's civil society makes it hard to play a decisive role in the designing and implementation of the reform agenda.

Implications for the EU's democracy promotion in the southern Mediterranean

The persistence of authoritarianism in the region challenges EU foreign policies that aim, as mentioned above, at supporting democratic reform in the region in general and in Egypt in particular. Besides the 'Gamal group', which is involved in the political and economic cooperation agenda due to its increasing role in representing the Egyptian government, this analysis of Egypt's 'agents of change' shows different groups with whom cooperation could prove potentially effective. On this basis, projects with syndicates (such as the Judges' Club and the Press Syndicate) might have priority over projects with the 'closed community' of westernized NGOs, with limited access to society. Cooperation with heterogeneous movements such as Kifaya should, however, be approached with caution by the EU, as it is difficult to evaluate how Kifaya will develop; it may well falter or blossom due to the diversity and inconsistency of the group. For a long-term EU foreign policy objective, this might be a further obstacle for implementing a consistent agenda. In order to find adequate partners for cooperation in matters of politics, economy, and society, the EU's development and economic aid/cooperation needs more monitoring before launching projects. There is a need for closer coordination and cooperation with all active institutions and actors on the ground to evaluate the potential, objectives, and background of counterparts (for EU projects) in Egypt. Prior to the launching of projects, prospective cooperation partners should be evaluated closely with regard to their 'variety', 'capability', and understanding of 'reform'.

As a consequence of the diversity of Egyptian reform actors, the EU should also diversify its partners. There is no contradiction in deepening contact with the political wing of the Muslim Brotherhood in terms of political and civil society dialogue, at least with those who abide by the principles of political participation. Arguably, the Brotherhood should not be considered as part of the problem, but more as part of the solution for the sake of Egypt's long-term stability. The objective of the EU's democracy promotion programme should be to make clear in its diplomatic ties with the Egyptian regime that any further attempts to exclude the Brotherhood from the political process will not result in a sustainable, stable political system. It may be that the latter can be improved and sustained by an inclusive approach that implies letting in popular actors, such as the Muslim Brotherhood. Engaging them in politics and political decision-making may trigger an open public debate and an EU–Egyptian cooperative relationship as tools to boost the legitimacy of the whole political system.

Conclusion

All reform actors in Egypt have the 'variety–capability gap' in common. In the case of oppositional 'agents of change', this gap leads to a lack of capability to alter the reform agenda despite substantial public backing. In the case of reform actors within the regime (such as the 'Gamal group'), we can see a high degree of capability to design the reform agenda, but only half-hearted attempts to mobilize public support. Both the MB, with its public support but limited capability to alter the agenda directly, and the dominant 'Gamal group', with its minor commitment to mobilize the people, support the notion of a 'variety–capability gap'. Additionally, the empirical analysis presented in this article has shown that the extent of repressive action on behalf of the regime changes according to the public support of actors from the opposition. While the Brotherhood – as the most popular opposition actor – faces all the means of a repressive authoritarian state, other reform actors with more limited public support are more likely to be targeted by strict regulations. Sometimes they even serve as an important and welcome element in the controlled pluralism allowed in an authoritarian state (with secular opposition parties). The fundamental flaw of Egypt's authoritarian system is the lack of mechanisms which ensure that the different elements of the opposition have the ability not only to articulate their views, but also to act on them. This lack of inclusiveness is best described by the words of Springborg: '[Egypt] is the type of state that allows a relative freedom of expression, but not freedom of action'.[58] As long as the regime adheres to a controlled inclusiveness of the political scene that excludes its adversaries, the 'variety–capability gap' remains valid.

In terms of policy implications for external actors such as the EU, the categorization of Egypt's reform actors with their diverse backgrounds and actor capabilities sheds light on the balance needed between the EU's normative ideals in regard to promoting democracy in the southern Mediterranean (i.e. the MENA region in a wider sense) on the one hand, and the stark reality of which actors the EU should engage with on the ground, on the other. Diversifying cooperation partners might be a first step in improving the coherence of EU foreign policy in this region. As the empirical analysis in this article has shown, the diverse background and actor capability of potential cooperation partners in Egypt stress the need for an improved assessment of state, power, and politics with the constituting actors on the ground in order to ensure a sound implementation of EU's core interests in the MENA region.

Notes

1. Capability is primarily based on the organizational capacity of a certain group to aggregate its objectives, to put the latter into a coherent policy, and to participate in the political arena. In this article, capability is measured in terms of its actual impact on the reform agenda with no comprehensive empirical assessments of the individual organizational capacity and other important qualities for political actors (such as flexibility, credibility, and quickness), cf. Demmelhuber, *EU-Mittelmeerpolitik und der Reformprozess in Ägypten.*
2. In Arabic, the word for reform is 'islah'. It has two meanings: in modern standard Arabic, the term 'islah' is used in a general sense similar to the meaning of the Latin 'reformare'. In contemporary Islamic literature, the content is more diverse and refers to the orthodox reformism of the type that emerges in the writings of late nineteenth-century reformers Mohamed Abduh, Rashid Rida, and their students, cf. *Encylopaedia of Islam*, Vol. IV. Leiden: E.J. Brill, 1978, 141–71.
3. For the case study of Egypt, cf. Kienle, *A Grand Delusion.*
4. Cf. Francesco Cavatorta's contribution to this Special Issue.
5. A majority of the NDP in the Maglis al-Sha'b (lower house of parliament) could only be achieved by the joining of the so-called 'NDPendents'. Upset by the official decision of the NDP committees about which candidate should be fielded in the 222 constituencies, many ran as independent candidates and were able to defeat the official NDP candidates in many constituencies. This lack of party discipline was to be avoided later, but it failed in the 2005 parliamentary elections as well.
6. For the latest biographical update on Gamal Mubarak, cf. Steiner, 'Gamal Husni Mubarak'.
7. The floating of the Egyptian pound (LE) in January 2003 under the disputed government of Prime Minister Ebeid must be seen as the informal trigger for the current reform process.
8. Richter, 'Finishing Off Law 1991/203 and Beyond', 205.
9. These 'young' professionals included Rashid Mohamed Rashid (Ministry of Trade and Industry), Mahmoud Mohieddin (Ministry of Investment), Youssef Boutros

Ghali (Ministry of Finance), Tarek Kamel (Ministry of Communication and Information Technology), Essam Sharaf (Ministry of Transport), Ahmed Darwish (Ministry of Administrative Development), Ahmed el-Maghrabi (Ministry of Tourism), Sameh Fahmi (Ministry of Oil), and Fayza Abul-Naga (Ministry of International Cooperation), cf. Gamal Essam el-Din, 'Reshuffle Postponed', *al-Ahram Weekly* 762 (29 September–5 October 2005).

10. Demmelhuber and Roll, 'Herrschaftssicherung in Ägypten', 26.
11. Gamal Tai'a, 'Ahmad Ezz … wa milyar al-bursa', *Ruz al-Youssef*, 6 June 2006; Ahmad Fakri, 'Maglis idara al-gam'iyya al-lati tahkumu misr', *al-Ghad*, 29 October 2006.
12. Hamzawy, 'Understanding Arab Political Reality', 3.
13. Pierre Prier, 'Rumeurs de succession au pays des pharaons', *Le Figaro*, 4 May 2007.
14. Author's interview (confidential) with a young member of the Muslim Brotherhood, Cairo, March 2008.
15. *al-Akhbar* (Lebanon), 19 February 2007. Author's translation from Arabic.
16. These developments must be seen in the context of the students' association elections of November 2006. The security apparatuses tried to thwart the Brotherhood's election campaigns, thus prompting many students to set up 'Free Students Associations' in order to rival the newly elected student associations, cf. Azuri, 'The Egyptian Regime vs the Muslim Brotherhood'.
17. Zollner, 'Prison Talk'.
18. Sixty-one per cent of the 144 nominated candidates won (88 mandates), cf. Hamzawy and Brown, 'Can Egypt's Troubled Elections Produce a More Democratic Future?', 4.
19. Between 2000 and 2005, 80% of all queries, interpellations, and questions in the Maglis al-Sha'b put forward by independent parliamentarians affiliated to the Muslim Brotherhood dealt with cultural, social, and moral issues. This pattern is likely to continue along with an increased self-defined role of the MB as guardian of the government, cf. Gamal Essam el-Din, 'One More Episode', *al-Ahram Weekly* 822 (30 November–6 December 2006).
20. Ibid.
21. Michael Slackman, 'Egypt Debates the Symbol of the Veil', *International Herald Tribune*, 5 February 2007; Mahmud Muhammed, 'Nuwwab al-watany yattafiqun ma'a al-ikhwan 'ala iqala Faruk Hosni', *al-Masri al-Youm*, 22 November 2006.
22. See Are Hovdenak's contribution to this special issue on the Palestinian case.
23. el-Ghobashy, 'The Metamorphosis of the Egyptian Muslim Brothers', 382ff.
24. Demmelhuber and Roll, 'Herrschaftssicherung in Ägypten', 25f.
25. In this case study of Egypt, syndicates are professional associations of people with the same official job title.
26. The Syndicates Law of 1993 was enacted after several syndicate elections were won by Islamist candidates affiliated to the Muslim Brotherhood. Law 100 gives the government the ultimate power to appoint governing boards of unions and syndicates, to manage the election procedures for the governing boards, and to declare syndicate elections invalid, cf. Wickham, 'Islamic Mobilization and Political Change'.
27. The Egyptian Organization for Human Rights, *The Situation of Human Rights in Egypt*.
28. That is to say, the Engineers', Doctors', Lawyers', Pharmacists', and Scientists' Syndicates, cf. Kassem, *Egyptian Politics*, 112.
29. Author interview with Nasser Amin, Director of the Arab Center for the Independence of the Judiciary and the Legal Profession, Cairo, 28 February 2007.
30. Saad Mahmoud, 'Judge Lashes Out at Gov't and Opposition', *The Egyptian Gazette*, 22 February 2007.
31. Oxford Business Group, *Emerging Egypt 2007*, 12ff.

---

134   *T. Demmelhuber*

32. For an overview of the judges' role in Egyptian history and an analysis of the 'moment of reform' in 2005, see el-Ghobashy, 'Egypt's Paradoxical Elections'.
33. Ebeid, *Parties, Parliament and Democracy in Egypt*, 86.
34. Euchner, 'Opposition'.
35. International Crisis Group, 'Reforming Egypt', 14.
36. The SCC ruling was finally overruled by the constitutional amendments of spring 2007.
37. The debate on the supervisory role of the judiciary during national elections began with a lawsuit filed by an independent candidate for the parliamentary elections in 1990, Gamal al-Nasharti. See Kassem, 'The 2000 Elections', 38.
38. The original Law 40/1977 was amended by Law 170/2005. It established the Political Parties Affairs Committee (PPAC). It is a regime-affiliated committee (associated to the Maglis al-Shura, the upper house of parliament) with full competence to decide over the licensing and possible freezing of parties. The committee is chaired by the speaker of the Maglis al-Shura, who currently serves as General Secretary of the NDP. Dominated by the NDP, it lacks the necessary independence to perform its duties, cf. International Crisis Group, 'Reforming Egypt', 7.
39. Visibility is restricted to the parties' newspapers. All opposition parties are based in Cairo with hardly any party structures in the rest of the country. (Only al-Wafd has a comprehensive network of party offices across the country. Author's interview with Mahmud Abaza, party leader of al-Wafd, Cairo, 25 June 2008.)
40. In 2007 there were promising internal democratic procedures in al-Ghad. See Maram Mazen, 'Ehab El Khouly Wins al-Ghad's Party Presidency', *The Daily Star Egypt*, 7 March 2007.
41. For a comprehensive analysis on this issue, see Stacher, 'Parties Over'.
42. Comprehensive coverage in *al-Quds al-'Arabi*, 1 January 2006.
43. The slogan 'Kifaya' stands for 'al-haraka al-misriyya min agli al-taghyir' ('The Egyptian Movement for Change').
44. 'A Declaration to the Nation' and 'The Egypt We Want', published on the movement's website, http://harakamasria.org.
45. 'Forum on the Middle East and Africa', conference organized by FRIDE (Fundación para las Relaciones Internacionales y el Diálogo Exterior), Madrid, 17 December 2004. Ibrahim was quoted in a report which emerged from this forum.
46. William Safire, 'Kifaya!', *New York Times*, 27 March 2005.
47. Author's interview with Adam Morrow, freelance writer, Cairo, 20 February 2007.
48. It remains to be seen how Kifaya's approach to regional and international issues is subject to change under the new general coordinator, Abdel Wahab Messiri. See Yasmine Saleh, 'Kefaya to Focus on Political Reformation Rather than Demonstrations', *The Daily Star Egypt*, 28 January 2007.
49. March and April 2007 witnessed increased activism of Kifaya in the face of fierce opposition to the constitutional amendments pushed through by the regime; Cynthia Johnston, 'Kifaya Movement Says Referendum Fixed', *The Daily Star Egypt*, 22 March 2007.
50. Vairel, 'Quand "assez"! ne suffit plus'.
51. Sarah Leah Whitson (Middle East Director, Human Rights Watch), quoted in *Human Rights News*, 'Egypt: Blogger's Imprisonment Sets Chilling Precedent'.
52. BBC News, 'Egypt Blogger Jailed for Insult'.
53. Esraa al-Shafei, 'Democracy is Possible, Arab Bloggers Assure us Every Day', *The Daily Star Egypt*, 22 February 2007.
54. Author's interview with Sahar Hamouda, Deputy Director of Alex-Med Research Centre, Alexandria, 19 November 2006.

55. Author's interviews with Nehad Rageh, Project Director at the Egyptian NGO Support Center, Cairo, 1 November 2006 and 23 March 2008.
56. The focus on human rights as a legitimate working field for NGOs was legalized in 2000 by ministerial decree, Human Rights Watch, *Egypt: Margins of Repression*, 9.
57. Author's interview with Bahey el-Din Hassan, Director of the Cairo Institute for Human Rights Studies, Cairo, 20 November 2007.
58. Springborg as quoted in Rania al-Malky, 'Political and Social Protest: A 30-Year Review', *The Daily Star Egypt*, 26 April 2007.

Bibliography

Azuri, L. 'The Egyptian Regime vs. the Muslim Brotherhood'. *The Middle East Media Research Institute*, 5 February 2007, http://www.memri.org/

BBC News. 'Egypt Blogger Jailed for Insult', 22 February 2007, http://news.bbc.co.uk/2/hi/6385849.stm

Demmelhuber, Thomas. *EU-Mittelmeerpolitik und der Reformprozess in Ägypten. Von der Partnerschaft zur Nachbarschaft*. Baden-Baden: Nomos, 2009.

Demmelhuber, Thomas, and Stephan Roll. 'Herrschaftssicherung in Ägypten. Zur Rolle von Reformen und Wirtschaftsoligarchen'. *SWP-Studie*. 20th ed. Berlin: German Institute for International and Security Affairs, 2007.

Ebeid, Mona Makram. *Parties, Parliament and Democracy in Egypt*. Cairo: AUC Press, 2003.

el-Ghobashy, Mona. 'Egypt's Paradoxical Elections'. *Middle East Report* 238 (2006): 20–9.

el-Ghobashy, Mona. 'The Metamorphosis of the Egyptian Muslim Brothers'. *The International Journal of Middle Eastern Studies* 3 (2005): 373–95.

Euchner, Walter. 'Opposition'. *Handlexikon zur Politikwissenschaft*, ed. W. Mickel, and Wolfgang. (pp. 322–25). Munich: Ehrenwirth, 1983.

Hamzawy, Amr. 'Understanding Arab Political Reality'. *Policy Outlook April 2005*. Washington, DC: Carnegie Endowment for International Peace, 2005.

Hamzawy, Amr, and Nathan J. Brown. 'Can Egypt's Troubled Elections Produce a More Democratic Future?'. *Policy Outlook December 2005*. Washington, DC: Carnegie Endowment for International Peace, 2005.

Human Rights News. 'Egypt: Blogger's Imprisonment Sets Chilling Precedent', http://hrw.org/english/docs/2007/02/22/egypt15379.htm

Human Rights Watch. *Egypt: Margins of Repression. State Limits on Nongovernmental Organization Activities* vol. 17, p. 8. Cairo, 2005.

International Crisis Group. 'Reforming Egypt: In Search of a Strategy'. *Middle East and North Africa Report* 46 (2005).

Kassem, Maye. 'The 2000 Elections: New Rules, New Tactics'. *Elections in the Middle East. What Do They Mean?*, ed. A. Hamdy, and Iman. (pp. 38–49). Cairo: AUC Press, 2004.

Kassem, Maye. *Egyptian Politics: The Dynamics of Authoritarian Rule*. Boulder: Lynne Rienner Publishers, 2004.

Kienle, Eberhard. *A Grand Delusion. Democracy and Economic Reform in Egypt*. London: I.B. Tauris, 2000.

Oxford Business Group. *Emerging Egypt 2007*. London, 2006.

Richter, Frederik. 'Finishing Off Law 1991/203 and Beyond: The Egyptian Privatization Programme during 2005'. *L'Égypte dans l'année 2005*, ed. Florian Kohstall, 203–26. Cairo: CEDEJ, 2006.

Stacher, Joshua A. 'Parties Over: The Demise of Egypt's Opposition Parties'. *British Journal of Middle Eastern Studies* 2 (2004): 215–33.

Steiner, Johannes. 'Gamal Husni Mubarak'. *Orient* 3 (2006): 311–22.

The Egyptian Organization for Human Rights. *The Situation of Human Rights in Egypt - Annual Report 2002*. Cairo, 2003, http://www.eohr.org/annual/wr02/ar1.htm (Chapter IX: 'The Right to Form Parties, Associations and Unions').

Vairel, Frédéric. 'Quand "assez"! ne suffit plus: Quelques remarques sur Kifaya et autres mobilisations égyptiennes'. *L'Égypte dans l'année 2005*, ed. Florian Kohstall, 109–36. Cairo: CEDEJ, 2006.

Wickham, Carrie Rosefsky. 'Islamic Mobilization and Political Change: The Islamic Trend in Egypt's Professional Associations'. *Political Islam. Essays from Middle East Report*, ed. Joel Beinin and Joe Stark, 120–35. Berkeley: University of California Press, 1997.

Zollner, Barbara. 'Prison Talk: The Muslim Brotherhood's Internal Struggle during Gamal Abdel Nasser's Persecution 1954 to 1971'. *The International Journal of Middle Eastern Studies* 3 (2007): 411–33.

'Divided they stand, divided they fail': opposition politics in Morocco

Francesco Cavatorta

School of Law and Government, Dublin City University, Dublin 9, Ireland

The literature on democratization emphasises how authoritarian constraints usually lead genuine opposition parties and movements to form alliances in order to make demands for reform to the authoritarian regime. There is significant empirical evidence to support this theoretical point. While this trend is partly visible in the Middle East and North Africa, such coalitions are usually short-lived and limited to a single issue, never reaching the stage of formal and organic alliances. This article, using the case of Morocco, seeks to explain this puzzle by focusing on ideological and strategic differences that exist between the Islamist and the secular/liberal sectors of civil society, where significant opposition politics occurs. In addition, this article also aims to explain how pro-democracy strategies of the European Union further widen this divide, functioning as a key obstacle to democratic reforms.

Introduction

The democratization literature on the Middle East and North Africa (MENA) has recently begun to focus attention on the behaviour and actions of parties and movements operating under authoritarian conditions. Similar analyses were in the past conducted by using the theoretical tools of transitology, whose main assumptions were first set out in the mid-1980s in the work of Schmitter and O'Donnell,[1] and which served as a key theoretical framework to explain processes of democratization. In addition to its academic value, some decision-makers used findings to inform their policies when 'crafting' democracy.[2] However, in recent times, many of the original findings have come under criticism in light of new theoretical contributions and empirical evidence.[3] Perhaps more importantly, many scholars now realize that 'democratization got stuck in many transition countries',[4] requiring different theoretical approaches to analyse existing political systems.

With the controversial exceptions of Israel, Turkey, and arguably Lebanon, the MENA stands out for its relative lack of consolidated or established democracies, despite various processes of ongoing liberalization initiated in the late 1980s and 1990s. Given the persistence of authoritarianism,[5] it has become more fruitful to abandon the rigidity of the transition paradigm and concentrate on the examination of opposition dynamics without linking them to the 'teleology of transitology'.[6] As Pripstein-Posusney argues, 'there is a paucity of comparative literature on opposition strategies under pseudo-democratic conditions',[7] where façade democratic institutions often provide cover for the unaccountability and authoritarianism of the principal decision-makers,[8] and an analysis of opposition dynamics may reveal processes that the literature on democratization does not appear to capture. The specific focus of such studies is on cross-ideological co-operation between opposition actors. In this context, there is the theoretical expectation that under authoritarian constraints opposition groups, irrespective of their ideological positions and policy preferences, will pool their resources to try to pressurize the regime into reforming the political system because they all share the common objective of eliminating the authoritarian player to open up the political space. This is to be expected because it is only the removal of authoritarian constraints that will allow genuine opposition actors to put forth their visions of a new society freely. There is substantial empirical evidence from Eastern European and Latin American cases to suggest that such a theoretical assumption carries considerable validity.[9] In addition, it is important to emphasize that international actors play a significant role in generating 'pooling dynamics' among opposition groups. The European Union has been traditionally very active in processes of democratization,[10] by sponsoring opposition groups in order to help them create the circumstances for political pluralism, as the more recent cases of Serbia and Georgia also demonstrate.

This article argues that in the MENA, contrary to some claims, effective unity of the opposition does not occur and it postulates that there is much more competition than cooperation among opposition groups. This is particularly true when one examines the fractious relationships between secular/liberal movements on the one side and Islamist ones on the other. The article attempts to explain why the MENA deviates from the expected behaviour of alliance-building between genuine opposition groups. The analysis concentrates on the Moroccan case and examines the divisions within the opposition not only in the context of ideological differences and tactical considerations, but also in light of the preponderant role that the EU plays in reinforcing such divisions through its direct policies of democracy promotion and its wider Euro-Mediterranean Partnership framework.

While there are methodological problems in selecting only one case study, the broad similarities that exist between many countries in the region, in terms of the widespread existence of authoritarianism, the presence of similar political opposition dynamics with a dominant Islamist current and a less popular secular-liberal one, and the role of the EU as an external promoter of regional policies of democratization and market liberalization, might allow for useful generalizations.

Morocco is a useful case study because of the nature of its political system, based on the controversial concept of *alternance*[11] implemented by the late King Hassan II. It is precisely in such contexts, where the previous exclusionary rules of participation have been relaxed in order to create a shift towards more pluralism, as attested by the inclusion of an Islamist party into the political system and the growth of autonomous social movements and civil society organizations, that we might witness the emergence of a unified opposition demanding significant and meaningful democratic institutional changes, such as the revision of the current constitution.

Theoretical discussion

Under pseudo-democratic conditions, where a degree of pluralism is introduced in the hope of re-legitimizing the authoritarian system, it is logical to assume that genuine opposition actors, irrespective of their ideological and policy differences, will coalesce, if only temporarily, to put pressure on the regime to accede to their demands for more democratic change. Such an assumption is theoretically sound because opposition groups under an authoritarian regime are likely to suffer from the same constraints on their political activities and are likely to share the same desire for the authoritarian player to be removed. Thus, it seems legitimate to hypothesize that such circumstances would lead to identifying the regime as the common, principal 'enemy'. This would in turn be expected to lead to the creation of some sort of united front, electoral alliance or umbrella organization to deal with the ruling elites and negotiate or demand, depending on their strength and resources, political reforms. The creation of a viable alternative to the regime in place is paramount because an authoritarian system can survive without much legitimacy.[12] Thus, in past transitions to democracy, such umbrella organizations were indeed created and alliance-building was common. Acting as rational actors, opposition parties in authoritarian regimes often form electoral alliances to unsettle the predominance of the ruling party and are at times quite successful, through this alliance, in triggering wider political reforms.[13]

Thus, the pooling of resources is expected to take place because there is a common objective to be achieved and differences can be briefly set aside, as the removal of the authoritarian player is the most pressing common goal. Ideological differences and policy disputes are also momentarily set aside because if the authoritarian player remains in control such debates are of only academic interest. It follows that the assumption regarding the inevitability of coalition-building among opposition groups carries considerable theoretical weight in the sense that it constitutes rational behaviour for political groups wishing to reform the existing system.[14]

Furthermore, there is a significant amount of empirical evidence to support the claim that coalition-building is likely to occur when one examines the experiences of Eastern Europe and Latin America. In his examination of the democratization of the then Czechoslovakia, Olson points out that all the opposition groups and leading civil society movements 'were submerged ... in the formation of the Civic Forum of Prague, and the Public Against Violence in Bratislava. Both were amorphous reform groupings, united for the single purpose of removing communists from power. Having quickly achieved their goal, they as quickly lost the source of their cohesion'.[15] The Polish transition showed similar traits as the 'lay left' opposition were joined by Catholic activists within the umbrella group established prior to the arrival of *Solidarnosc* on the scene. *Solidarnosc* itself was a vast collection of groups and individuals with different agendas, but with the common intent of removing the communists from power.[16] The post-transition divisions within the movement, which led to the creation of a number of political parties claiming a *Solidarnosc* legacy, testify to the ideological heterogeneity of the movement. The experience of some Eastern European countries is by no means unique and the Chilean opposition was also able to achieve a considerable degree of unity to remove Pinochet by bringing together a number of different social movements and parties with very little in common in terms of ideology and policy preferences.[17]

Given the strength of both the theoretical assumptions and the extent of supportive empirical evidence, we might expect that similar behaviour would occur in other authoritarian contexts where a certain degree of liberalization is introduced and where there are a number of active opposition groups. Both these conditions are present in many MENA countries, which, at different times over the last two decades, have experienced some political liberalization and the emergence of opposition actors. It is plausible to argue both that other regions' democratization experiences are applicable to the MENA as well to contend that the region should not be treated as unique when it comes to social fragmentation, civil society activism, and opposition dynamics.[18]

Indeed, a number of scholars point out that coalition-building has been in place for some time and continues to characterize MENA political systems when these become more open, pointing again to the existence of trends found in other regions. For example, in Jordan the Islamist Islamic Action Front (IAF) participated in the Higher Committee for the Coordination of National Opposition Parties (HCCNOP) with leftist and secular parties.[19] In Egypt, the Muslim Brotherhood has a history of striking electoral alliances with secular opposition parties, as it did with the Wafd and Labour party[20] in the 1980s, while more recently 'Islamists are part of the pro-democracy Kifaya coalition'.[21] In Algeria, the Islamist Front Islamique de Salut (FIS) and a number of secular, leftist movements agreed on a common platform of demands during the civil war, highlighting the proximity of views between ideological rivals on democratic procedures.[22] In Tunisia, secular intellectuals and political parties with an anti-Islamist ethos made a rapprochement towards Islamists in order to highlight the repressive measures of the regime for the international community.[23] More recently, Lebanon experienced the emergence of an unexpected alliance between Hezbollah and Michel Aoun's party.[24] In Yemen, the Islamist Islah party cooperated with its secular counterparts.[25]

However, alliance-building has not been deep or effective to any significant extent and it can be argued that it has been mainly of a tactical nature. This is indeed the crucial point. Alliances in MENA countries seem to be very tentative and ad hoc; opposition movements manage to build coalitions in order to put pressure on the regime on a specific issue, but the short-term nature of their accords never develops into more wide-ranging programmes for change. This is particularly evident in the absence of a truly sustained dialogue between opposition Islamists and secular-liberal and leftist movements, whose relationships are fraught with difficulties and suspicions. Thus, rapprochements never seem to go beyond the achievement of limited results, fail to be sustained over time, and are consequently generally weak. It is the absence of sustainability of these experiences that characterizes most opposition politics in the MENA and it is therefore important to explore why such coalition-building dynamics fail to be effective when, under similar circumstances, other coalition-building efforts in different areas of the globe consolidated successfully.[26] If the MENA is unique in this respect, then what are the conditions of its uniqueness?

All this presents a significant academic puzzle and, at the same time, poses a challenge for domestic and international actors genuinely interested in and committed to democratic change. The absence of a significant degree of unity among opposition movements partially contributes to explaining how authoritarian regimes in the region have been able to remain in power despite the legitimacy crisis that many suffer from.

There are two major explanations that focus on the inability of the opposition to have a more central role in the lengthy processes of democratic transition in the region, but they are mostly concerned with the capabilities of the regime rather than the deficiencies of the opposition. Firstly, as Eva Bellin argues, 'authoritarianism has proven exceptionally robust in the Middle East and North Africa because the coercive apparatus in many states has been exceptionally able and willing to crush reform initiatives from below'.[27] This points to the efficiency of the regimes in stifling opposition, which, weakened by constant repression, is therefore unable to make coherent demands because it is first and foremost preoccupied with its own survival. Albrecht offers a different explanation and focuses his attention on strategies of selective co-optation, which divide opposition groups. Some opposition figures and movements are periodically integrated into the regime, but they are unable to influence policy-making decisions and are almost entirely dependent on the authoritarian leader for survival and for benefits.[28]

The focus on repression and co-optation overemphasizes the material and legitimacy resources necessary for the authoritarian regimes to implement such strategies and overlooks both the strength of opposition actors and the dynamics that often characterize their relationships. It follows that the absence of coalition-building cannot solely be explained by focusing on the regimes' strengths. First of all, a number of authoritarian regimes do not possess sufficient material and legitimacy resources necessary to effectively repress and/or co-opt opposition all of the time.[29] This is evident in the regimes' attempt to recapture legitimacy through the introduction of 'façade' democratic changes such as multiparty elections for legislatures that are virtually emptied of any meaningful policy-making power and autonomy. Secondly, the importance of ideology in polarized authoritarian societies should be taken into account. As hinted by Pripstein-Posusney, it is ideological disagreements that are usually to blame for the failure of both electoral and non-electoral coalitions between opposition actors in authoritarian contexts.[30] Thirdly, in order for the co-optation of opposition groups by the ruling elites to be successful, one needs to rely on the willingness of actors to be co-opted through incentives that are greater than the positive inducements of coalition-building.

Following on from the previous discussion, this article hypothesizes that coalition-building does not occur because of ideological differences and tactical considerations between opposition actors, played out in a context where the international dimension has become a crucial variable in how domestic political and economic arrangements are advanced.[31] The opposition groups in the MENA are considerably more divided than their counterparts in other transitional countries on the type of post-authoritarian society that they would like to construct because their belief systems are often very different, sometimes simply irreconcilable. While it could be argued that such ideological and policy differences often also characterized other societies, the contention of this article is that the strength of Islamist ideological discourse and its potential, practical translation into legislation about, for example, women, minorities or religious schooling, is very much perceived to be inimical to the construction of some form of western-style liberal-democracy, which is the ultimate objective of other sectors of the opposition and of the international community. While the division of the opposition into a secular/liberal/leftist camp and an Islamist one might seem arbitrary, it is analytically useful because, ultimately, the question of the creation of an Islamic state, which all Islamists want, is divisive and the views about it potentially irreconcilable. In this sense, Islamism deserves to be taken seriously as an ideological project. Islamists typically have a rather clear ideological script to which they refer, striving to translate their ideological position into specific policies, as Pace clarifies in her contribution to this special issue. It is true that there are a number of competing 'Islamisms' to be accounted for, but divisions within political Islam are tactical rather than ideological, particularly when it comes to the objective of creating the Islamic state, whatever that may mean to different Islamist groups.[32]

During transitions to democracy outside the MENA, opposition parties and movements were significantly divided over issues related to the institutional set-up of the country, the electoral system to be adopted, and the type of economic development to be undertaken. In the MENA these issues are equally divisive, but, in addition, there is the very controversial issue of the role of religion in shaping public policy in all domains of political, social, cultural, and economic interaction. To some extent, all issues are ultimately informed by the ideological position on the role of religion in politics. This is very problematic for the linkage between liberalism and democratic procedures. Furthermore, Western states are opposed to any role for Islamists in the decision-making process regarding the future of the countries in the region, as Volpi highlights in his contribution. Thus, the opposition of the international community to political Islam has a significant influence on how domestic actors interact with each other because of the resources that external actors can distribute in the domestic political game.

A further issue to deal with is the paradox of a 'democratic discourse' that all MENA opposition groups adopt. What is striking when one examines their public pronouncements is that all opposition movements, Islamists included, utilize very similar discourses when outlining their position. For instance, in Morocco, the discourse of the Islamist Justice and Charity Group is favourable to procedural democracy[33] as the only way for the country to exit the crisis it finds itself in, just like a number of secular and liberal social movements which claim that democratic procedures and protection of human rights are the only solution to the country's ills. Thus, there is a rhetorical consensus on democracy, human rights, justice, accountability, and independence, which would indicate that they all strive for the same objectives and should, therefore, find it easy to come to an accommodation.[34] Such concepts, however, take on very different meanings depending on which group is using them illustrating the paradox of all groups who use a democratic discourse without agreeing on basic definitions of its fundamental concepts. This demonstrates how only an ideological understanding of their use can explain why, despite such rhetorical consensus, that there are no practical and concrete measures taken to translate it into coalition-building. This further paradox is at the heart of the political debate in the MENA region where opposition movements regularly accuse each other of 'lying their way to power'. Non-Islamist opposition actors for whom democratic political change equates to the elimination of religion from public life are very sceptical of the pro-democracy stances of Islamist parties and prefer to side with the authoritarian rulers in the hope of obtaining limited advantages rather than choosing full co-operation with a political player they do not trust.[35]

Tactical considerations compound these ideological differences. In transitions elsewhere, it was almost impossible for opposition actors to know *a priori* what their level of popular support was likely to be once free and fair elections were called. This scenario does not exist in the MENA, as past elections in the region have been extremely significant because they have shown that Islamism enjoys much – although variable levels of – support.[36] The same cannot be said for either the ruling parties or, more importantly, for the secular opposition parties. Given the poor performances of secular leftist and liberal parties, it should not come as a surprise that cooperation with Islamists is a very contentious issue for them. Most activists in the secular camp are convinced that Islamist movements would often do extremely well in free and fair elections and they are afraid of the potential institutional and legislative changes that Islamists would introduce, rolling democratic achievements back.[37] Thus, it would not make sense for secular/liberal/leftist groups to work closely with Islamists against the ruling regime because a genuine process of democratization might

well not benefit them, but instead aid a feared competitor. In this scenario, it is also
no surprise that Islamist movements in recent times have expressed the wish to
cooperate with the secular elements of the opposition in order to secure both
acceptance and some form of democratic legitimacy. When it comes to the Islamists' strategy, they seem to consider coalition-building as a welcome development if done on their own terms, but there is no incentive to truly compromise
on key issues, given that they expect to win free and fair elections, which will
give them the opportunity to dominate the new institutions.[38]

This article examines Morocco in order to analyse the validity of such a framework in explaining why effective and long-lasting coalitions do not occur in the
country. In order to substantiate the hypothesis that ideological difference is the
main variable explaining absence of coalition-building, there should be sufficient
evidence to demonstrate that ideology and references to very different belief
systems are at the heart of the political discourse of the opposition actors. In
addition, it should be demonstrated that references to such belief systems are
not simply made in order to claim some form of legitimacy, but are a crucial
part of policy formation. Finally, there should be evidence that the actions and
activities of international actors, specifically the European Union, reinforce such
a divide and contribute to the persistence of authoritarianism.

Opposition politics in Morocco

Morocco is today categorized as a 'liberalised autocracy',[39] where the ultimate
decision-maker, the king, is unelected and unaccountable, but also where a multi-
party system exists alongside a degree of individual freedoms. The system as a
whole rests on the centrality of the monarchy, but some political institutions and
large sectors of society display a degree of pluralism that challenges the authoritarianism of the system.

Morocco has always maintained at least some façade of pluralism,[40] but under
King Mohammed VI, who gained the throne in 1999, there has been a relaxation
of the most authoritarian aspects of the regime and this has encouraged more openness and more participation in the political process,[41] leading to the emergence of a
number of outspoken opposition actors. Looking at the institutional level, there are
a number of political parties that are formally independent from the monarchy and
argue for changes that would see the introduction of accountability for the principal decision-makers. However political parties, including the Socialist Union and
the Islamist Party of Justice and Development (PJD),[42] have largely been co-opted
in so far as they have to recognise the primacy of the king if they wish to be integrated into the system.

Thus, it is only by looking at the broader social level that one sees the emergence of movements dedicated to reforming radically all aspects of Moroccan
politics and society. It is in the realm of civil society where the confrontational attitudes of different opposition groups are the clearest. As Michael Willis highlights,
political parties in North Africa are highly discredited in the eyes of many citizens

and do not perform the basic tasks that political parties should be carrying out.[43] Thus, to a significant extent, 'opposition politics' takes place within civil society and, therefore, opposition dynamics should be examined in this context. In addition, the European Union, through its policies for the region, has explicitly designed democracy promotion strategies on strengthening civil society because it believes that it is only through increased civil society activism that democratic reforms will be introduced and sustained.[44]

The activism of civil society in Morocco has been examined in some detail elsewhere,[45] but it is worth reiterating here that there is a strong presence of both secular/liberal groups (among the most active organizations are women's rights groups) and Islamist ones, in particular al Adl led by Sheikh Yassine, which is probably the largest Islamist movement in the country.[46] The level of co-operation between the two sectors of civil society is quite limited. On issues such as prisoners' rights, there is some convergence between the two camps, as there is on some foreign policy matters, such as the Palestinian–Israeli conflict. Such convergence is at times explicit and takes the form of mass demonstrations, such as the pro-Palestinian march in July 2006 in Rabat.[47] The potential for convergence on more explicitly domestic, political issues is there,[48] but it is never fully exploited and divisions tend to emerge quickly and strongly, reinforcing the separation already in existence. All alliances are temporary and focused on specific issues without spill-over effects into more comprehensive coalition-building.

The explanation for the inability and unwillingness of these groups to co-operate more fully with each other and establish a common platform of minimal demands for change is largely due to the radically different visions that they have for Morocco. Such different and, crucially, competing visions are the product of three interconnected factors. First of all, the respective ideological programmes, positions, and values have their roots in two systems of beliefs that seem to contradict one another to the point of conflict. Secondly, such ideological conflicts are reinforced by the activities and beliefs of external actors, specifically the European Union, attempting to promote a particular version of democracy. Finally, there are tactical considerations related to perceived strength of all actors involved.

As in other post-colonial societies, two different ideological poles of reference uneasily co-exist in Morocco: an imported European liberal secularism and an Islamism based on indigenous traditions and interpretations. While this might be a crude differentiation in light of the surge of post-Islamism,[49] it is important to emphasize that the worldviews and sources of legitimacy of these two poles make it extremely complicated to have a workable synthesis along Turkish lines, which, some contend, is in a state of crisis of itself. On matters related to democracy, democratization, and human rights, these two poles of reference differ quite substantially. Both ideological referents claim that a 'new', more democratic and more just Morocco can be built if the prescriptions of their respective ideologies are correctly followed.[50] Both desire radical change and wish to construct a more equitable society, where the leadership is accountable to the people. On closer inspection, the language of both is indeed similar, but the 'content' which is to constitute this 'new' country radically differs. The debate mainly centres on the role of religion in the public sphere, on which all other issues, ranging from individual freedoms to economic policy, depend for a resolution.

The focus on Sheikh Yassine's (the leader of the outlawed Islamist movement, the Justice and Charity Group) group is valid because of the dominance of the group within the Islamist camp in Morocco, particularly after the snubbing that the PJD, the main Islamist ideological rival, received from voters in the September 2007 elections.[51] The Justice and Charity Group refuses to engage in what it perceives to be a rigged political system, which does not take into account the will of Moroccans. Judging by the low voter turnout at the September 2007 legislative elections, it could be inferred that many ordinary Moroccans share this view.

If one examines the rhetoric of Sheikh Yassine, it emerges that he has nothing but contempt for the modernity the West espouses,[52] which is precisely the type of modernity that many among the secular and liberal Moroccans (such as Nourredine Saoudi, a leading civil society activist, who argues that the rise of Islamism is a danger for Morocco)[53] aspire to. In fact, according to Maddy-Weitzman, 'Yassine [views] modernity and its globalised culture as superficial and even bestial'.[54] In particular, he rejects the notion that any political, economic, and social system can be based on absolute rationality because 'a modern notion of progress founded on reason and committed entirely to efficiency'[55] is bound to lead to disastrous results such as Nazism and the breakdown of the fabric of society. According to Lauzière, 'Yassine undertakes what can be called an epistemological and spiritual *dawa*, in which he attempts to debunk the rational assumptions that have characterised philosophical modernity since the Enlightenment'.[56] Thus, instead of aping Western modernity, Yassine wishes for Muslims to revert back to Islam and the notions it provides in order to construct a society that is certainly rational, but where the spiritual and the divine also have a place because it is only through spiritual connections that society can truly be just and well-balanced. Such criticism of current Western modernity does not represent an exception within the world of Islamism and is the starting point of the critique that Yassine and other Islamist thinkers put forward when analysing the state of their respective societies. According to them, Muslim polities have been bastardized by 'occidentalizing elites' and reduced to spiritual rubble. The solution to the material and spiritual ills of Morocco that Yassine identifies, such as very poor social indicators, a weak position in the international system and widespread corruption, is obviously a return to Islam and, more specifically, the creation of an Islamic state. In his Memorandum to King Mohammed VI, Yassine writes: 'we reject all that risks to make us part way with our very own *raison d'être*: Islam'.[57] It is, therefore, the 'applied' spirituality of Islam that will rescue Morocco with its principles of social justice and moral behaviour. The problem with such language and ideological drive is that they do little to reassure secular opposition groups because they are vague in terms of the crucial aspects of who is to govern society and on what legitimacy one is to govern. Yassine offers dogmatic certainty at a time when 'it is easy to see liberal-democracy not as the crowning achievement of civilisation but as manifestation of a laissez-faire, morally bankrupt modernity'.[58] For this he might be appealing to some, but appears dangerous to others. The appeal of his rhetoric should not be underestimated, as he is the leader of an Islamist movement with a large and dedicated following. Despite his Sufi-imbued discourse, Yassine's political Islam is quite representative of mainstream Islamist movements elsewhere, particularly when it comes to condemn what are perceived the most deleterious aspects of Western modernity and offers 'Islam as the solution'.[59]

Yassine's religious discourse does not necessarily make al Adl an enemy of democracy *per se*.[60] In fact, Yassine argues that the only concrete way out of the current crisis is for Morocco to hold genuinely free and fair elections, which would produce accountable, political representatives. Yassine states, 'democracy, understood as the freedom and the right of the people to choose their own government, is for us the only way out of the authoritarian darkness'.[61] However, and this is where secular liberal groups again criticize and fear al Adl, he goes on to argue that there is a distinction between the procedures of democracy and the corollaries to these procedures, such as secularization and indifference to spiritual values, which he strongly rejects. The endpoint of any transition is for Yassine 'a democratic process in which Islam is established [in power]',[62] but it is not specified how this would take into account the positions of those who claim that Islam should be relegated to the private sphere. Furthermore, Yassine seems to leave the door wide open to the possibility that the future leaders of Morocco might also have to invoke religious legitimacy in order to govern, which would, according to his secular critics, defeat the very purpose of democratization. After all, the King already rules because of his religious legitimacy, and Zaghal points out how Yassine challenges the monarchy precisely on religious grounds, making political contestation religion-dependent rather than excluding it and focusing on individual rights and full, popular sovereignty.[63] On this point, the divergence between opposition groups with different ideological references is very significant. Al Adl does not yet participate in institutional politics and calls instead for radical reforms that would be initiated with the election of a 'Council of the People of Morocco', a popularly elected constitutional assembly that would discuss the future of the country and the institutional choices to be made.[64] This might in theory be acceptable to other groups, but would not solve the issue of religious legitimacy to rule.

In some respects, the positions and activities of al Adl should not be seen as inherently incompatible with what secular and liberal associations believe and do, such as delivering essential social services, promoting accountability of officials, defending the rights of political prisoners and advocating genuine democratic change. Yassine's critique of the ills of Moroccan society is shared by liberal and leftwing circles, particularly when it comes to discussing the country's very poor social indicators. The same United Nations statistics that Yassine uses to make his case for Islamism are also used by secular and liberal associations to highlight the problems of Morocco. In addition, just like al Adl, a number of different organizations are involved in charitable work and are politically active in their attempt to combat corruption and protect human rights. However, the ideological references and, hence, the endpoint of a Moroccan political transformation, are so different that any formal coalition-building is prevented.

Leftist liberal secular groups are much smaller in numbers than the Islamist associations connected to Yassine or to the PJD, and are generally founded and run by members of the French-educated elite. This is particularly true of women's associations, whose work is highly controversial in Islamist circles. Their values and references, are steeped in the legacy of the Enlightenment and anchored to rational, Western modernity, according to which religious values might be personally important, but should be categorically excluded from public policy-making. The colonial experience ended in Morocco in 1956, but the intellectual legacy of France is still very much present, and while there is certainly a degree of respect for Islam as a system of religious beliefs, there is the conviction that there should not be 'submission' to it in terms of political positions as argued by, for instance, the Socialist Party.[65] Thus, the endpoint of a potential transition in Morocco for secular-liberal groups is a secular state where Islam is completely taken out of politics and privatized. The rhetorical question in secular circles is, 'if Islam were not excluded, how could it be institutionalized without a return to authoritarianism or the creation of new types of discrimination?' For instance, what status would be adopted for the Moroccan Jews, given Yassine's barely concealed anti-Semitism?[66] As Pratt argues, 'many women's rights activists are concerned about cooperation with Islamist groups because they believe that an Islamic state represents one of the greatest obstacles to women in gaining equal rights'.[67] The secularists' fear of political Islam is summed up in the words of a former leftist political prisoner now engaged in human rights issues, who stated that 'the vast majority of Islamists do not subscribe to the universal values of democracy and simply want to use the procedures of democracy to come to power and impose a theocratic regime on the rest of society'.[68]

Different ideological references explain the mutual accusations that both sectors of civil society fling at each other. On the one hand, Islamist groups accuse the modernizing elites and the secular liberal and leftists groups of having adopted the former colonialists' lifestyle and values, which allow them to maintain their privileged status, and of attempting to force these values on the rest of Moroccan society. On the other, Islamists are accused of intolerance and lack of sincerity in their pronouncements in favour of democracy and human rights.[69] The tensions that arose between the two camps at the time of the reform of the family code and in the aftermath of the Casablanca bombings of May 2003 testify to these profound divisions. Such ideological positions are interpreted not simply as rhetorical devices, but are perceived to be true beliefs upon which these movements would act in terms of legislation if they were permitted to do so, as the legislative changes introduced by other Islamist parties when in power show.[70] Thus, Yassine's insistence on the application of *sharia* law is viewed not simply as consistent with his ideological discourse, but as a concrete, political demand, which other opposition groups find unacceptable because their references are not in Islam, but in liberal, Western thinking.

If we add to this the importance of tactical considerations, it should come as no surprise that effective and sustained co-operation does not occur. The electoral advances of the PJD frightened secular movements, even though the 2007 parliamentary elections saw them gain 'only' second place. In addition, the potential arrival of al Adl on the electoral scene might further polarize things. The secular groups' fear of electoral marginalization is a powerful incentive not to build coalitions.

The democracy promotion measures that the international community and the European Union (EU) in particular set forth are highly problematic in this context because they simply reinforce the divisions between the two sectors of civil society, rather than promoting their rapprochement. The EU implements a double strategy to promote democratization in Morocco.[71] The first pillar is trying to engage the regime in a series of reform processes that would lead it to adopt democratic changes over a number of years because of its interactions with the EU, which provides financial help to key reform sectors of the institutional and economic set up of the country. The second pillar is the fostering of civil society activism, which, building on the experience of Eastern Europe,[72] is believed to be a necessary building bloc of democracy because of its ability to make demands on the authoritarian regime from below. So far this strategy has been a comprehensive failure[73] and, paradoxically, Morocco is probably more authoritarian today than it was five years ago. This new, authoritarian turn is partly due to international circumstances, which impacted quite significantly on Morocco with the 'arrival' on the scene of suicide terrorism, but it is also the product of the failure of the EU as a whole to put significant pressure on the regime to implement serious changes due to EU preference for securitization over normative change, which have become even more significant in the context of 'the war on terror'.

Channelling aid and funds for reform through the regime's institutions is certainly a mistake because the availability of external resources facilitates the task of blocking demands for change. However, the negative impact of the EU is much more significant at the level of civil society because of the fact that its policies are based on the perception that Islamism poses a problem rather than an opportunity. Islamism as a whole represents a challenge not only because of its potentially antagonistic stances *vis à vis* the West, but because it offers a view of democracy and a vision of society perceived to be at odds with the European experience and interpretation of what constitutes democracy. The values and the type of democracy that the European Union exports is inevitably linked to the experience and the ideology upon which democracy was first established in Europe, how it developed, and how it merged liberalism with democratic procedures. It is thus quite logical that the European Union provides funds to those associations that are seemingly ideologically close to its views, while also supporting similar values on the other side of the Mediterranean. In the case of Morocco, 11 million dirhams (US$1.5m) were handed out in 2006 to civil society groups: not one was an Islamist organization.[74]

This poses a double problem. Firstly, the secular and liberal groups in Morocco such as Feminine Solidarity, cannot count on as many activists as the Islamist groups and hence the people involved constitute a minority of those who are politically active in opposition. In addition, the accusation of being anti-Islamic for the work they do (caring for single mothers) further puts pressure on them and their operations.[75] Secondly, the EU does not only promote democracy, but pursues other objectives, such as the economic integration of Morocco into a free trade area, which may further impoverish ordinary Moroccans.[76] Thus, the beneficiaries of European support expose themselves to the criticisms of Islamists because they not only import 'un-Islamic' values, but also because by their activism they arguably contribute to the country's continuing poverty. In sum, support of only a certain sector of the opposition and close interaction with the regime make the EU a problematic actor rather than a facilitator of genuine democratic change.

In addition, the European Union refrains from engaging with Islamists. By implication, this labels Islamists as 'undesirable', as if they had nothing to contribute to the pro-democracy debate and were not the potential representatives of the majority of Moroccans. The popularity of Islamism is evident, but the EU ignores it and treats political Islam solely as challenge. Thus, the EU prefers to either cosy up to the regime or only deal with opposition movements that largely share the same values, forgetting that such values, in the eyes of many ordinary Moroccans, simply represent the continuation of a form of cultural, economic, and political colonialism.[77]

The inability and the unwillingness of European policy-makers even to conceive of the possibility that an alternative might exist to liberal democracy, such as an Islamic one, reinforces the domestic divisions among opposition groups in Morocco and, while the intervention of the international community is welcomed by the secular/liberal groups, it is resented by Islamists. As the spokesperson of al Adl argued, 'there is fundamentalism today in the West',[78] by which he implied that there is a strong bias against Islamists and Islam.

Conclusion

During processes of liberalization it might be expected that opposition groups, irrespective of their differences, would coalesce to achieve the one, common objective that stops them from operating freely: the institutional elimination of the authoritarian gate-keeper. The expectation was confirmed in a number of cases in the transitions of Eastern Europe and Latin America, but such sustained co-operation does not seem to characterize the MENA. There is a degree of co-operation on some specific issues, but there is no formalized coalition. The absence of such co-operation in the case of Morocco is all the more surprising because of a tradition of limited political pluralism and the presence of Islamist movements that have either been institutionalized (the PJD), or have strongly committed themselves to change through peaceful means (al Adl).

The divisions are particularly strong between secular, liberal leftist groups engaged in democratization and human rights work, and Islamist associations connected to al Adl and the PJD. The explanation for the absence of formal coalitions between the two sectors rests on three interconnected factors. First, the ideological divide between the two sectors of society is so significant that they fear each other more than they fear the continuation of authoritarian rule. The strength of Islam as an ideological reference frightens secular and liberal groups, just as the attachment of the latter to the values of the Enlightenment and European modernity unsettles Islamists. The ideological divide is so profound that both sectors are aware of the fact that specific, probably unwelcome, policies would flow from such ideological stances and they are not prepared to accept each other's potential victory were the rules of the game modified. Secondly, the democracy promotion strategies of the European Union and of its member states reinforce such a divide, because they promote only a very exclusivist understanding of democracy, which is appealing only to one sector of society and not to the other. Funding follows for those who already have accepted and internalized the values of liberal democracy, thereby excluding Islamism and its representatives. Finally, tactical considerations play a role insofar as the perception of who will benefit from genuine democratization impedes coalition-building and entrenches positions. The historical experience of Iran, where leftists, liberals, and Islamists co-operated to overthrow the Shah, is a precedent that secular groups might not wish to repeat given the final outcome of the revolution.

These divisions suit the authoritarian leader, who is able to play one sector of the opposition against the other, depending on the issue, and is thereby able to remain the sole and unaccountable arbiter of the political system by carefully managing repression and co-optation. For the international community, this is quite a positive outcome as stability is guaranteed; for the secular, liberal opposition, a degree of influence is also guaranteed as long it ultimately rallies to the regime; and for Islamists, the current situation is akin to the continuation of colonial rule by an indigenous elite, although some sectors of institutionalized Islamism benefit from co-optation.

The Moroccan case is quite paradigmatic of trends that exist elsewhere in the MENA. Divisions within civil society remain prominent in Egypt, Jordan, and Algeria, leading authoritarian regimes to successfully implement policies of 'divide and conquer'. Through its policy instruments, the European Union provides the ideal external support for the continuation of such divisions, leading Islamists to increasingly lose hope that the EU might be different from the United States. Civil society dynamics are an important indication of the nature of political relationships within any polity. When it comes to the MENA, such relations are fraught with difficulties and suspicions, leaving one quite pessimistic about the possibility of civil society being a driving force for democratic transformation.

Notes

1. O'Donnell and Schmitter, *Tentative Conclusions*.
2. Di Palma, *To Craft Democracies*.
3. For a critical analysis of democratization understood simply through domestic factors see Yilmaz, 'External-Internal Linkages'; Haynes 'Comparative Politics and "Globalisation"' and Cavatorta, 'Geopolitical Challenges'. For a critical analysis of democratization as elite-bargaining see Welzel, 'Democratization as an Emancipative Process'.
4. Dauderstädt, 'Dead Ends of Transition', 9.
5. Hinnebusch, 'Authoritarian Persistence'.
6. Carothers, 'The End of the Transition Paradigm'.
7. Pripstein-Posusney, 'Multi-Party Elections', 47.
8. Schlumberger, 'The Arab Middle East'.
9. On Czechoslovakia see Olson, 'Democratization and Political Participation'; on Poland see Stokes, *The Walls Came Tumbling Down*; and on Chile see Oxhorn, *Organising Civil Society*.
10. See Whitehead, 'Democracy by Convergence'; Tovias, 'The International Context of Democratic Transition' and Pridham, 'Democratic Transition'.
11. For an examination of the policy of *alternance* see Willis, 'After Hassan'.
12. Przeworski, 'Some Problems in the Study of Transition'.
13. See Franklin, 'Political Party Opposition' and Howard and Roessler, 'Liberalizing Electoral Outcomes'. I am grateful to Hendrik Kraetzschmar for pointing me to this literature.
14. See endnote above for references to this literature.
15. Olson, 'Democratization and Political Participation'.
16. Stokes, *The Walls Came Tumbling Down*, 30.
17. Oxhorn, *Organising Civil Society*.
18. Norton, *Civil Society in the Middle East* and Berman, 'Islamism, Revolution and Civil Society'.
19. Clark, 'The Conditions of Islamist Moderation'.
20. Pripstein-Posusney, 'Multi-Party Elections', 50.
21. Pratt, *Democracy and Authoritarianism*, 134.
22. Impagliazzo and Giro, *Algeria in Ostaggio*.
23. Labidi, 'La longue descente'.
24. I am grateful to Peter Seeberg for pointing this out.
25. Schwedler, *Faith in Moderation*.
26. Kraetzschmar, 'The Profitability of Opposition Cooperation'.
27. Bellin, 'The Robustness of Authoritarianism', 139.
28. Albrecht, 'How Can Opposition Support'.
29. Schlumberger and Albrecht, 'Waiting for Godot'.
30. Pripstein-Posusney, 'Multi-Party Elections', 50.
31. See Haynes, 'Comparative Politics and "Globalisation"' and Cavatorta, 'Constructing an Open Model'.
32. Cavatorta, 'The Role of Democratization'. Some groups wish to impose it from above; others would prefer to build it from below, while others still would like it to be sanctioned through electoral procedures. While the nature of the Islamic state would be different depending on the way in which it will be built, specific features such as the role of religion in public policy would remain central for all and this is what secular/liberal groups find unacceptable.
33. See Yassine, *To whom it is concerned*, 2000, available in English at http://www.radioislam.org/yassine/meng.htm

34. For other examples see Cavatorta and Elananza, 'Political Opposition in Civil Society'.
35. For an overview of how secular groups prefer regime co-optation to alliances with Islamist ones, see Brumberg, 'Islamists and the Politics of Consensus' and Cook, 'The Right Way'.
36. The events of the past two decades, ranging from the Egyptian Muslim Brotherhood's electoral successes in the 1980s to the landslide victory of the Islamic Front in Algeria in 1991, and from the spectacular electoral advances of the Moroccan Party for Justice and Development in 2002 to the victory of Hamas in January 2006 in the Palestinian elections, provide ample evidence of the strength of Islamism at the ballot box.
37. See Khalil, 'Egypt's Muslim Brotherhood'.
38. A number of Islamist movements seek recognition to operate as political parties in order to have access to policy-making power. See for instance a report on the Muslim Brotherhood in the *Daily News Egypt*, 14 January 2007, at: http://www.dailystaregypt.com/article.aspx?ArticleID=4972
39. Brumberg, 'The Trap of Liberalised Autocracy'.
40. Leveau, 'Morocco at the Crossroads'.
41. Vermeren, *Le Maroc en Transition*.
42. For an analysis of the PJD, see Mohsen-Finan and Zeghal, 'Opposition Islamiste et Pouvoir Monarchique'.
43. Willis, 'Political Parties in the Maghrib'.
44. See the regional strategy paper of the Euro-Med Partnership for 2002–2006 available at http://ec.europa.eu/external_relations/euromed/rsp/rsp02_06_en.pdf and the analysis of EU's democracy promotion strategies by Annette Junemann, available at http://www.liv.ac.uk/ewc/docs/Junemann.pdf
45. See Sater, 'The Dynamics of State and Society' and Chomiak, 'Civil Society in Transition'.
46. For studies on the movement see Entelis, 'Un Courant Populaire'.
47. A report on the march can be found in *Le Journal Hebdomadaire*, No.264, 15–21 July 2006, 12.
48. For a detailed study on the level of actual and potential co-operation between Islamists and secular/liberal groups, see Cavatorta, 'Civil Society, Islamism and Democratisation'.
49. Bayat, *Making Islam Democratic.*
50. Both Islamism and liberalism are treated as political ideologies, although their proponents would probably claim that they are not ideologies, but only reflect the nature of society.
51. For an analysis of the elections and their significance see Storm, 'The Parliamentary Elections in Morocco'.
52. Yassine, *Winning the Modern World*.
53. Interview by e-mail with the author, 13 August 2005.
54. Maddy-Weitzman, 'Islamism, Moroccan-Style', 46.
55. Yassine, *Winning the Modern World*, 7.
56. Lauzière, 'Post-Islamism and the Religious Discourse', 252.
57. See Yassine, *Memorandum*, 2000.
58. Julian Baggini, 'This is What the Clash of Civilisations is Really About', *The Guardian*, 14 April 2007, http://www.guardian.co.uk/comment/story/0,,2057060,00.html. I am indebted to Michelle Pace for pointing this article out to me.
59. See, for instance, the interview of the Egyptian Muslim Brotherhood's Supreme Guide Mohamed Mahdi Akef in *al Ahram Weekly*, 15–21 December 2005.
60. Cavatorta, 'Neither Participation nor Revolution'.
61. Yassine, *Memorandum*.

62.   Maddy-Weitzman, 'Islamism, Moroccan-Style', 48.
63.   Zeghal, *Les Islamistes Marocains*.
64.   Author's interview with F. Arsalane, spokesperson of the *Al Adl*, Rabat, August 2005.
65.   See the party's website at http://www.usfp.ma/
66.   Maddy-Weitzman, 'Islamism, Moroccan-Style'.
67.   Pratt, *Democracy and Authoritarianism*, 138.
68.   Author's confidential interview, Casablanca, August 2005.
69.   See for instance the following editorials: 'What Do the Islamists Want?', *La Vie Economique*, 24 January 2003, and by A. Dilami, *L'Economiste*, 17 January 2003.
70.   The case of the FIS in Algeria when running local councils in 1990/1991 is a clear example. When in charge of local councils FIS elected representatives began requiring women to wear the veil, banned satellite dishes and forcibly closed bars.
71.   See Pace, 'Norm Shifting from EMP to ENP'.
72.   Tempest, 'Myths from Eastern Europe'. Some scholars refute the claim that civil society activism was so important for democratization in Eastern Europe, but policy-makers seem to believe those myths.
73.   Youngs, 'European Approaches to Security'.
74.   See EU website: http://www.delmar.ec.europa.eu/fr/quoi_de_neuf/20061004.htm
75.   For a description of this association see Howe, *Morocco. The Islamist Awakening*.
76.   For an analysis of the dichotomy between Morocco as a middle-income country and its very poor social indicators see Ivan Martin, 'Morocco: The Basis for a New Development Model?' published at http://www.realinstitutoelcano.org/analisis/947.asp
77.   See interview with Nadia Yassine at http://www.nadiayassine.net/en/page/10513.htm
78.   Author's interview with F. Arsalane, spokesperson for *Al Adl*, Rabat, August 2005.

Bibliography

Albrecht, Holger. 'How Can Opposition Support Authoritarianism? Lessons from Egypt'. *Democratization* 12 (2005): 378–97.
Bayat, Asef. *Making Islam Democratic*. Stanford: Stanford University Press, 2007.
Bellin, Eva. 'The Robustness of Authoritarianism in the Middle East'. *Comparative Politics* 36 (2004): 139–57.
Berman, Sheri. 'Islamism, Revolution and Civil Society'. *Perspectives on Politics* 1 (2003): 257–72.
Brumberg, Daniel. 'Islamists and the Politics of Consensus'. *Journal of Democracy* 13 (2002): 109–15.
Brumberg, Daniel. 'The Trap of Liberalised Autocracy'. *Journal of Democracy* 13 (2002): 56–68.
Carothers, Thomas. 'The End of the Transition Paradigm'. *Journal of Democracy* 13 (2002): 5–21.
Cavatorta, Francesco. 'Civil Society, Islamism and Democratisation. The Case of Morocco'. *Journal of Modern African Studies* 44 (2006): 203–22.
Cavatorta, Francesco. 'Constructing an Open Model of Transitions. International Political Economy and the Failed Democratisation of North Africa'. *Journal of North African Studies* 9 (2004): 1–18.
Cavatorta, Francesco. 'Geopolitical Challenges to the Success of Democracy in North Africa: Algeria, Tunisia and Morocco'. *Democratization* 8 (2001): 175–194.
Cavatorta, Francesco. 'Neither Participation nor Revolution. The Strategy of the *Jamiat al-Adl wal-Ihsan*'. *Mediterranean Politics* 12 (2007): 379–95.
Cavatorta, Francesco. 'The Role of Democratization in Reducing the Appeal of Extremist Groups in North Africa and the Middle East'. *Countering Terrorism and Insurgency in*

the 21st Century. Combating the Sources and Facilitators, ed. James Forest, 2007, Praeger Security International.

Cavatorta, Francesco, and Azzam Elananza. 'Political Opposition in Civil Society. An Analysis of the Interactions of Secular and Religious Associations in Algeria and Jordan'. *Government and Opposition* 43 (2008): 561–78.

Chomiak, Laryssa. 'Civil Society in Transition: the Experiences of Centres for Abused Women in Morocco'. *Journal of North African Studies* 7 (2002): 55–82.

Clark, Janine. 'The Conditions of Islamist Moderation: Unpacking Cross-Ideological Cooperation in Jordan'. *International Journal of Middle East Studies* 38 (2006): 539–60.

Cook, Stephen. 'The Right Way to Promote Arab Reform'. *Foreign Affairs* 84 (2005): 91–102.

Dauderstädt, Michael. 'Dead Ends of Transition: Rentier Economies and Protectorates'. *Dead Ends of Transition*, ed. Michael Dauderstädt and Arne Schildberg. Frankfurt: Campus Verlag, 2006.

Di Palma, Giuseppe. *To Craft Democracies*. Los Angeles: University of California Press, 1990.

Entelis, John. 'Un Courant Populaire Mis à l'Ecart'. *Le Monde Diplomatique* 49 (2002): 22.

Franklin, James. 'Political Party Opposition to Non-competitive Regimes: A Cross National Analysis'. *Political Research Quarterly* 55 (2002): 521–46.

Haynes, Jeffrey. 'Comparative Politics and "Globalisation"'. *European Political Science* 2 (2003): 17–26.

Hinnebusch, Raymond. 'Authoritarian Persistence, Democratization Theory and the Middle East: An Overview and Critique'. *Democratization* 13 (2006): 373–95.

Howard, Marc, and Philip Roessler. 'Liberalizing Electoral Outcomes in Competitive Authoritarian Regimes'. *American Journal of Political Science* 50 (2006): 365–81.

Howe, Marvine. *Morocco. The Islamist Awakening and Other Challenges*. Oxford: Oxford University Press, 2005.

Impagliazzo, Marco, and Mario Giro. *Algeria in Ostaggio. Tra esercito e fondamentalismo, storia di una pace difficile*. Milano: Ed. Guerini e Associati, 1997.

Khalil, Magdi. 'Egypt's Muslim Brotherhood and Political Power: Would Democracy Survive?'. *Middle East Review of International Affairs* 10 (2006): 44–52.

Kraetzschmar, Hendrik. 'The Profitability of Opposition Cooperation in Authoritarian Elections: A Cross-national Survey'. Paper presented at the British Society for Middle East Studies Annual Conference, Leeds, UK, 4–6 July 2008.

Labidi, Kamel. 'La longue descente aux enfers de la Tunisie'. *Le Monde Diplomatique* 53 (2006): 10–11.

Lauzière, Henri. 'Post-Islamism and the Religious Discourse of Abd Al-Salam Yassin'. *International Journal of Middle East Studies* 37 (2005): 241–61.

Leveau, Rémy. 'Morocco at the Crossroads'. *Mediterranean Politics* 2 (1997): 95–113.

Maddy-Weitzman, Bruce. 'Islamism, Moroccan-Style: The Ideas of Sheikh Yassine'. *Middle East Quarterly* 10 (2003): 43–53.

Mohsen-Finan, Khadija, and Malika Zeghal. 'Opposition Islamiste et Pouvoir Monarchique au Maroc. Le cas du Parti de la Justice et du Développement'. *Revue Française de Science Politique* 56 (2006): 79–119.

Norton, Augustus Richard. *Civil Society in the Middle East*. Leiden: Brill, 1995/1996.

O'Donnell, Guillermo, and Philippe Schmitter. *Tentative Conclusions about Uncertain Democracies*. Baltimore: Johns Hopkins University Press, 1986.

Olson, David. 'Democratization and Political Participation: The Experience of the Czech Republic'. *The Consolidation of Democracy in East-Central Europe*, ed. Karen Dawisha and Bruce Parrott, 150–96. Cambridge: Cambridge University Press, 1997.

Oxhorn, Philip. *Organising Civil Society.* Pennsylvania: Pennsylvania State University Press, 1995.

Pace, Michelle. 'Norm Shifting from EMP to ENP: The EU as a Norm Entrepreneur in the South?'. *Cambridge Review of International Affairs* 20 (2007): 659–75.

Pratt, Nicola. *Democracy and Authoritarianism in the Arab World.* Boulder, Colorado: Lynne Rienner, 2007.

Pridham, Geoffrey. 'Democratic Transition and the International Environment'. *Transitions to Democracy*, ed. Geoffrey Pridham. Aldershot: Dartmouth, 1995.

Pripstein-Posusney, Marsha. 'Multi-Party Elections in the Arab World: Institutional Engineering and Oppositional Strategies'. *Studies in Comparative International Development* 36 (2002): 34–62.

Przeworski, Adam. 'Some Problems in the Study of Transition to Democracy'. *Transitions from Authoritarian rule. Comparative Perspectives*, ed. Guillermo O'Donnell, Philippe Schmitter, and Laurence Whitehead. Baltimore: Johns Hopkins University Press, 1986.

Sater, James. 'The Dynamics of State and Society in Morocco'. *Journal of North African Studies* 7 (2002): 101–18.

Schlumberger, Oliver. 'The Arab Middle East and the Question of Democratization: Some Critical Remarks'. *Democratization* 7 (2000): 104–32.

Schlumberger, Oliver, and Albrecht Holger. 'Waiting for Godot: Regime Change Without Democratization in the Middle East'. *International Political Science Review* 35 (2004): 371–92.

Schwedler, Jillian. *Faith in Moderation: Islamist Parties in Jordan and Yemen.* Cambridge: Cambridge University Press, 2006.

Stokes, Gale. *The Walls Came Tumbling Down. The Collapse of Communism in Eastern Europe.* Oxford: Oxford University Press, 1993.

Storm, Lise. 'The Parliamentary Elections in Morocco, September 2007'. *Electoral Studies* 27 (2008): 359–64.

Tempest, Clive. 'Myths from Eastern Europe and the Legend of the West'. *Democratization* 4 (1997): 132–44.

Tovias, Alfred. 'The International Context of Democratic Transition'. *West European Politics* 7 (1984): 158–71.

Vermeren, Pierre. *Le Maroc en Transition.* Paris: La Découverte, 2004.

Welzel, Christian. 'Democratization as an Emancipative Process: The Neglected Role of Mass Motivations'. *European Journal of Political Research* 45 (2006): 871–96.

Whitehead, Laurence. 'Democracy by Convergence and Southern Europe: A Comparative Politics Perspective'. *Encouraging Democracy. The International Context of Regime Transition in Southern Europe*, ed. Geoffrey Pridham. Leicester: Leicester University Press, 1991.

Willis, Michael. 'After Hassan: A New Monarch in Morocco'. *Mediterranean Politics* 4 (1999): 115–28.

Willis, Michael. 'Political Parties in the Maghrib: The Illusion of Significance'. *Journal of North African Studies* 7 (2002): 1–22.

Yassine, Abdessalam. *Winning the Modern World for Islam.* Iowa City: Justice and Spirituality Publishing, 2000.

Yilmaz, Hakan. 'External-Internal Linkages in Democratization: Developing an Open Model of Democratic Change'. *Democratization* 9 (2002): 67–84.

Youngs, Richard. 'European Approaches to Security in the Mediterranean'. *Middle East Journal* 57 (2003): 414–31.

Zeghal, Malika. *Les Islamistes Marocains.* Paris: Editions La Découverte, 2005.

Islamist moderation without democratization: the coming of age of the Moroccan Party of Justice and Development?

Eva Wegner and Miquel Pellicer

Mohammed V University, Rabat, Morocco

This article studies a novel factor relevant for the moderation of an Islamist party: the degree of dependency on a social movement organization. This question is examined in a case study analysing the evolution of the relationship between the Moroccan Islamist party, Party of Justice and Development (PJD), and its founding social movement organization. Over time, the PJD has been gaining autonomy, becoming more moderate and simultaneously gaining strength. Contemporaneously, liberalization in Morocco has been partially reversed, partly as a result of the rising Islamist strength. These findings suggest that it is the strength of the Islamist opposition, rather than its ideological rigidity, that makes MENA rulers reluctant to liberalize. We study the implications of these findings for European Union policy towards Islamist parties in the MENA region.

Introduction

The literature on democratic transitions has frequently argued that the moderation of oppositional actors is an important requisite for successful democratization processes. According to this literature, moderation is required to defuse the 'fear of the masses' of incumbent elites. This argument has been subsequently put into question by showing important, successful transitions where the opposition was far from moderate, such as in Portugal.[1]

In scholarship on the Middle East and North Africa (MENA), the moderation of the Islamist opposition has recently received considerable attention.[2] As a leading scholar writes, Islamist moderation has emerged as '*the* issue at stake in debates on Islamist political participation'.[3] This literature focuses on whether the inclusion of Islamist organizations in the formal political processes leads to their ideological moderation. Moderation is typically defined narrowly as 'becoming truly committed to democratic practices'.[4] Whether moderation is a requisite for democratization in the MENA or not is rarely made explicit in this literature, although it often seems to be assumed implicitly.[5] (In the following, we will refer to this literature as the 'inclusion-moderation literature'.)

Regardless of whether moderation is actually required for democratization or not, it appears to be relevant for Western decision-makers. In particular, the timidity of democracy promotion efforts by the European Union (EU), and Western actors more generally, towards the MENA is frequently attributed to the ideological nature of Islamist movements. To the extent that Islamists are not 'moderate', it is believed that pursuing an energetic democracy promotion policy could backfire by bringing to power actors that would hold illiberal and possibly anti-democratic and anti-Western positions[6] (see Hovdenak's article on Hamas in this special issue).

This article studies the moderation of one strand of the Islamist opposition in Morocco and discusses implications more widely for EU policy toward rulers and the Islamist opposition in the MENA. In contrast to the inclusion-moderation literature, we do not focus particularly on Islamist positions towards democratic practices but define Islamist moderation as an increasing flexibility towards core ideological beliefs. We consider our definition more appropriate as it does not presume that Islamists are per se anti-democratic. Like the inclusion-moderation literature, we study the effect of inclusion on moderation: the constraints flowing from participation in formal political processes are supposed to promote bargaining, compromise, and the pursuit of small policy gains, all of which require that the content of the ideology is negotiable. We focus on a novel channel of moderation that relates to the interactions between an Islamist party and an Islamist social movement. We also examine, briefly, the implications of this moderation for political reform in Morocco.

A relevant, and often overlooked, characteristic of Islamist parties in the MENA is that, even when founded by an Islamist social movement organization (ISMO), they are distinct from these organizations. The evolution of a party's relationship with an ISMO affects the party's margin for political moderation. At least initially, a party depends on an ISMO's resources for mobilization and support. Being dependent, a party has to give voice to its founding organization's demands and policy stances.[7] This is not contentious in the beginning, as both organizations share similar interests, mainly to increase protection from repression and to promote the Islamist agenda.[8] However, while a party operates in the institutional arena, an ISMO does not and, therefore, is not subject to those institutional constraints that apply to political parties such as building coalitions and compromise with other political parties to advance their policy goals. In the hegemonic authoritarian regimes of the MENA, political parties, moreover, have constantly to signal loyalty to the regime and acceptance of its legitimacy to rule in order to avoid repression. As a social movement actor, an ISMO can thus typically afford to remain more committed to its core agenda. As a result of these different environments, electoral participation can lead to an increasing gap between the two actors' agendas: Over time, the priorities of party leaders and members may increasingly be dictated by the logics that rein in the institutional arena and by loyalty to a party rather than to a social movement organization. In this process, a party may reform or trade central programmatic points.[9] This process, however, will be limited to the extent that the party maintains a strong dependency on the movement. Thus, the degree of dependency of a party on its founding organization is likely to be relevant for its margin for moderation.

Against this background, this article investigates the relationship between the Party of Justice and Development (PJD) and its founding organization, the Movement of Unity and Reform (MUR) in Morocco. The article covers the period from 1992, when the palace tolerated the integration of the Islamists into a dormant political party, up to 2007, when the latest parliamentary elections were held in Morocco. It focuses especially on the period from 1997–2004, when the emancipation process of the PJD from the MUR took place. The case study in this article is based on two field research trips, the first in 2003–2004, and the second in 2007.[10] It shows that, over that period, the PJD became more independent and moderate partly by acquiring independent mobilization resources, and also stronger in terms of popular support. The article shows that the Moroccan regime responded to these developments by deliberalizing, suggesting that the regime cared more about strength of the Islamic opposition than its level of moderation.

Based on the case study, the last section of the article speculates about policy implications for actors who want to promote Islamist moderation and political liberalization in the MENA. It focuses on the consequences of providing resources to Islamist parties, for instance, by giving advice on professional electoral campaigning or, more generally, by publicly considering them as legitimate opposition actors. The actual policy of the EU towards Islamists in the MENA region is contrasted with the lessons extracted from the case study.

The article is organized as follows. The second section studies the growing autonomy of the PJD from the MUR. The third section analyses the PJD's moderation process, while the fourth examines the response of the regime to the increasing strength of the PJD. The fifth discusses the implications of our findings for EU policy towards Islamist parties, and the sixth section is the conclusion.

The emancipation process of the PJD

The PJD is the offspring of one of the two principal Islamist movement organizations in Morocco.[11] Its inclusion occurred at a moment of political reforms, among them two constitutional reforms that attributed more power to political parties and parliament but did not affect the authoritarian nature of the political regime.

The Islamist organization which gave birth to the PJD emerged from the Islamic Youth Association, an organization founded around 1970.[12] The founder of the Islamic Youth Association, Abdel Karim Muti', an inspector of the ministry of education, was influenced by the radical ideas of the second leader of the Egyptian Muslim Brotherhood Sayyid Qutb.[13] Mirroring Qutb's beliefs about

Egyptian society, Muti' considered Moroccan society to be in a state of pre-Islamic ignorance against which the use of violence was legitimate to achieve an 'Islamic state'. The Islamic Youth recruited its members mostly in universities and in secondary schools. After the implication of some members in the assassination of Omar Benjelloun, editor of the socialist party newspaper and prominent Moroccan Marxist intellectual, in 1975, the organization was banned and officially dissolved in 1976. Muti' fled into exile and was – in absence – condemned to a life sentence; the militants of the organization remaining in Morocco were persecuted.

The majority of the activists founded a new organization, al-Jama'a al-Islamiyya (The Islamic Group) in 1981 (which became the MUR in 1996). Its founders Mohamed Yatim, Abdallah Baha, and Abdellilah Benkirane were later Members of Parliament and members of the General Secretariat of the Party of Justice and Development. Since the mid-1980s, a reformist vision and a comprehensive approach to society emerged and solidified within this organization. Violence as a means to achieve political goals was explicitly condemned; the political and religious legitimacy of the monarchic regime was officially accepted; and the organization adopted internal democratic structures.[14]

The Moroccan Islamists had thus already reformed their positions regarding the use of violence and democratic principles before participating in the political process. Other positions mirror those promoted by many Islamist groups in the Middle East and North Africa. According to a charter published in the late 1980s, the organization's goals were to renew the understanding of religion, to advocate the implementation of shari'a law, to achieve a comprehensive cultural renaissance, to work on accomplishing the unity of Muslims, to confront ideologies and ideas which they believed were subversive to Islam, and to raise the educational and moral level of the Moroccan people. These objectives were to be attained by individual, public, cultural, social, economic, political, and educational activities.[15]

From the 1980s, the organization engaged in a discussion on the desirability and potential means of political participation. Different options for its implementation were considered. The preferred one, the creation of its own political party, was rejected by the authorities in 1992. Instead, the palace tolerated the taking over of a dormant political party (the Movement Populaire Constitutionnel Démocratique – MPCD) by leaders and members of the MUR. This arrangement was made official in 1996 at an extraordinary party congress of the MPCD, during which MUR leaders were appointed to the party's highest body, the General Secretariat. This party was renamed the Party of Justice and Development in 1998.

Initially the party depended strongly on the MUR for human, propaganda, and infrastructure resources. From the late 1990s onwards, the PJD slowly decreased its dependency on the MUR. An important precondition was that no formal links were established between the two organizations: party membership was not made conditional on MUR membership and no quotas for office were reserved for MUR members. In the late 1990s, MUR committees debated the question of a total fusion with the party, but eventually voted against it.[16] The MUR's Shura

Council then adopted a 'document of complementarity' that laid out the intended division of labour. The PJD was defined as a political organization dealing with all political issues of the country and defending 'Islamic causes' in the institutions, whereas the MUR was meant to focus on vocation/mission (*da'wa*) and education. The two organizations were to be linked by consultation, co-operation, and co-ordination, and by their joint objectives and principles.[17] From then on, their relation was labelled a 'partnership'.

The increasing distance between the two organizations materialized particularly along two dimensions: First, the PJD increased its independent mobilization resources, and, second, it established boundaries in relation to its environment through the institutionalization of the party organization. Independent mobilization resources consisted of financial and human resources, and ancillary organizations of the party. Financial resources were partly provided by the Moroccan state through funding of the party's electoral campaign. However, the party also raised money through the reallocation of at least 22% of the Members of Parliament's (MP) salary (which the party had made mandatory) and membership fees.[18]

Independent human resources were gained through new party members who were not affiliated to the MUR. By 2004, the PJD had increased its membership to between 12,000 and 15,000 members.[19] While there is no way to assess directly the proportion of MUR members among these, we can infer a trend of a decreasing proportion of MUR members among PJD members from different types of data. First, a survey of party congress deputies from 2004 shows that one-third of them had joined the PJD after 1999.[20] Knowing that the majority of MUR members initially interested in party politics joined the party between 1992 and 1999, we can assume that a large number of the newcomers were not affiliated to the MUR. Most likely, the proportion of newcomers was actually higher, since a survey from the party congress tends to be biased towards members with a higher degree of seniority. Second, by 2002, there was a large proportion of non-MUR members among the PJD's local and provincial party leaders, electoral candidates, and MPs. This was shown in the profiles of the PJD's 179 candidates for the 2002 parliamentary elections, published by the MUR's journal *Al-Tajdid*, which listed the candidates' affiliations with other organizations and their position in the party. These profiles show that among these candidates, only one-third of those who were part of the PJD's 'intermediate leadership' (National Council and/or members of the provincial secretariats) and only a quarter of those holding office in the PJD's local secretariats were also MUR members. For the PJD's candidates and deputies, this trend was even more marked. Out of the 179 candidates, only 56 were affiliated to the MUR. As for the MPs, out of the 42 MPs in 2002, only 22 were MUR members.[21] This contrasts sharply with the profiles of the 14 deputies from 1997, who were all MUR members except for one. Finally, even some of the party members affiliated to the MUR may be best considered as PJD human resources. This proves to be the case, as will be shown below, since such members may shift their loyalty to the party.

More independent resources also came from developing parallel structures to the MUR: a 'Commission for Women and the Family' and a youth organization, the 'Youth of Justice and Development'. Both of these can be regarded as competing organizations to the MUR's (much more powerful) Organization for the Renewal of the Female Conscience and its Youth committee, respectively. In contrast, the PJD's Forum du Développement, founded in 2002, has no MUR counterpart. It is a forum of cadres who are either members or supporters of the party. Its tasks are to develop party policies, to support the parliamentary group, and to give technical and political training to the party's deputies. These ancillary organizations are exclusively financed by the party.

By 2002, the PJD's independent resources for electoral mobilization had improved considerably in comparison to the 1997 campaign, for which the party had entirely relied on the MUR. This was even more the case for the elections in 2003. In the 2003 campaign for the communal elections, the PJD's national office aimed to co-ordinate and unify the local campaigns and provided the local sections with a remarkable amount of independent propaganda resources.

The second crucial step towards autonomy was the institutionalization of the PJD's party organization. In a general way, institutionalization implies the establishment of boundaries *vis-à-vis* the environment.[22] For a party, these boundaries are particularly sharpened when rules are formalized and abided by, so that there is less scope for an informal impact of other organizations on the party. Moreover, institutionalization implies the strengthening of the role of the party organization for providing legitimacy to party leaders at all levels of the organizational hierarchy and, ultimately, to tie their loyalty and interests to the survival of the party rather than the movement organization.

In the case of the PJD, the formalization of party rules at all levels was consciously enacted through two revisions of the party's by-laws in 1999 and 2004. At the beginning, the competences and prerogatives of different party bodies were only loosely defined; in practice, electoral candidates were nominated by the party leadership and the latter was appointed rather than elected. The vagueness of the original by-laws – a rather obscure, one-page document – left much space for informal external influence.[23] In contrast, the 2004 by-laws define the relationship and prerogatives of the different bodies in detail: complicated procedures apply for choosing the candidates both for parliamentary and local elections and for party office.

Moreover, a commitment to internal democratic practices, and the respect for procedures and their transparency enforced the effect of formalization on party autonomy. This commitment to transparency of procedures and to internal democratic structures, as part of the party's message and identity, has been relevant to the party since the late 1990s. For instance, at the opening session of the 1999 congress, Al-Mukri al-Idrissi Abu Zaid, a member of the General Secretariat, emphasized that a political party that did not respect its own rules could not protest against the state's lack of rule of law.[24] As another party leader put it more recently, a rule can be more or less good, but the most important thing is that the rules for selection are clear and transparent and applied to everybody.[25] In the same fashion, provincial secretaries cite the party rules to defend contested decisions *vis-à-vis* the base, for instance, regarding the selection of electoral candidates,[26] and party members mention democracy and transparency as a reason for joining the party.[27] Crucially, the very fact that the General Secretariat formalized an extension of its powers through the 2004 by-laws, instead of keeping the vagueness of its prerogatives, shows that 'democratic legitimacy' and transparency are highly valued in the PJD.

The combination of detailed decision-making procedures with the commitment for respecting these procedures worked as strong boundaries *vis-à-vis* the MUR, leaving little space for extra-organizational nominations and decisions. Indeed, the legitimacy of party leaders and party decisions now has an intra-organizational source. One example is the General Secretariat. Even if all the initial MUR architects of the political inclusion of the Islamist movement still hold office in the PJD's General Secretariat, this is not because they are appointed in their function as MUR leaders. Their legitimacy now formally emanates from being elected by the party members in the congress and the National Council, and party leaders are accountable to party institutions.

These developments may, ultimately, also shift the loyalty of office holders away from the MUR and towards the party. In the case of the General Secretariat, interviews revealed that, by 2003, there were essentially three ways in which the current and former affiliation with the MUR was treated. First, there was a stronger loyalty to the MUR. Party activities and decisions were based on whether they were deemed beneficial or not for the MUR.[28] A second way of addressing the issue was a sort of stated separation of loyalties, where the logic of action was seen as depending on the respective organizational context.[29] In this case, it is not clear what would happen if conflicts arose between these two loyalties. Finally, in some cases, the commitment to the party clearly took precedence. An example of this came from a member of the General Secretariat who had given up his MUR office position. He treated his MUR affiliation as similar to his affiliation with a labour union and his presidency of a study association. In his words, he was 'a member of many things'.[30]

In sum, the PJD has increased its autonomy considerably since its first electoral participation in 1997. This was a consequence of the strengthening of the party's independent capabilities for mobilization and of changing the structural characteristics of the party organization to decrease the informal impact of the MUR on an initially weak organization which had no clearly defined boundaries. It is noteworthy that – except for the automatic state funding – all these were deliberate decisions of the party leadership. This is telling for how the party viewed itself. Had it been content with simply being the parliamentary branch of the MUR, there would have been no need for the party to have its own organizations linking it to social groups, no need for independent human resources, nor to invest so much in the party organization. Initially, this investment in the party organization is likely to have resulted from the MUR's illegality as it increased the benefits of investing in the legal structures. However, even after the legalization of the MUR, the PJD's investment in mobilization capabilities and party institutionalization continued at the same, if not greater, pace.[31]

Party autonomy and moderation

The PJD's gradual autonomy from the MUR facilitated an increasing flexibility of the party *vis-à-vis* their previously shared agenda. Generally, party autonomy facilitates such flexibility, as no extra-institutional actor can enforce its positions on the party. As mentioned above, the key difference between party and social movement organization is that the former operates under the constraints of formal politics, whereas the latter does not. As long as the movement organization, as an extra-institutional actor, controls the party, the moderation of the party is either impossible (in case of total dependency), or too costly from a support point of view. Thus, moderation is only possible to the extent that the party has sufficient autonomy or that the movement organization endorses moderation itself, as a result of other factors.

We operationalize moderation as stemming from institutional constraints by comparing the attitude of the PJD and of the MUR towards different decisions of the PJD that involved compromise on the Islamist agenda. Thus, we use the degree of disagreement/conflict between the two actors as an indicator of the party's moderation. In the following, we discuss party decisions and MUR attitudes regarding the support of, or the participation in governance with, left parties, the rise of technocrats in the party, and the policies implemented by PJD local councillors to assess the party's moderation over time.

Indeed, in the early years of the PJD's parliamentary presence (1997–1999), when the party was fully dependent on the MUR, no conflicts appear to have occurred.[32] The initial support the PJD lent to the Left-led *alternance* government in 1998 was supported by the MUR as a necessity for consolidating former King Hassan II's toleration of the Islamists' electoral participation. Everyone wanted to show that the Islamists were not a 'current of refusal' but a constructive and conciliatory movement that supported the King's decision to form a consensual government.[33]

In 2000, the first problems materialized in the context of this support. The *alternance* government aimed to modernize the Moroccan personal status code (family laws). Supporting the government, the PJD would have had to endorse a bill that the MUR (in fact, the entire Moroccan Islamist movement) strongly opposed and had mobilized against since the spring of 2000. The Islamists mainly opposed the abolition of polygamy and the right of women to arrange marriages without a 'marital tutor'; but the protest was also conducted as a general campaign against the 'secularist and francophone elites' and 'foreign powers' which supported the project in order to strip the country of its Islamic identity and heritage (see also Powell's article on Tunisia in this special issue). Moreover, this occurred in the context of another ideological conflict about a bill on micro-credits, where the government refused an amendment the PJD wanted to introduce. This amendment provided the possibility of introducing Islamic modes of financing, that is loans without interest, alongside conventional means of financing. From the PJD's perspective, the Islamist mobilization against a government it supported posed heavy problems. Eventually, its National Council voted in favour of going over to the opposition in autumn 2000, thus bringing the party in line with the Islamist agenda. However, it is noteworthy that the vote in the National Council was very narrow. The decision against further support of the government was taken with a difference of only 11 voices out of 280, showing already a decreasing, ideological rigidity of many representatives of the intermediate leadership.[34]

After the 2002 parliamentary elections, the issue of cabinet participation was again raised. The PJD had increased its seats from 14 to 42 and would have obtained around six to seven ministries if it had joined government.[35] The MUR's concern that that the PJD would join an 'un-Islamic' government were publicly expressed by the MUR's president. About one month after the elections, while the discussion about the constitution of the government was underway, Ahmed Raissouni, the MUR's president from 1998 to 2003, gave an interview to the PJD's newspaper *Al-'Asr*. In this interview, he claimed the PJD's electoral success for the MUR, stating that 'The reputation of the party and its popularity are the fruit of this movement [the MUR], which directed all its efforts and its activities towards this party'.[36] Additionally, while saying that he did not speak 'in the name of the party', Raissouni issued conditions for cabinet participation: He 'could not imagine' that the party would participate in a government that did not clearly engage itself in respect of the Islamic identity of the country and the reinforcement of the Arabic language. In particular, he stated that the party should refuse to participate in a government which rejected the establishment of *zakat* (obligatory alms) and loans without interest. In view of the aforementioned profiles of the PJD's deputies from 2002, Raissouni's concerns about the PJD's betrayal of the Islamic cause were probably somewhat justified. By linking a reminder about the PJD's dependency to advice about acceptable and non-acceptable conditions of cabinet participation, Raissouni intended to define thresholds of compromise for the party and to make the party adhere to the Islamists' core ideology. The very fact that this reminder had to be made via public channels, however, also indicated clearly that, by 2002, the MUR was not able to control the party directly.

That the PJD did not join the cabinet in 2002 was certainly an acknowledgement of the MUR's threat. At the same time, it is noteworthy that the party had also strong, non-ideological incentives not to join the cabinet and that those party leaders and MPs who were against cabinet participation seldom mentioned ideological reasons for not joining the cabinet. Rather, they feared a decrease in future electoral strength caused by being part of a government that was unlikely to improve the socio-economic grievances of those new voters whose support it had gained in the elections. Along the same lines, party leaders were aware that cabinet participation would make it more difficult to maintain its image as non-corrupt challengers of the Moroccan elite. Therefore, joining government would have come at the price of losing not only the MUR's support, but also that of new sympathizers who had voted for the party in the 2002 elections. Moreover, just as in 2000, the decision to join the opposition benches was far from being unanimous among party members and leaders. There were essentially three reasons given by those wanting to maintain support for the government in 2000 and those wanting to join it in 2002. A first group feared that the PJD would increase its electoral strength in opposition and, thus, scare the regime. A second and a third either saw no crucial programmatic differences between the PJD and the other Moroccan parties', maintaining that ideological policies were a luxury that could be promoted once the basic work was done (that is, decrease poverty, etc.), or wanted to acquire more governmental expertise for the future.[37]

After the 2003 municipal elections, the PJD changed its attitude towards government. As already mentioned, the PJD had organized its electoral campaign independently and made use of its own (new) propaganda resources in these elections. After the elections, the party formed local governmental alliances with all the existing Moroccan parties. This very pragmatic approach towards local government was the consequence of a clear orientation of the party leadership towards institutional politics and their appreciation of what this required. Most importantly, the leadership's decision was due to its perception that – after the terrorist attacks of 16 May 2003 – the PJD should demonstrate through participation in government that it was not 'a party of refusal'.[38] At that time, the PJD also tried to distance itself more clearly from the MUR and denounced MUR leaders for speaking in the name of the party.[39] an obvious hint to MUR leader Ahmad Raissouni, who had restated his rejection of government participation with the left and, moreover, questioned the King's ability to fulfil his role as Commander of the Faithful.[40]

A second perspective where we can see how the increasing distance from the MUR allowed institutional considerations to dominate party decisions, can also be found in the context of the 2003 communal elections. After 16 May, the power of a pragmatist, technocratic faction inside the General Secretariat and the National Council grew considerably. A prominent representative of this faction was a leading member of the party's ancillary organization, Forum du Développement. While a MUR member, he became fully absorbed with institutional considerations for policy-making: For example, he argued that it was too easy to denounce the government for privileging the macro-economic equilibrium when this was a constraint imposed by international actors. Moreover, he strongly criticized the Islamists' inclination to populism and unrealistic policy promises for winning 'the crowd's' support and stressed the necessity of a 'culture of expertise and of figures' and feasible policy propositions that were 'scientifically valid'.[41]

Importantly, the increasing power of the technocrats among the leadership allowed them to implement an idea they had previously pursued unsuccessfully during the 2002 parliamentary elections: to bring the party's cadres from the back row into the centrality of politics. Technocrats were 'parachuted' into electoral lists' pole positions. From the perspective of the party leaders, the technocrats were to provide the living evidence of the PJD as a party of serious and conciliatory people who knew how to deal with a budget and deliver improvements, and who could establish good relations with the authorities.

The following example of a PJD vice-mayor illustrates how these experts approach politics in the framework of local governance. The vice-mayor pursued concrete projects, the implementation of which he favoured over faithfulness to Islamist ideology. Immediately after his appointment, this vice-mayor drafted a project for social housing to improve the living conditions in the poorest neighbourhoods. After overcoming the initial suspicion of the mayor and the governor, his project was set in motion. It was financed through loans with interest. Acknowledging the contradictions with the Islamist claim against usury – the very claim that, as shown before, was a no-go for the MUR's president – he stated: 'I don't even realize, for me that's fine, this is not really what we are concerned about.' Clearly, he accepted this type of financing as a necessary condition, knowing that, otherwise, the project would not materialise at all. In his words: 'Now, we realize that it is not enough to have principles to be able to set up a budget. The citizens judge you on the basis of your efficiency.'[42]

This is, of course, only one example and not all those elected in the communal elections have the same profile. However, given the strong intervention of the General Secretariat in favour of the experts in the communal elections, and the fact that this faction is now dominating the General Secretariat, we suggest that this approach reflects a more general trend. Moreover, the increasing involvement in local governance has also begun to have an impact on those without a technocratic profile. The PJD's councillors reportedly started to get interested in advice regarding taxes, budgets, street lighting, waste, etc.[43]

In summary, as party autonomy grew, the PJD was increasingly capable of taking independent decisions that revealed a pragmatic attitude towards the Islamist agenda. Whereas in 2000 and 2002, the MUR's position won over the party, this was no longer the case in 2003. Of course, the institutional pressure on the party increased considerably after the terrorist attacks of May 2003. Nevertheless, autonomy is what enabled the party to respond to this pressure by only considering its own interests, even dropping key aspects of the Islamist agenda where necessary. Eventually, the MUR withdrew its support for the PJD, possibly the strongest indicator of the extent of the PJD's moderation over the last decade. Whereas in 2002, the MUR had aimed to bring the PJD in line by threatening to cut its support, in 2007, the support was actually cut. In the 2007 elections, there was no campaign on the PJD's behalf, not even an endorsement to vote for it.[44]

Islamist moderation and deliberalization

As shown above, the PJD became more and more ideologically flexible during the last decade. Not fully explicitly but unmistakably, many studies assume that

Islamist moderation will make democratization in the MENA more likely. Although the mechanism by which this process is supposed to take place is not analysed, the assumption appears to be that Islamists' moderation would deflate fears of the political elite that Islamists would abuse democratic processes to install an Islamist dictatorship.[45]

In contrast, the PJD's moderation was not followed by a notable increase in civil and political liberties. On the contrary, since the beginning of the 2000s, there has been a trend towards reversing earlier political liberalization measures. This was shown in a more repressive approach, first, towards more critical social and political actors in general and, second, towards the PJD in particular.

An important symbol of the general trend towards deliberalization was the reversal of the newly acquired principle of nominating a political prime minister, that is, the head of the strongest party. Instead, Mohamed VI, who had followed Hassan II on the throne in 1999, nominated Driss Jettou, the previous minister of interior without party affiliation. Besides this, human rights abuses increased and press freedom decreased. For example, a 2004 report by Amnesty International highlighted Morocco's poor record, denouncing a sharp rise in reported cases of torture or ill-treatment in the context of 'counter-terrorism' measures from 2002.[46]

As for the PJD, the regime increasingly intervened in party affairs, especially after 2003. First, the regime tried to neutralize the PJD's more critical figures, especially the outspoken head of the PJD's parliamentary group and member of the General Secretariat, Mustapha Ramid. In July 2003, Ramid had already offered his resignation in protest against the 'anti-democratic ways in which the party was treated and the odious instrumentalization of the May 16th attacks'.[47] At that time, the party leadership refused to accept his resignation. However, in October 2003, the minister of interior increased the pressure and Mustapha Ramid eventually had to resign as head of the parliamentary group.[48] In the same vein, it was made clear to the leadership that Ramid must not become the party's Secretary General.[49] Second, the PJD was forced to reduce its coverage of electoral constituencies in an unprecedented way in 2003. Originally, the PJD had intended to cover around 50%, just as in the 2002 parliamentary elections. In the 2003 elections, however, after some 'negotiations with the ministry of interior'[50] the party was only allowed to contest around 18% of the contested seats. Moreover, a system of partial coverage was enacted. That is, in big cities, the constituencies were covered in such a way that the party could not win a majority of the seats, i.e. the presidency, in any city. Although the PJD could cover all constituencies in the 2007 parliamentary elections, strong gerrymandering and a new electoral law guaranteed that, while the PJD won most votes, it gained five seats less than the winning Istiqlal party.

Why did the regime repress an ever more moderate PJD? An important factor was certainly the increase in the PJD's strength. Since its first electoral participation in 1997, the PJD had increased its electoral support from 14 to 42 seats in 2002. Although in 2007 the PJD ultimately only gained an additional five seats, it was widely believed before the elections that it would gain up to 40% of the vote.[51] In Morocco, where governments are typically composed of around five parties that fight over resources and ultimately resort to the King for arbitration, gaining 40% of the votes might have allowed the PJD to lead a small government coalition and to assert the prerogatives of party government, parliament, and political parties *vis-à-vis* the monarchy. If an elected government is assertive and defends its prerogatives, it is uncomfortable for the regime, irrespective of the policies pursued by any particular party. However moderate the PJD might have been in office, for the regime, a party with such strength would have hampered the pursuit of divide-and-rule politics, an important pillar of regime stability in Morocco. Even if – in contrast to the MENA republics – the electoral landslide of an oppositional party is not an immediate threat to regime survival, an important pillar of rule in MENA monarchies is precisely the division and fragmentation of political forces, which facilitate the control and manipulation of the opposition and allow the monarch to act as the supreme arbitrator of politics.[52] The supremacy of the monarchy in the political game is thus based on the absence of a united opposition or one particularly strong oppositional actor. Moreover, the very fact that the Moroccan king has kept such tight control in the past over who would be allowed representation in the institutions (and in what proportion) demonstrates a strong concern about the balance inside these institutions.

In sum, any possible effect of the PJD's moderation on democratization was cancelled out by its increase in strength that was threatening the regime (for this point, see also Cavatorta's contribution in this issue).

The EU and the promotion of Islamist moderation

The promotion of democracy is a stated goal of the EU's external policies in general, and of the Barcelona process in particular.[53] Although the EU has yet to develop a systematic approach towards Islamist parties, in view of European concerns about terrorism and radicalization, it is logical to assume that Islamist moderation and inclusion in the political process ought to be an EU goal as well. Moreover, an – admittedly awkward – illustration of the goal of moderation is the EU's stance towards the electoral victory of Hamas in January 2006 (see also Hovdenak's and Pace's contributions in this special issue on Hamas and EU democracy promotion). The three conditions that the EU, alongside the government of the USA and the United Nations (UN), established for recognizing the Hamas government (recognition of Israel, renunciation of violence, and acceptance of existing peace accords) can be understood as an – unsuccessful – attempt to force moderation.

Besides showing that the EU indeed needs a policy towards Islamist political parties, an important lesson of this failed policy towards Hamas is that Islamist moderation cannot be mandated by an external actor. This applies particularly to actors such as the Islamists, who derive part of their legitimacy from their autonomy from Western influence. Thus, the EU, as an external actor, can be thought to have relatively little, direct influence over moderation processes and should seek to influence such processes indirectly.

Our case study suggests that one way of doing so could be through the provision of resources to Islamist political parties. A key implication of the Moroccan case is that an increasing pragmatism of Islamist parties can result from an increase in party autonomy from the Islamist movement and that this autonomy was fostered by the party's accumulation of its own resources. Drawing on the findings of the Moroccan case study one could speculate that external actors could contribute to these processes by providing resources to the party, for instance, by offering technical training to MPs and party members, improving their campaigning skills or, more generally, by publicly considering them as part of the legitimate opposition.

Whether the EU would see this channelling of resources to Islamist parties as beneficial or not is likely to depend on how moderate the party already is. The EU would probably not wish to empower a party if it considers it 'radical' in the first instance. If, conversely, the party is already moderate, empowering it would seem to be in the EU's interests, in the same way that it would typically seek to strengthen civil society actors in authoritarian regimes countries.[54]

This could be done by emulating the example of the United States. The US government-funded National Democratic Institute, for instance, provides training for Moroccan parties – including the PJD. Such a policy should be complemented by pressures for political liberalization to ensure that the regime does not respond to the Islamists' increasing strength with repression. Particular attention should be paid to preventing the party from being banned, as this would, at the very least, neutralize the gains of moderation. For the EU, including the PJD in civil society forums in the context of the Euro-Mediterranean Partnership (EMP), would officially recognize the party as a legitimate actor, thereby working as a shield against repression, and making it more difficult for the party to be banned.

Current EU policy towards Morocco shows a different picture. EU policy towards the Islamists – to the extent that it exists – is one of avoidance. Islamists have never benefited from funding in the framework of the EMP. In view of the PJD's legality, this would, however, be possible. Moreover, the agenda of the PJD is to some extent close to the EU's in that it promotes transparency, aims at upgrading representative institutions, and even promotes women in public and party office more energetically than the majority of the other Moroccan parties. However, the consensus among EU policy-makers appears to be to avoid the Islamist issue for as long as possible. In contrast, the EU strongly supports the Moroccan regime with material and legitimacy resources. To date, Morocco is one of the main benefactors among southern countries of the EMP.[55] As to legitimacy resources, the EU provides them, for instance, with praise for the Moroccan 'democratisation process [and] transparent and democratic general elections' at a time when NGOs report deliberalization.[56] Similarly, the renewed praise for the 2007 elections as 'democratic, transparent, and fair' by the EU and its member states stands in sharp contrast to an actual turnout of 37%, and an electoral law designed to ensure the supremacy of the monarchy in the political process.

Concluding remarks

This article has focused on only one particular channel for moderation – autonomy – which is surely not the only relevant one. However, as our case study showed, this channel can be important and its implications are undoubtedly worth considering seriously. These implications will obviously apply best for the Moroccan case. Nevertheless, we believe that the channel uncovered is of some generality and could potentially apply to other places as well. In that case, of course, the particular context needs to be taken into account.

There are important cases (for instance, Egypt) where the regimes refuse to legalize an Islamist political party and Islamists, thus, contest elections as independent candidates. In such cases, obviously our suggested path to moderation could not be set in motion. Those representing the party inside the political institutions will always be fully subject to the decisions of external leaders. In such cases, the EU's efforts could then be directed towards pressurising the regime for party legalization.

Party legalization may not in all cases lead to party autonomy as smoothly as was the case with the PJD. For instance, our research suggests that all the crucial decisions of the Jordanian Islamic Action Front (IAF) are, 15 years after its foundation, in reality taken by the Muslim Brotherhood. In this case, however, the social movement organization formalized its control over the party through a document that obliges IAF members who are members of the Muslim Brotherhood to vote for decisions previously taken by the IAF's Shura Council.[57] Nevertheless, a faction inside the IAF is currently striving for more autonomy, namely through the recruitment of new members who are not affiliated to the Muslim Brotherhood. In some situations, therefore, certain conditions may make the evolution towards autonomy slower or more difficult, relative to the Moroccan case.

Finally, our article shows that moderation does not automatically lead to a greater willingness of ruling elites to democratize. Indeed, an ideologically flexible opposition is not enough to induce autocrats to democratize. Nancy Bermeo shows that moderation is not a necessary condition for democratization.[58] Our case study shows that it is not sufficient either. For the EU, this implies that if moderation *and* democratization are relevant goals in the MENA region, each will have to be promoted for its own sake.

Notes

1. See Nancy Bermeo's discussion of the literature in her article 'Myths of Moderation'.
2. See, for instance: Clark, 'The Conditions of Islamist Moderation'; Schwedler, *Faith in Moderation*; Robinson, 'Can Islamists be Democrats?'.

3. Schwedler, 'Democratization, Inclusion and the Moderation of Islamist Parties', 59, emphasis in the original.
4. See Schwedler, *Faith in Moderation*, 149.
5. Clark, for instance, writes that 'questions concerning whether the inclusion of Islamist political parties is leading to their ideological moderation and, as a result, the deepening of democracy, have become important and expanding areas of study in the literature on the Middle East' ('The Conditions of Islamist Moderation', 541). More generally, the fact that moderation is defined in relation to democratic practices and that its importance is motivated by the 'paradox of democracy' whereby possibly non-democratic actors may subvert democracy suggests that the Islamists' ideological rigidity is indeed perceived as a barrier for democratization in the Middle East. See Schwedler, *Faith in Moderation*, chapter 1.
6. Youngs, 'The European Union and Democracy Promotion in the Mediterranean'; Jünemann, 'Support for Democracy or Fear of Islamism?'; Sharp, 'US Democracy Promotion in the Middle East'.
7. For the implications of such an 'external sponsor' of a political party, see Panebianco, *Political Parties: Organization and Power.*
8. There are some issues that are typically part of the agenda of Islamist groups, such as the promotion of conservative morals, of personal status laws that are in line with supposed Qu'ranic principles, and of shari'a law. In accordance with the vagueness of the religious texts on which Islamist groups draw, the actual content of the ideology of Islamist parties or movement organizations as well as the role ascribed to shari'a is not immutable and varies across organization, country, and time. For a good overview of variations of Islamist ideology, see Krämer, *Gottes Staat als Republik.*
9. Of course, this development may not apply in all cases: some social movements may eventually become more moderate while some of these parties may never do so. The history of other social movement parties in general, however, shows that the large majority of such parties eventually drop a fundamentalist, ideologically driven agenda. See, for instance, Offe, 'Reflections on the Self-Transformation of Movement Politics', or Hanagan. 'Social Movements'.
10. The 2003–2004 field research was carried out by Eva Wegner; field research in 2007 was undertaken by both authors.
11. The other strand is Sheikh Yassine's Justice and Charity organization (al-'Adl wal-Ihsan). This organization is barred from participation in political institutions. Its exclusion is 'self-chosen' as it refuses the conditions of political participation: to accept both the religious legitimacy of the monarchy and its dominant role in politics.
12. The dates given for the founding of the Islamic Youth Association range from 1969 to 1972.
13. Sayyed Qutb (1906–1966) is considered one of the most influential Islamist theorists and activists in the twentieth century. In the 1950s and 1960s, he became the mastermind of the Egyptian Muslim Brotherhood. He is especially known for his view of Islam as a general religious, moral, social, and political system in his book *Mile Stones* in 1964. According to Qutb, shari'a is supposed to be the sole base of government and social relations in an 'Islamic state'. Accordingly, Qutb rejected the extant Arab regimes and advocated not only proselytizing and exemplary behaviour but also violence to achieve the true Islamic society. He was sentenced to death in 1966.
14. For the history of the Movement of Unity and Reform, see Tozy, *Monarchie et Islam politique au Maroc.*
15. The charter is cited in Shahin, *Political Ascent*, 189.
16. *Al-Tajdid*, Special Issue on the Movement of Unity and Reform (December 2002), 4.
17. Ibid., 16.

18. The party received four million dirhams for the 1997 elections, 17m dirhams for the 2002 elections, and another 4m dirhams for the 2003 communal elections (figures provided by the PJD's treasurer). The membership subscription is collected once a year. Working members (those who have been active for more than one year and have the right to vote in the party's internal elections) pay 200 dirhams (around €20). Participating members (those who have just joined to the party and still have to prove their commitment) pay 100 dirhams (around €10).

19. While it was impossible to get precise figures, these were given by party leaders during author's interviews with members of the PJD's general secretariat, Rabat, 4 September 2003 and 17 November 2003.

20. Data collected at the PJD's party congress in 2004. See Wegner, *The Inclusion of Islamist Movements*. Data is available from the authors upon request.

21. Profiles published daily in *Al-Tajdid* from 12 to 26 September 2002. Data available from the authors upon request.

22. Panebianco, *Political Parties: Organization and Power.*

23. The 1997 by-laws were published in the PJD's newspaper *Al-'Asr*, 10 October 1997, 4.

24. *Al-Tajdid*, Editorial, 'The PJD and the Present Responsibilities', 1 December 1999, 1.

25. Author's interview with member of the PJD's general secretariat, Rabat, 12 December 2003.

26. Author's interview with member of a PJD local secretariat, Khenitra, 9 November 2003.

27. Author's interviews with delegates at the PJD's party congress, Rabat, 8–11 April 2004.

28. Author's interview with a member of the PJD's general secretariat and the MUR's executive bureau, Rabat, 12 November 2003.

29. Author's interview with a member of the PJD's general secretariat and member of the MUR's executive bureau, Rabat, 17 November 2003.

30. Author's interview with a member of the PJD's general secretariat, Rabat, 4 September 2003.

31. See Wegner, *The Inclusion of Islamist*, chapter 3.

32. In the 1997 parliamentary elections, the PJD covered around 50% of the electoral districts and won nine (out of 325) seats. In the autumn of 1999, after by-elections and the defection of two MPs from other parties, the figure increased to 14. According to the US Embassy's *Country Report on Human Rights Practices*, most independent observers concluded, however, that the 1997 election results were heavily influenced, if not predetermined, by the government. In the more transparent 2002 elections, the PJD covered again around half of the electoral districts and increased the number of seats to 42 (out of 325). In 2007, the party covered all districts except one and won 47 seats.

33. Author's interview with a member of the PJD's general secretariat, Rabat, 7 March 2003.

34. At that time, the National Council was composed of the PJD's MPs, the General Secretariat, and the leaders of local and provincial secretariats.

35. This is calculated on the basis of the number of ministers allocated to parties with similar electoral results.

36. *Al-'Asr*, 7 November 2002, 5, author's translation.

37. Author's interviews with PJD MPs and party leaders, Mohammedia and Rabat, 1 March 2003, 9 November 2003; 12 November 2003, 11 December 2003.

38. Author's interview with a member of the PJD's general secretariat, Rabat, 4 September 2003.

39. Interview with Abdelilah Benkirane, member of the general secretariat and former MUR leader, *La Vie Économique*, 16 June 2003.

40. *Aujourd'hui Le Maroc*, 12 May 2003, 1.
41. Author's interview, Rabat, 6 November 2003.
42. Author's interview, Rabat, 12 April 2004.
43. Conversation with a member of the PJD's Forum for Development at the party congress, Rabat, 8 April 2004.
44. Authors' interviews with PJD leaders, Rabat, 1, 2, and 3 November 2007.
45. For an illustration of this, see Schwedler, *Faith in Moderation*, chapter one, Schwedler, 'Democratization', and Clark, 'The Conditions'.
46. Cf. http://www.amnesty.org/en/library/asset/MDE29/004/2004/en/dom-MDE 290042004en.html
47. *Al-Ayam*, 18 July 2003, 1.
48. See, *Le Journal Hebdomadaire*, 7–13 December 2003, 1–2.
49. Author's interview with a PJD member, Rabat, 12 April 2004.
50. Author's interview with a PJD leader, Rabat, 12 November 2003. The party later portrayed the reduction of the coverage as its own, autonomous decision. See Wegner, 'Islamist Inclusion and Regime Persistence'.
51. At the time of writing, it is not clear whether the weak result of the PJD (as compared to the expectations) was the outcome of vote-buying – as claimed by the PJD – or of weaker electoral support for the PJD than expected. Whatever the truth, for our argument, it is not the result as such that matters, but what everybody believed before, namely that the PJD would be by far the strongest party after the elections.
52. Richards and Waterbury, *A Political Economy of the Middle East*, 297–98.
53. See the EU's external relations' website at http://ec.europa.eu/external_relations/ human_rights/intro/index.htm, and for the 1995 Barcelona declaration, see http:// ec.europa.eu/external_relations/euromed/index_en.htm
54. See Wegner, 'Authoritarian King and Democratic Islamists'.
55. For EU policies towards Morocco, see among others, Haddadi, 'The EMP and Morocco' and Haddadi 'Two Cheers for Whom?'.
56. See European Commission, 'Euro-Med Partnership: Morocco. National Indicative Programme 2005-2006', June 2004, 1.
57. Interview with a member of the IAF's executive bureau, Amman, 14 June 2007.
58. Bermeo, 'Myths of Moderation'.

Bibliography

Bermeo, Nancy. 'Myths of Moderation: Confrontation and Conflict during Democratic Transitions'. *Comparative Politics* 29 (1997): 305–22.
Clark, Janine A. 'The Conditions of Islamist Moderation: Unpacking Cross-Ideological Cooperation in Jordan'. *International Journal of Middle East Studies* 38 (2006): 539–560.
Haddadi, Said. 'The EMP and Morocco: Diverging Political Agendas'. *Mediterranean Politics* 8 (2003): 73–89.
Haddadi, Said. 'Two Cheers for Whom? The European Union and Democratization in Morocco'. In *The European Union and Democracy Promotion: The Case of North Africa*, ed. Richard Gillespie and Richard Youngs, 149–69. London: F. Cass, 2002.
Hanagan, Michael. 'Social Movements. Incorporation, Disengagement, and Opportunities – A Long View'. In *From Contention to Democracy*, ed. Mario G. Giugni, Doug McAdam, and Charles Tilly, 3–30. Lanham, MD: Rowman & Littlefield, 1998.
Jünemann, Annette. 'Support for Democracy or Fear of Islamism? Europe and Algeria'. In *The Islamic World and the West: An Introduction to Political Cultures and International Relations*, ed. Kai Hafez, 103–26. London: Brill Academic Publishers, 2000.

Krämer, Gudrun. *Gottes Staat als Republik*. Baden Baden: Nomos, 1999.

Offe, Claus. 'Reflections on the Self-transformation of Movement Politics: A Tentative Stage Model'. In *Challenging the Political Order. New Social and Political Movements in Western Democracies*, ed. Russell J. Dalton and Manfred Kuechler, 232–50. Cambridge: Polity Press, 1990.

Panebianco, Angelo. *Political Parties: Organization and Power*. Cambridge: Cambridge University Press, 1988.

Richards, Alan, and John Waterbury. *A Political Economy of the Middle East*. 2nd ed. Boulder, CO: Westview Press, 1998.

Robinson, Glenn E. 'Can Islamists be Democrats? The Case of Jordan'. *Middle East Journal* 51 (1997): 373–87.

Schwedler, Jillian. 'Democratization, Inclusion and the Moderation of Islamist Parties'. *Development* 50 (2007): 56–61.

Schwedler, Jillian. *Faith in Moderation. Islamist Parties in Jordan and Yemen*. Cambridge: Cambridge University Press, 2006.

Shahin, Emad Eldin. *Political Ascent. Contemporary Islamic Movements in North Africa*. Boulder, CO: Westview Press, 1998.

Sharp, Jeremy. 'US Democracy Promotion in the Middle East: The Islamist Dilemma'. *CRS Report for Congress* RL33486 (2006).

Tozy, Mohamed. *Monarchie et Islam politique au Maroc*. Paris: Presses de Sciences Po, 1999.

US Department of State. *Morocco Country Report on Human Rights Practices for 1998*. http://www.usembassy.ma/themes/CivilSociety/us.htm

Wegner, Eva. 'Authoritarian King and Democratic Islamists in Morocco'. *The Challenge of Islamists for EU and U.S. Policies: Conflict, Stability, and Reform*, ed. Daniel Brumberg and Muriel Asseburg, 53–8. Washington/Berlin: USIP/ SWP, 2007.

Wegner, Eva. 'The Inclusion of Islamist Movements Into Political Institutions: The Case of the Moroccan Party of Justice and Development'. European University Institute, 2006, PhD thesis.

Wegner, Eva. 'Islamist Inclusion and Regime Persistence: The Moroccan Win-Win Situation'. In *Debating Arab Authoritarianism: Dynamics and Durability in Non-Democratic Regimes*, ed. Oliver Schlumberger, 75–93. Stanford: Stanford University Press, 2007.

Youngs, Richard. 'The European Union and Democracy Promotion in the Mediterranean: A New or Disingenuous Strategy?'. *Democratization* 9 (2002): 40–62.

Promoting democracy in Algeria: the EU factor and the preferences of the political elite

Ayşe Aslıhan Çelenk

Department of International Relations, Erciyes University, Kayseri, Turkey

The aim of this study is to analyse the reasons for the shortcomings of the EU as an agent of democracy promotion in Algeria. Instead of focusing solely on the EU, the study proposes that it was the interaction between EU-level problems and domestic, political factors which led to the shortcomings of the EU's conditionality in Algeria. The security priorities, the potential threat of Islam, and the perceived potential of instability resulting from democratization made the EU less eager to apply conditionality for political change in Algeria. The preferences and interests of France and the way in which the Mediterranean partners are perceived by the EU also affected the EU's impact at the domestic level. However, the powers and choices of the political elite (especially the army and the president) are argued to be the major determinants of the EU's impact, as this elite controls the channels through which the EU seeks to influence the democratization of Algerian politics. The main argument advanced in this study is that it was the simultaneous processes of re-definition of the security concerns at the EU level and the empowerment of the authoritarian elite in Algeria, which led to the shortcomings of the EU's conditionality for democratization.

Introduction

The effectiveness of the EU as a global political actor has been extensively discussed, especially since the 11 September attacks in the United States, when the Union failed to speak with a common voice regarding the war in Iraq and the member states were divided among themselves in terms of their opinions and actions about the responses to the threat of terrorism.[1] The EU has launched various initiatives to deal with the challenges of successive enlargements throughout its history and to establish good relations with its neighbours. One of these initiatives covers the Middle East and North Africa within the context of EU–Mediterranean relations. The Euro-Mediterranean Partnership (EuroMed, or EMP) was a foreign policy move that set ambitious objectives from the beginning for establishing political, economic, and cultural cooperation in the Mediterranean region, and various instruments were developed in order to realize this cooperation.[2]

One of the objectives of the EU in the Mediterranean is to promote democracy, human rights, and the rule of law in the countries of the region in order to have a more secure international environment.[3] This article examines, through an institutionalist perspective, to what extent the EU has achieved this objective in the Algerian context by using the 'misfit model of Europeanization'.[4] In order to understand how EU conditionality works in promoting democracy in Algeria, the nature of the EU's pressure for initiating institutional change is analysed. Then, the article investigates the way in which EU-level pressures are interpreted and processed at the domestic level. The interaction between the EU's impact and domestic political processes and actors is taken as the basic factor to determine the prospects for democratization in Algeria and the article focuses on analysing the dynamics of this interaction.

The first part of the article explains the theoretical framework, based on institutionalism and models of Europeanization. The concept of Europeanization is used to refer to various processes within European politics in the literature.[5] Within the context of this study, it is essentially understood as the process of exporting political norms and economic practices advocated by the EU, such as democracy, pluralism, and a free market economy[6] and forms of government, to EU neighbours. The theoretical framework is developed further in the second part, with a discussion of the nature of EU-level pressures for democratization in Algeria, which are mainly the EMP and the European Neighbourhood Policy (ENP). In this part of the article, the absence both of a Country Report as well as an Action Plan with regard to Algeria, within the ENP framework, will be dealt with as part of the shortcomings of the EU's democracy promotion policies in Algeria. In the third part, the way in which the EU's impact is dealt with in the Algerian context is analysed and the colonial legacy, the threat of political Islam, and the impact of the political elite are identified as the main factors in this process. The article concludes with some comments on the limitations of the EU's conditionality in Algeria and an analysis of the interaction between the EU's impact and domestic factors.

The theoretical framework: Europeanization and institutionalization

The concept of Europeanization has come to refer to various processes within the course of European integration. For instance, it may refer to the changes in the territories of Europe through enlargement; development of institutionalized governance at the European level by means of policy co-ordination and coherence; central penetration of national and sub-national systems of governance by European-level institutions; exporting forms of political organization and governance beyond European borders; or a political project of creating a unified and politically stronger Europe.[7] The case of democracy promotion in Algeria can be considered as a form of Europeanization, of exporting norms and values of political organization beyond European borders.[8] Defined in this way, the process of Europeanization starts with pressures for change from the European level and, in exchange for certain benefits or more integration, the domestic, political level is expected to respond to this pressure for change. The way in which the domestic level does respond to this pressure depends on the existing institutional setting and the mediating factors, such as the preferences and strength of the major political actors and the institutional culture and norms, which determine the prospects for change as a result of the EU's impact.[9] In other words, the institutional culture of each setting determines to a considerable extent how much resistance the EU will face in exporting political values and practices to its neighbours and the overall prospects for success.

As the 'misfit model'[10] of Europeanization suggests, the way in which EU-level pressures affect the state level depends on the historical and political context, and the preferences and powers of the major political actors. In other words, the misfit model suggests that: (1) there exists a difference between the EU policy preferences and the domestic practices of the states; and (2) the EU presses for change at the domestic level in exchange for certain benefits of institutional adjustment to the EU practice. In the case of democracy promotion, the EU perceives a difference between its understanding of governance and that of the partners, which is crucial for its security, and tries to remedy this 'misfit' by offering some incentives and applying pressure for democratization. However, the domestic institutional setting determines the distribution of resources among domestic political actors and how the EU affects that distribution.[11] When the costs of responding to the EU pressure for change are higher, domestic political actors tend to resist EU-level pressure. In the Algerian case, the colonial legacy, perceptions about political Islam, and the preferences of the military and the president, as the major elite political actors, are the domestic determinants of the way in which EU's democracy promotion policies affect the country.[12]

In terms of promoting democracy in Algeria, the main frameworks for the EU have been the EMP and the ENP. At the domestic level, the major factors mediating the EU's impact have been the colonial ties of Algeria with France, the experience of the country with Islamism, and the preferences of the political elite. In order to analyse the outcome of the interaction between these factors and the prospects for democratization in Algeria, both aspects need to be examined thoroughly, but first of all, we need to understand the nature of the EU-level pressures for change.

The Euro-Mediterranean Partnership and promoting democracy in Algeria

Although the EU initiated economic and political relations with the region in the 1960s, the Mediterranean region only became of strategic importance for the EU in the late 1980s, with the southern enlargement of the Community to include Greece, Spain, and Portugal and with the end of the Cold War. The southern enlargement of the European Community provided an opportunity for cooperation among Mediterranean countries and created a suitable environment for the EU to increase its influence in the region.[13] The new security understanding in the post-Cold War period also increased the importance of the Mediterranean. This new and broader security understanding included economic, political, and social instabilities as forms of threat, in addition to direct military threats, and required new solutions based on international and regional cooperation for these problems.[14] Within this context, democracy promotion as a means of achieving stability became one of the security objectives of Europe,[15] and formed one of the basic premises of the EU's policies towards the Mediterranean. An increase in shared political values and the spread of democratic norms were considered important means of achieving regional security[16] and the EU has developed various instruments to this end.

For the Mediterranean region in general, and for Algeria in particular, the main framework of democracy promotion is the EMP,[17] launched in 1995 as a result of the joint French-Spanish initiative at the Barcelona Conference. The Barcelona Declaration provided the official basis for the relationship of the EU with its Mediterranean partners and aimed at strengthening democracy and respect for human rights, sustainable economic development, and promoting inter-cultural dialogue.[18] The political and security components of the declaration required the Mediterranean partners to 'develop the rule of law and democracy in their political systems, respect human rights and fundamental freedoms and guarantee the effective legitimate exercise of such rights and freedoms'.[19] Within the official framework of the EMP, the EU exerts pressure for further democratization through the conditionality principle. In other words, the continuation of the EU's relation with each Mediterranean partner is conditional on the commitment of the partners to the principles in the Barcelona Declaration.[20] They imply that suspension of economic and political relations with the Mediterranean partners is a measure that the EU could use to apply more pressure in terms of promoting democracy in the Mediterranean.

The different strategies of the EU 'to induce authoritarian states to achieve democratic transition or consolidation'[21] establish the EU's democracy promotion policies, which are based on conditionality and incentives. Within the Euro-Med framework, political conditionality, financial and economic incentives, and norm diffusion are the basic strategies for democracy promotion[22] and, for the most part, the EU promises to fulfil its financial commitments to Mediterranean partners as long as adequate progress is achieved in terms of political reform.[23] The democracy promotion policy of the EU can be characterized as mainly a 'top-down'[24] approach, in which governments of the partner states are the main targets. In this approach, financial conditionality based on aid is the main instrument and the suspension clauses in the association agreements with each partner serve as the pressure for democratization, despite the fact that the economic and financial partnership is not framed in terms of human rights.[25] Since the main instrument of political conditionality is the reward of ultimate EU membership, this instrument cannot be considered as effective in the Mediterranean. In the case of the Mediterranean, one way of using political conditionality as a means of promoting democracy can be to provide tangible incentives, such as security cooperation, which would be more useful for the domestic political elite than the political disincentives of democratization.[26] In other words, the benefits, which the political elite will receive in exchange for applying the EU conditionality for democratization, have to compensate for the loss of political power, which the elite will likely experience at the domestic level as a result of democratization. In Euro-Mediterranean cooperation, the EU mostly provides financial aid in order to offer support for political reform in the partner states; this has shortcomings in terms of providing sanctions when the suspension clauses in the association agreements are not activated.

In order to deal with the new international and security challenges that arose with the 2004 enlargement, in 2003 the EU designed a new official framework for dealing with its new neighbours, which is called the ENP. The ENP stresses the importance of common values, namely democracy and human rights, the rule of law, good governance, market economy principles, and sustainable development,[27] for the development of good relations between the EU and its neighbours, including the Mediterranean region. In terms of promoting democracy in the Mediterranean, the ENP introduced a new instrument in the form of increased bilateral relations, (previously signed) association agreements and action plans, designed specifically for each partner country.

The EMP and the ENP provide official frameworks for promotion of democracy in Algeria. While the EMP provides the regional context for the relations, the ENP is based on bilateral relations in order to better promote internal reforms. However, since Algeria has been reluctant to participate in the ENP framework, the conditionality of the association agreement and the Barcelona process has been the major instrument of the EU to promote democracy in Algeria. However, as this study aims to reveal, these instruments have had certain shortcomings in terms of generating institutional change in the Algerian case. Before analysing the limitations of the democracy-promotion policies of the EU in Algeria, the domestic political setting, over which the EU seeks to exerts its influence and pressure, needs to be understood.

Democratization and the preferences of the Algerian political elite

Algeria was a French colony from 1830 to 1954, when the War of Liberation began, and, after eight years of war, Algeria declared its independence in 1962. The major legacy of the colonial experience and the war of liberation was the strong, centralized state structure designed by the military and civilian elite,[28] which affected the prospects for democratization in Algeria. The supremacy of the military and the authoritarian nature of government were the consequences of the leading role of the army in the independence struggle and in the period of reconstruction thereafter. The military, the bureaucratic elite, and the president formed the three pillars of the centralized state structure[29] and power became concentrated in the hands of these interdependent institutions. The special importance of the army in Algerian politics has been evident in the post-liberation history of the country.[30] It was the army which overthrew the first president of Algeria, Ahmed Ben Bella, with a coup in 1965 and replaced him with Houari Boumediene. In this period, the National Assembly was dissolved and the Constitution was suspended by the military. After 10 years of authoritarian rule under FLN (National Liberation Front, the extension of the army into the political sphere as a party), the country returned to the constitutional system in 1975. However, the army retained its control over politics by being represented in the major political institutions.

The political role of the army was challenged during the Chadli Benjedid era (1979–1988). Benjedid succeeded Boumediene, and during his presidency Algeria went through a process of political liberalization,[31] which in turn led to the resurgence of political Islamism alongside different ideologies. The political climate of strikes, protests, and bloody clashes between various groups and the military, along with the rise of the Front Islamique du Salut (FIS) as the main opposition party and the popular support given to the FIS, brought the army back into politics. The perceived threat of political Islam led to the suspension of the elections and, once again, the army intervened in politics in 1992.[32]

During the 1988–1992 period, the ruling elite sustained the non-democratic governing structures of the state and prevented full democratization of the country. This was despite the efforts of various civil society organizations, including those run by students, women, Islamists and labour unions.[33] These circumstances enabled the army to carry out the 1992 coup and to strengthen its position within the political elite.[34] In time, the military became the 'vanguard against militant Islam'[35] and remained ready to take over power in case of the re-emergence of the threat of Islamism in the country. As David Sorenson argues, during this period, every significant aspect of politics required the approval of the military, which retained its control over the party and the bureaucracy.[36] However, after defeating the Islamists in the late 1990s, following a lengthy civil war during which more than 100,000 people died, the army returned to barracks. The transfer of political power to civilians, nonetheless, did not initiate a process of democratization in the country, as the presidential authority replaced the army as the new centre of political power.

Abdelaziz Bouteflika was first elected as the president of Algeria in 1999 and again in 2004 for his second term. With the disappearance of Islamic insurgency and the withdrawal of the army from politics, political powers were gradually transferred and concentrated in the office of the president,[37] which exacerbated concerns about the prospects for democratization in Algeria. After consolidating his power during his first term, Bouteflika revealed tendencies towards presidential authoritarianism during his second term in the post-2004 period.[38] These tendencies included constitutional amendments, which increased the presidential term from five to seven years, and enabled the president to be elected for a third term, while also giving the president himself the right to choose the vice-president. In addition, the president and his close circle were exempted from prosecution for their actions in office,[39] thus dramatically minimizing their accountability.

The political powers of the army and the president, which stem both from the colonial legacy and the threat of political Islam, make the preferences and decisions of the political elite crucial in terms of the external promotion of democracy in Algeria and the way in which EU conditionality functions within the Algerian context. The authoritarian tendencies initiated by the army and maintained by the president make the political elite the primary actors dealing with the EU. The perceptions of the domestic political elite about the values the EU wants to promote, and the nature of the pressure, determine to what extent the EU can realize the objective of democracy promotion in Algeria.[40] The fact that the country has other policy options, because of its ties with the global economy and its strength as a supplier of energy, decreases the impact of EU pressure and it thus becomes easier for the Algerian political elite to dismiss EU conditionality.[41] The existence of other alternatives for finding a place in the global order has enabled the Algerian government to refuse to take part in the ENP framework, as the incentives provided were not considered as important stakes for political reform. As the centres of power in the country, the political elite are able to filter and process EU pressure in terms of democratization and to influence the EU's potential, if any, impact. Thus, when assessing whether the EU has been a successful actor in terms of promoting democracy in Algeria, it is crucial that the internal dynamics are taken into consideration.

The limitations of EU conditionality in Algeria

The major sources of the limitations of EU conditionality in Algeria are the inherent paradoxes of the security concerns and aims of the EU;[42] the clash between the national interests of the member states (especially those of the former colonial power, France) and local community interests; the challenges of the international environment after 9/11; and the way in which the Mediterranean is perceived and conceptualized within the EU.

Since the launching of the Barcelona Process, the EU has often been criticized for being highly rhetorical in its aims, lacking concrete and effective policy initiatives. The reason for this criticism is the fact that the security concerns of the EU and the ideal of democracy promotion have often contradicted each other in the Mediterranean region. 'Despite its professed claims in favour of democracy, Europe gives the impression that it does not wish its emergence in the South, because it suspects what the outcome would be, and does not want to take the risk of having its suspicion confirmed'.[43] In other words, the unpredictable outcomes of democratization are, in fact, perceived as a threat to the stability and security of the region, which are crucial for the continuation of economic and political cooperation between the EU and the Mediterranean partners. The economic and political interests of the EU member states lead the EU to cooperate with the ruling political elite at the nation-state level and the status quo is thus preserved.[44] In the case of Algeria, the EU prefers stability over promoting democracy, and the authoritarian regime is in fact tolerated or even welcomed, regarded as the lesser of two evils, given the possibility of the likely alternative: a radical Islamist regime.[45] Instead of intervention, the EU has followed, and still follows, a policy of containment in Algeria[46] and the conditionality aspect of the EMP is not applied in this case (nor in any other Mediterranean case). In fact, despite internal violence and authoritarian tendencies in the country, the EU proceeded with negotiations of the association agreement with Algeria, which was eventually signed at the Valencia Conference in 2002. Moreover, the fact that the most effective instrument of Euro-Mediterranean cooperation – the MEDA funds – were never considered for suspension, even though steps towards democratization were not taken in Algeria,[47] shows that the ideal of democracy promotion may be sacrificed by the EU under certain conditions.

The priorities of the EU in terms of its Algerian policy can be inferred from the community strategy prepared for the 2007–2013 period. While acknowledging that 'it is rather premature to anticipate the adoption of an action plan'[48] for Algeria, the Commission has identified certain areas for assistance in Algeria. According to the Strategy Paper, the priorities of the EU are 'the justice system reform, improvement of economic growth and employment conditions and the improvement of public services'.[49] While various concrete projects to these ends are to be assisted by the EU, there exists no special programme for democracy promotion in the strategy of the EU until 2013.

The distribution of MEDA funds also reveals the priority of economic and security concerns over the policy of democracy promotion in the Mediterranean in general, and in Algeria, in particular. While the bulk of the MEDA funds were reserved for poverty reduction and commercial cooperation,[50] during the periods between 1995–1999 and 2000–2006, Algeria was the sixth-highest beneficiary of the funds with a total of €500 m, most of the aid being reserved for economic liberalization.[51]

The north–south divide within the EU has also contributed to the shortcomings of the EU's democracy promotion in Algeria.[52] For the southern EU members, such as France and Spain, initiating democratization was perceived as destabilizing the region, while northern members like Sweden, pushed for more political pressure. Southern member states opted for the status quo and commercial cooperation instead of using political conditionality for democratization.[53] The top-down understanding of reform also makes the democratization efforts of the EU dismissible by the Algerian political elite. The idea of promoting 'European' values and standards, with little differentiation according to national and local concerns and cultures, as well as the asymmetrical relationship between the EU and the southern partners, together legitimize the choice of the political elite to ignore the pressure coming from the EU for political reform.[54]

The legacy of colonial ties between France and Algeria has also affected EU policy. Because of historical ties, France tried to keep the EU at arm's length from any political intervention in Algeria,[55] as the country was perceived as a French foreign policy domain. After the launching of the EMP in 1995, the Algerian domain was gradually opened up to wider EU influence. However, the security concerns and foreign policy priorities of France continued to have a significant influence on the EU's approach towards Algeria. As the first bilateral partner and the largest donor to the country,[56] French priorities in Algeria, such as the modernization of the public sector,[57] have shaped the strategies of the EU in terms of initiating change in Algeria. Moreover, colonial ties also contribute to the consolidation of the asymmetrical relationship between the EU and Algeria, since EU attempts at political reform are perceived as different forms of Western interventionism at the domestic level.[58] As Entelis has pointed out, 'France has too complex and controversial a relationship with its former colony to act in a democratically meaningful way'.[59] In other words, for the political and economic interests of France in Algeria, which in time also affected EU policies, the continuous existence of the authoritarian regime and its stability is preferred over democratization, which could lead to the emergence of an Islamist government.[60] The fear of the consequences of an Islamist government, the possibility of a consequential large-scale refugee movement, the stability of energy exports to Europe, and the fear of spillover of terrorism and political violence from Algeria, are some of the main reasons why France opts for stability instead of democracy promotion. This choice, in turn, affects the direction of EU pressures for democratization in the country.[61]

The 11 September attacks on the United States also had an impact on the policies of the EU as a democracy-promoting actor. After 9/11, Euro-Mediterranean relations went through a process of 'securitization'.[62] In this period, as new security concerns based on the threat of global terrorism emerged, Western governments began to reassess and restructure the state–individual relationship and redefine the boundaries of individual liberties and democracy. During this internal reassessment period, promotion of democracy became of secondary importance in the international realm and security concerns became much more critical.[63] This reassessment of priorities decreased the EU's pressures in terms of democratization and 'the fear of giving too much political space to Islamic fundamentalism has acted as a powerful deterrent'[64] in realizing the initial aims of the Barcelona Process.

> Since 2001, the EU has increasingly used its economic and political leverage to encourage Arab governments to cooperate with the EU on controlling illegal migration and sharing information on counter-terrorism, and less on encouraging democratic reform in those countries.[65]

In other words, after the 11 September attacks, it is possible to observe a reprioritization of interests and targets in the Mediterranean for the EU, where democracy promotion policies were pushed to the backstage.

In 2005, while the EU allocated €800 m for controlling illegal migration in the Southern Mediterranean, only €10 m of aid was reserved for promoting regional democracy.[66] These numbers reveal a decline in the willingness of the EU to provide financial assistance, which had been one of its most important policy instruments for promoting democracy, and a re-prioritization of its interests in the region. Moreover, the security environment after 9/11 enabled the Algerian political elite to legitimize their authoritarian policies, with the stated purpose of fighting Islamist terrorism.[67] In addition, after 9/11, the Euro-Mediterranean framework lost its priority in terms of coping with security threats, and inter-state cooperation and bilateral relations once again became more important than multilateral forms of cooperation.[68] The French-Algerian Security Cooperation Framework, which was revived in 2003, is one of the examples of the bilateral cooperation initiatives in the Euro-Mediterranean area, which were preferred to multilateral cooperation activities.[69]

EU perceptions of political Islam in the Mediterranean partner states have also affected the extent to which the EU's conditionality has worked in the Algerian case. As Bicchi and Martin argue, 'the EU's call for more democracy and human rights in the Arab world clashes with the EU's attempt to avoid any opposition in relation to parties and NGOs proposing an agenda construed in Islamist terms'.[70] The fact that the EU does not engage in any kind of dialogue, even with moderate or reformist Islamic/Islamist actors within the framework of intercultural dialogue, and leaves the distribution of the funds to the discretion of national governments, shows that the EU prefers to cooperate with the political elite and (co-opted) civil society representatives, considered by the political elite to be 'legitimate' systemic actors.

One criticism directed towards the EMP from Algeria is that it lacks a certain level of differentiation when dealing with partner countries: 'Algiers insists that it should not be forced to accept a one-size-fits-all agreement that would be inappropriate given Algeria's size, potential and extra-ordinary position as an energy exporter'.[71] Although the association agreements signed with each partner aimed to remedy this situation, a single framework and a single set of principles are still applied to all of the Mediterranean partners; hence in a way, certain values are being imposed without taking the context-specific factors into consideration. The EU's one-sided approach diminishes the credibility and impact of the Union as the promoter of democracy in the region and may negatively affect Mediterranean partners' perceptions. The rift between the EU and the Mediterranean partners, which became apparent in the Barcelona meeting of November 2005 (the ten-year anniversary of the Barcelona Process), is a consequence of the reaction of Mediterranean partners to this policy approach of the EU. The original agenda of the Barcelona Meeting was to establish a code of conduct for countering terrorism in the Mediterranean. However, the outcome of the meeting was only a presidency declaration,[72] revealing the different opinions on each side of the Mediterranean regarding the fight against terrorism. Especially after 11 September, the EU was heavily criticized by Mediterranean partners for forcing its own agenda and security and perceptions of threat onto the partner countries.[73] In fact, the heads of state of the Mediterranean partners, with the exception of the Palestine National Authorities and Turkey, were absent at this meeting, which is a testament to the failure of the EMP in realizing its initial objectives. Algeria was one of the leading countries to oppose an agenda being imposed on the Mediterranean; it was also a country which was very resistant to EU engagement in its internal affairs.[74]

The last factor, which limits the conditionality of the EU in promoting democracy in Algeria and in the Mediterranean, is the way in which the EU constructs and conceptualizes the region. From the beginning of its relations with the Mediterranean, the EU perceived the Mediterranean as 'the other' through which it defined its own identity as being more politically and economically advanced. In other words, the Mediterranean region signified the cultural, political, and geographical boundaries of the EU and it was perceived as a neighbour which needed the support of Europe and European values to achieve stability and development.[75] This 'otherness' of the Mediterranean was implicitly accepted in the context of the principle of exporting 'shared values' and practices to the region and this situation affected the way in which the EU was perceived at the nation-state level. The EU, which was perceived as an outsider, chose to cooperate with the state elite in the Algerian case and did not target the grassroots level, thus missing the opportunity to initiate a process of democratic transformation in the country. This was partly due to the fact that the state elite could play the gate-keeper role in any contact between the EU and civil society institutions. The projects funded by the EU mostly focused on the technical aspect of governance and provided assistance for infrastructure building and training and the EU's aid was distributed to civil society organizations by the government,[76] which prevented the EU's impact for democratization from passing through the filter of the Algerian state elite.

Theory revisited: the EU factor, domestic political actors and prospects for democratization in Algeria

The promotion of democracy within the framework of the Barcelona Process can be considered as a form of Europeanization, defined as the spread of European values (as noted earlier) to other parts of the region. While focusing on the success or lack of success in EU efforts at promoting democracy in Algeria, the interaction between the EU's impact and the domestic political context has been taken as the main determining factor. In other words, the EU itself has been bound and affected by the historical and political context of the country and the preferences of the Algerian political elite, while trying to press for more democracy in Algeria. As Roberto Menotti notes,

> While the Barcelona Process addresses a desire for reform, there is no comparable clarity on short-term policies designed to manage the risks and opportunities when and where they arise. The EU has not been able to overcome the 'Algerian

syndrome', the belief that premature elections can lead to an Islamist victory and civil war, as they did in Algeria in 1992.[77]

The Algerian case suggests that when the EU is faced with the choice between initiating change and maintaining stability, it opts for stability even at the expense of the ideal of promoting democracy in the Mediterranean region. This concern for stability decreases the pressure on the political elite to initiate reform in the country. In fact, the fear that greater political liberalization could lead to a transfer of power into the hands of alternative power groups serves as a justification for both the authoritarian tendencies of the ruling elite and the non-interference policy of the EU,[78] and the political elite gain more space to pursue their own interests. In the absence of any consent on the part of the Algerian political elite, attempts by the EU to promote democracy fail to create the desired impact in terms of reaching the grassroots level.

In the Algerian case, it is possible to argue that security priorities and the concerns of the EU about the political and economic stability of the country and the preferences of the member states have decreased the intensity of pressure for democratization in Algeria. This lack of determination on the part of the EU has been combined with a process that empowers the Algerian, authoritarian political elite (the army and the president) and further weakens any prospects for democratization. The lack of political incentives on the part of the EU, in the absence of prospects for membership or deeper cooperation, and the existence of other policy options based on the importance of Algerian resources for the European economy, reduce the ability of the EU to exert pressure and to use political conditionality for promoting democracy in the country.

The prospects for institutional change depend on a variety of factors, including the way in which the change is initiated, the existing institutional setting, where change is initiated, and the agents of change, that is, the major political actors. In the case of democratization in Algeria, EU policies have had various shortcomings in terms of combining rhetoric with reality, the authoritarian character of the state as well as the increasing strength of the political elite, who, as potential agents of change, resist EU pressure for democratization. As a result, the EU's conditionality has, in terms of initiating political change, been rather limited in the Algerian case.

Conclusion

The main aim of this article has been to analyse the main factors which led to the failure of the EU's democracy promotion policies in Algeria. Instead of focusing on the EU aspect of the problem alone, the article has proposed a model which takes into account domestic political factors resisting change. It was argued that the EU's conditionality has not worked in Algeria due to the result of simultaneous processes of re-prioritization of security objectives in the EU and empowerment of the authoritarian political elite in Algeria, which has mainly manifested itself through the actions of the army and the increased powers of the president.

The discrepancy between the political objectives of the Barcelona Declaration and actual practices has occurred as a result of the changes in the European security environment, the economic interests of the Mediterranean members of the EU, and the policy preferences of France, which has colonial ties with Algeria. The perception of the Mediterranean partners as 'the other' also diminished the power and credibility of the EU as a promoter of democracy and human rights. The top-down approach of the EU, which prefers to cooperate with the ruling political elite instead of the grass-roots level, the half-hearted commitment of the EU to the policy of democracy promotion, and the tendency to dismiss incentives provided by the EMP, make it easier for the Algerian political elite to evade EU pressures for political reform. For the southern members of the EU, and especially for France (the former colonial power), an authoritarian regime is preferred to a democracy, given the potential of an Islamist government, and the condition of political reform is not applied to economic and political cooperation agreements with Algeria, during times of military intervention and presidential authoritarianism.

While the EU has been re-thinking its security and political priorities, the political elite in Algeria has consolidated its power. As the main agent of change and the major source of power, the political elite has been able to filter the EU's impact before it reached the grassroots level and has, thus, been able to dismiss any pressures coming from the EU. The political elite preferred to maintain the authoritarian regime and deflected any impact by the EU at the domestic level. In the Algerian case, the shortcomings of the democracy promotion policies of the EU were not merely due to the problems stemming from the EU itself. The supremacy of the political and economic concerns of the individual member states, the lack of political incentives for reform, and the changes in the security environment of Europe were all effective in decreasing EU pressure for democratization in Algeria. However, the EU's democracy promotion policies were more easily dismissible in Algeria, because of the domestic political context with the increased powers of the authoritarian political elite and the existence of other policy options in international politics, such as partnership agreements with China on international judicial and criminal matters and economic and technical assistance, which had no conditionality, and expanded relations with the US.[79]

Notes

1. Schwarz, 'European Union Foreign Ministers Divided on Iraq War'.
2. See Barcelona Declaration, available at http://europa.eu/scadplus/leg/en/lvb/r15001.htm
3. Ibid.
4. Börzel, 'Europeanization and Territorial Institutional Change', and Börzel and Risse, 'When Europe Hits Home'.
5. For instance, it refers to the process through which supra-national institutions affect national and sub-national political practices, to diffusion of norms, rules, values, and practices or as it is understood in this study, to exporting forms of political organization and governance beyond European borders.
6. See Barcelona Declaration.

7. Olsen, 'The Many Faces of Europeanization'.

8. This notion can be inferred from the political and security cooperation basket of the Barcelona Declaration, which aims to create an area of democracy and peace and to guarantee the rights and freedoms of people in the Mediterranean region. The same notion can also be seen in 'Algeria Strategy Paper 2007–2013 and National Indicative Programme 2007–2010', http://ec.europa.eu/world/enp/pdf/country/enpi_csp_nip_algeria_en.pdf

9. Börzel, 'Towards Convergence in Europe?', 574; Börzel, 'Europeanization and Territorial Institutional Change', 143; Cowles, Caporaso, and Risse, 'Europeanization and Domestic Change', 6.

10. Ibid.

11. Börzel, 'Towards Convergence in Europe?', 577.

12. Roberts, 'Dancing in the Dark', 127.

13. Calabrese, 'Beyond Barcelona', 97.

14. Oljelund, *International Conference on European Security and Cooperation in the 21st Century*.

15. Dean, 'New Components of the European Security System', 106.

16. Youngs, *The European Union and the Promotion of Democracy* and Youngs, 'European Approaches to Security in the Mediterranean', 414.

17. The partnership agreement was signed between the 15 EU member states and 13 Mediterranean and North African countries. While Algeria, Cyprus, Israel, Egypt, Malta, Lebanon, Jordan, Morocco, Palestine Authority, Syria, Tunisia, and Turkey were partners, Libya participated as an observer country.

18. See Barcelona Declaration.

19. Ibid.

20. Tovias, 'The Regional Strategy Paper'.

21. Morisse-Schillbach, 'Patterns of Adaptation Towards EU Democracy Promotion'.

22. Ibid.

23. Tanner, *European Union Foreign and Security Policy*, 140.

24. Youngs, 'Europe's Flawed Approach to Arab Democracy'.

25. Pace, 'Human Rights Instruments in Euro-Mediterranean Relations'.

26. Schimmelfennig and Scholtz, 'EU Democracy Promotion in the European Neighbourhood', 8.

27. See the European Neighbourhood Policy, available at http://ec.europa.eu/world/enp/policy_en.htm

28. Entelis, *Algeria: The Revolution Institutionalized*, 158.

29. Entelis, 'Algeria: Technocratic Rule, Military Power', 93.

30. Ibid., 96–7 and Malley, *The Call From Algeria*, 128.

31. Entelis and Arone, 'Government and Politics', 184.

32. Tortter, 'National Security', 255.

33. Entelis, 'The Unchanging Politics of North Africa', 24.

34. Tortter, 'National Security', 256.

35. Sorenson, 'Civil-Military Relations in North Africa', 101.

36. Ibid.

37. Entelis, 'The Unchanging Politics of North Africa', 26.

38. Holm, 'Algeria: President Bouteflika's Second Term', 118.

39. Entelis, 'The Unchanging Politics of North Africa', 26.

40. Tanner, *European Union Foreign and Security*, 141.

41. Morisse-Schillbach, 'Patterns of Adaptation Towards EU Democracy Promotion', 12.

42. See Michelle Pace's article 'Paradoxes and Contradictions in EU Democracy Promotion in the Mediterranean: The Limits of EU Normative Power', in this issue.

43. Chourou, 'Security Partnership and Democratization', 188.

44. Lesser, 'Policy Toward Algeria After a Decade of Isolation', 10.
45. Ibid.
46. Ibid.
47. Youngs, 'The European Union and Democracy Promotion in the Mediterranean', 44.
48. European Commission, *Algeria Strategy Paper*, 2007.
49. Ibid.
50. Youngs, 'The European Union and Democracy Promotion in the Mediterranean', 56.
51. Morisse-Schillbach, 'Patterns of Adaptation Towards EU Democracy Promotion', 12.
52. Gillespie, 'A Political Agenda for Region-Building?', 4.
53. Ibid.
54. Börzel and Risse, 'One Size Fits All!'.
55. Daguzan, 'The Fate of Love and Hate France-Algeria'.
56. European Commission, *Algeria Strategy Paper*, 2007.
57. Ibid.
58. Tanner, *European Union Foreign and Security Policy*, 143.
59. Entelis, 'The Unchanging Politics of North Africa', 28.
60. Ciment, *Conflict and Crisis in the Post-Cold War Algeria*, 124.
61. Tanner, *European Union Foreign and Security Policy*, 138.
62. Joffe, 'The European Union, Democracy and Counter-Terrorism in the Maghreb', 150.
63. Volpi, 'Introduction: Strategies for Regional Cooperation in the Mediterranean', 119–20.
64. Smith, 'The Outsiders', 770.
65. Youngs, 'Europe's Flawed Approach to Arab Democracy'.
66. Ibid.
67. Morisse-Schillbach, 'Patterns of Adaptation Towards EU Democracy Promotion in the Maghreb', 12.
68. Volpi, 'Introduction: Strategies for Regional Cooperation in the Mediterranean', 119–20.
69. Ibid.
70. Bicchi and Martin, 'Talking Though or Talking Together?', 196.
71. Lesser, 'Policy Toward Algeria After A Decade of Isolation', 10.
72. Bicchi and Martin, 'Talking Though or Talking Together', 202.
73. Ibid.
74. Lesser, 'Policy Toward Algeria After A Decade of Isolation', 10.
75. Çelenk, 'The EU, NATO and Turkey's Mediterranean Policy', 557.
76. Youngs, 'Europe's Flawed Approach to Arab Democracy'.
77. Menotti, 'Democracy in the Middle East', 15.
78. Balfour, 'Re-thinking the Euro-Mediterranean Political and Security Dialogue', 18–19.
79. Algeria Events, 'Algeria-China: Strategic Cooperation Declaration Conclusion', and Zoubir, 'Algeria in the International Context'.

Bibliography

Algeria Events. 'Algeria-China: Strategic Cooperation Declaration Conclusion'. http://www.algeria-events.com/article552.html
Balfour, Rosa. 'Re-thinking the Euro-Mediterranean Political and Security Dialogue'. *ISS Occasional Paper No* 52 (2004).
Bicchi, Federica, and Mary Martin. 'Talking Though or Talking Together? European Security Discourses Towards the Mediterranean'. *Mediterranean Politics* 11 (2006): 189–207.

Börzel, Tanja. 'Europeanization and Territorial Institutional Change: Toward Cooperative Regionalism?'. *Europeanization and Domestic Change: Transforming Europe*, ed. G. Maria Cowles, James Caporaso, and Thomas Risse, 137–58. Ithaca: Cornell University Press, 2001.

Börzel, Tanja. 'Towards Convergence in Europe? Institutional Adaptation to Europeanization in Germany and Spain'. *Journal of Common Market Studies* 37 (1999): 573–96.

Börzel, Tanja, and Thomas Risse. 'One Size Fits All! EU Policies for the Promotion of Human Rights, Democracy and the Rule of Law'. Paper presented at the Workshop on Democracy Promotion, 4–5 October 2004, Stanford University.

Börzel, Tanja, and Thomas Risse. 'When Europe Hits Home: Europeanization and Domestic Change'. *European Integration Online Papers* 4 (2000), http://eiop.or.at/eiop/texte/2000-015a.htm

Calabrese, John. 'Beyond Barcelona: The Politics of the Euro-Mediterranean Partnership'. *European Security* 6 (1997): 86–110.

Çelenk, Ayşe Aslıhan. 'The EU, NATO and Turkey's Mediterranean Policy'. *The Geoeconomics and Geopolitics of Turkey*, ed. Nejat Doğan and Mehmet Öcal, 545–67. Ankara: Nobel, 2007.

Chourou, Bechir. 'Security Partnership and Democratization: Perceptions of the Activities of Northern Security Institutions in the South'. *Euro-Mediterranean Relations for the 21st Century*, ed. Hans Günter Baruch, Antonio Marquina, and Abdelvahab Biad, 183–96. Hampshire: Macmillan Press, 2000.

Ciment, James. *Conflict and Crisis in the Post-Cold War Algeria: The Fundamentalist Challenge*. New York: Facts On File Inc, 1997.

Cowles, Maria G., James Caporaso, and Thomas Risse, eds. Europeanization and Domestic Change. *Europeanization and Domestic Change: Transforming Europe*, 1–20. Ithaca: Cornell University Press, 2001.

Daguzan, Jean-François. 'The Fate of Love and Hate France-Algeria: An Inextricable Relationship'. http://209.85.129.132/search?q=cache:DceGqOk7EIgJ:www.liv.ac.uk/ewc/docs/Daguzan2002.doc+daguzan+the+fate+of+love+and+hate&hl=tr&ct=clnk&cd=1&gl=tr&client=firefox-a

Dean, Jonathan. 'New Components of the European Security System: The Roles of CFE, NATO, EC and the CSCE'. *The Future of the European Security: The Pursuit of Peace in the Era of Revolutionary Change*, ed. PhilipJ. Rogers, 105–21. Hampshire: Macmillan Press, 1993.

Entelis, John P. 'Algeria: Technocratic Rule, Military Power'. *Political Elites in Arab North Africa: Morocco, Algeria, Tunisia, Libya and Egypt*, ed. William I. Zartman, Mark A. Tessler and John P. Entelis, 92–143. London: Longman, 1982.

Entelis, John P. *Algeria: The Revolution Institutionalized*. Boulder, Colorado: Westview Press, 1986.

Entelis, John P. 'The Unchanging Politics of North Africa'. *Middle East Policy* 14 (2007): 23–41.

Entelis, John P., and Arone Lisa. 'Government and Politics'. *Algeria: A Country Study*, ed. Helen Chapin Metz, 173–235. Washington: Library of Congress, 1994.

Gillespie, Richard. 'A Political Agenda for Region-Building? The EMP and Democracy Promotion in North Africa'. *Institute of European Studies Paper* (2004), 040530.

Holm, Ulla. 'Algeria: President Bouteflika's Second Term'. *Mediterranean Politics* 10 (2005): 117–22.

Joffe, George. 'The European Union, Democracy and Counter-Terrorism in the Maghreb'. *Journal of Common Market Studies* 46 (2008): 147–71.

Lesser, Ian. 'Policy Toward Algeria After A Decade of Isolation'. *Mediterranean Quarterly* 12 (2001): 8–21.

Malley, Robert. *The Call From Algeria: Third Worldism, Revolution, and the Turn to Islam.* Berkeley: UCLA Press, 1996.

Menotti, Roberto. 'Democracy in the Middle East: Democratize but Stabilize'. *Middle East Quarterly* 13 (2006): 11–20.

Morisse-Schillbach, Melanie. 'Patterns of Adaptation Towards EU Democracy Promotion in the Maghreb: Tunisia and Algeria Compared'. Paper presented at the 6th Pan-European Conference, Turin, 12–15 September 2007.

Oljelund, Anders. 'European Security and Cooperation in the 21st Century'. Speech given at the *International Conference on European Security and Cooperation in the 21st Century.* İstanbul, 2001.

Olsen, Johan. 'The Many Faces of Europeanization'. *ARENA Working Papers* 01/2 (2002).

Pace, Michelle. 'Human Rights Instruments in Euro-Mediterranean Relations'. Euro-Mediterranean Human Rights Network. http://www.euromedrights.net/usr/00000026/00000027/00000028/001764.pdf

Roberts, Hugh. 'Dancing in the Dark: The European Union and the Algerian Drama'. *Democratization* 9 (2002): 106–31.

Schimmelfennig, Frank, and Hanno Scholtz. 'EU Democracy Promotion in the European Neighbourhood: Political Conditionality, Economic Development and Transnational Exchange'. *Challenges to Democracy in the 21st Century Working Paper* 9 (2007).

Schwarz, Peter. 'European Union Foreign Ministers divided on Iraq War'. World Socialist Website. http://www.wsws.org/articles/2002/sep2002/iraq-s05.shtml

Smith, Karen. 'The Outsiders: The European Neighbourhood Policy'. *International Affairs* 81 (2005): 757–73.

Sorenson, David. 'Civil-Military Relations in North Africa'. *Middle East Policy* 14 (2007): 99–114.

Tanner, Fred. *European Union Foreign and Security Policy: Towards a Neighbourhood Strategy.* London: Routledge, 2004.

Tortter, Jean R. 'National Security'. *Algeria: A Country Study*, ed. Helen Chapin Metz, 235–84. Washington: Library of Congress, 1994.

Tovias, Alfred. 'The Regional Strategy Paper'. www.femise.org/PDF/A_Tovias_1000.pdf

Volpi, Frederic. 'Introduction: Strategies for Regional Cooperation in the Mediterranean: Rethinking the Parameters of the Debate'. *Mediterranean Politics* 11 (2006): 119–35.

Youngs, Richard. 'European Approaches to Security in the Mediterranean'. *Middle East Journal* 57 (2003): 414–31.

Youngs, Richard. 'Europe's Flawed Approach to Arab Democracy'. Centre for European Reform. http://www.cer.org.uk/pdf/essay_youngs_arab_democracy.pdf

Youngs, Richard. 'The European Union and Democracy Promotion in the Mediterranean: A New or Disingenuous Strategy'. *Democratization* 9 (2002): 40–62.

Youngs, Richard. *The European Union and the Promotion of Democracy.* Oxford and New York: Oxford University Press, 2001.

Zoubir, Yahia. 'Algeria in the International Context'. Barcelona Chamber of Commerce. http://www.cidob.org/es/content/download/5686/55149/file/Ponencia+Zoubir+Anvari+2007.pdf

A clash of norms: normative power and EU democracy promotion in Tunisia

Brieg Tomos Powel

School of Law and Social Sciences, University of Plymouth, Plymouth, UK

As the European Union (EU) evolved as an international actor in the 1990s, it placed a commitment to promote certain values at the core of its foreign policy. These values include democracy, and alongside others such as a respect for human rights and the rule of law, they have resulted in the branding of the EU by some scholars as a 'normative power'. Democracy, however, is but one of many values promoted by the EU, and may not necessarily represent the most important in its relationship with Tunisia, where President Zine el Abidine Bin Ali and the ruling elite base their authority on claims championing stable development, modernization, and promoting secular values. Political actors advocating different values to the government are suppressed in the name of stability, leaving little space for a democratic opposition to develop. Evidence suggests that in the Tunisian context, stability is now increasingly preferred by EU policy-makers. This has a negative effect on both the potential for external support for political reform in Tunisia, and on the EU's wider claims to being committed to the promotion of democracy.

Introduction

> ... during the period of decolonization, certain colonized intellectuals have begun a dialogue with the bourgeoisie of the colonialist country. During this phase, the indigenous population is discerned only as an indistinct mass ... On the other hand, during the period of liberation, the colonialist bourgeoisie looks feverishly for contacts with the elite, and it is with these elites that the familiar dialogue concerning values is carried on. The colonialist bourgeoisie, when it realizes that it is impossible for it to maintain its domination over the colonial countries, decides to carry out a rear-guard action with regard to culture, values, techniques and so on.
>
> Franz Fanon, *The Wretched of the Earth*[1]

Written in the 1950s, Franz Fanon's words bear an intriguing relevance to the current relationship between Europe and Tunisia. Indeed, the consequences of the intellectual 'exchange' between both shores of the Mediterranean is such that many Tunisian intellectuals acquired their knowledge of the Maghreb, their own region and society, from French sources.[2] The Tunisian independence movement based its nationalist struggle on a combination of a familiarity with French culture, an advocacy of the French modernist character, and the promotion of a popular, Tunisian national identity.[3] These factors were combined in the post-independence period to create a new and exclusive *francisant* form of Tunisian identity, designed to mobilize the population behind the new government, which was rapidly conso-lidating Tunisian society around a single centre of power. Traces of this identity remain, continuing to stifle the development of popular opposition to the ruling elite.[4]

In recent years, Tunisia has developed a particularly close relationship with the EU. A 'partner state' since the launch of the Euro-Mediterranean Partnership (EMP or 'Barcelona Process') in 1995,[5] Tunisia was also the first Mediterranean state to initiate a bilateral Association Agreement with the EU (1998).[6] Central to the EMP are demands that Mediterranean partner states promote and strengthen practices of democratic government, with 'Association Agreements' acting as country-specific blueprints for intended reforms. Efforts to revitalize EU relations with its Mediterranean and Eastern European neighbours were consolidated in 2003 in the form of the European Neighbourhood Policy (ENP).[7] This sought to reinvigorate the EMP, particularly in light of the 11 September 2001 attacks and the subsequent international focus on the Middle East region. In 2004, Tunisia was amongst the first to agree on a bilateral 'Action Plan' with the EU as part of the ENP.[8] Despite these major policy initiatives, Tunisia continues to challenge those who seek meaningful, democratic government in the state. A recent report for Freedom House argues that political conditions in Tunisia con-tinue to lag behind impressive economic developments, and that the state presents 'a striking example of the institutionalization of the forms of democracy without any of the substance'.[9] Considering why the EU's efforts have not (as yet) been successful, this article examines the means by which the EU promotes democracy in Tunisia and why these may not be effective.

Methodologically, the article considers the discourse employed by the actors involved in the EU–Tunisia relationship. Thus, it draws on a number of interviews conducted with European and Tunisian individuals in 2005 and 2006. These indi-viduals include EU and Tunisian officials and independent NGO activists. Unless otherwise stated, all interviews were conducted in confidentiality, and the names of interviewees are withheld by mutual agreement. Moreover, a number of official policy texts which have emerged within the EMP and ENP frameworks are con-sulted, in addition to wider texts regarding more general EU and Tunisian govern-ment policies.

This article begins by considering the notion of normative power, a conceptual framework for understanding the EU as an international actor. It also outlines how normative power becomes a method for promoting democracy in other states. The article then turns to the specific case of Tunisia and the promotion of democracy in this North African state by the EU. This article contends that the promotion of democracy as a norm in Tunisia is stifled by the simultaneous and counter-productive promotion of stability. This is done by demonstrating how potential actors in the democratizing process are ostracized by both the EU and the Tunisian government in the name of stability. In the case of Tunisia, this particularly refers to Islamist political actors.

Framing EU democracy promotion in Tunisia

The EU does not have a stand-alone democracy promotion policy in Tunisia. Rather, Tunisia is included in wider multilateral EU policy initiatives (the afore-mentioned EMP and ENP). These initiatives combine EU political, economic, and cultural policies within multilateral frameworks supported by bilateral elements. It is interesting to note that the EMP includes non-EU states as 'equal' partners, brought together by the signing of the Barcelona Declaration in 1995. This declaration, on the one hand, binds its signatories to its contents, including commitments to political reform and democracy development.[10] The ENP, on the other hand, was created and initiated without the signatures or much substantive input from non-European states.[11] This framework now rep-resents the predominant structure for EU–Mediterranean relations, and the EMP now exists as part of this wider 'neighbourhood' dimension of EU foreign policy.[12] These two policies have institutionalized the EU–Mediterranean (and therein the EU–Tunisia) relationship. This institutionalization has provided a fra-mework within which democracy may be promoted in Tunisia. The first part of this section considers the academic debate on this method and on the concept of 'normative power Europe'. This is followed by an analysis of why these norms might be promoted, and concludes by arguing that, through normative power, the EU does nothing more than 'promote itself' in Tunisia. Thus, Fanon's obser-vation that the former colonialist bourgeoisie continues to promote its values and cultures in its former colonies still rings true, albeit in the guise of a new pan-European actor.

Normative power Europe

Debates over the nature of the EU as an international actor have paid particular attention to its non-military nature. In the 1970s, François Duchêne described the (then) EC as a 'civilian power,' alluding to the lack of a unified military arm.[13] By the early twenty-first century, questions have emerged regarding the EU's international identity and the effect of this identity on the nature of its foreign policy.[14] Notably, this debate has included discussion of the concept of 'Normative Power Europe', stemming from an article by Ian Manners in 2002.[15] In this work, the EU is conceived of as a particular type of international actor, predisposed to promote its values through its interaction with other actors. Manners' work has received considerable attention, including its role in the Mediterranean context; a debate which, in turn, has also drawn a further response from Manners himself.[16]

Key to understanding EU normative power, Manners argues, is the EU's existence as 'being different to pre-existing political forms', a difference which 'predisposes [the EU] to act in a normative way'. Specifically, this involves the promotion by the EU of the supposed 'core' European norms of peace, liberty, democracy, rule of law, and a respect for human rights through the EU's relations with other actors. To this he adds four secondary values of social solidarity, anti-discrimination, sustainable development, and good governance. According to Manners, all these norms have a European historical context.[17] Moreover, they are often portrayed as 'universal' in that they are considered valid or 'can be expected to gain approval in a free and open debate in which all those affected are heard'.[18] Indeed, normative power is 'defined on the basis of the universality of values, which in turn guarantees the (indirect) protagonism of third parties'.[19]

Norms are promoted through socialization achieved by including other actors within the same institutional frameworks as the 'self'.[20] Through the vigorous promotion of norms within these institutional frameworks, what begins as intentionally complicit behaviour by the actors gradually becomes routinized. Authoritarian regimes initially attempt to withstand this normative pressure by fielding a front of compliance. However, even these regimes become constrained by their commitments to institutional standardization, so that 'despite their original intentions they fall into a pattern defined by [the institution's] principles'.[21] Thus, through socialization, the norms of institutions, as defined by the EU in the case of the EMP and ENP, also become the norms of the actors.

Yet the issue of inclusiveness raises further questions regarding who is or indeed is not included. Federica Bicchi stresses that normative power must give voice to people outside of the EU.[22] Moreover, normative power also presents the risk that the exerciser of the power (that is, the EU) only 'speaks for' rather than 'gives voice to' those outside the EU. Thus, Bicchi suggests that the EU's actions should be assessed in two ways. Firstly, thorough scrutiny should be applied to the norms being promoted by the EU to assess their hypothetical inclusivity and their potential to be shared by those outside of the EU. Secondly, she calls for an empirical analysis of the inclusivity of the actual process of EU foreign policy-making. Therefore, central to this analytical exercise are questions regarding who might be the intended targets of the norm promotion and whether and to what extent should the EU consider the views of those actors who may be affected by EU normative power. Inclusivity then is not limited to those who may be directly involved with the EU, such as state governments themselves. Rather, it should be extended to those others who might also be subjects of the EU's exercise of normative power.

The normative power argument attracts its sceptics, particularly in the Mediterranean context. Richard Youngs, for example, argues that the EU's promotion of democracy and human rights varies depending on its strategic considerations.[23] Thus, democracy promotion becomes embroiled in processes of rational calculation, and EU commitments are inconsistently supported by its actions. Karen E. Smith also outlines inconsistencies with the application of (particularly) human rights elements of EU policy.[24] Smith stresses how the EU's emphasis on norms highlights the importance of its strategic and economic interests.[25] Partner states are often aware of this hypocrisy in EU democracy promotion. One Tunisian official stressed that the EU was only too eager to criticize any democratic discrepancy by Hamas in the Palestinian Territories, while being silent on alleged widespread human rights abuses during the 2005 Egyptian presidential and parliamentary elections.[26] However, these arguments rest on the conceptualization of normative power as a *reason* for action. In fact, normative power should also be considered as a *means* of achieving objectives different to, for example, military means. Thus, the analysis of the EU as a normative power may still be valid despite inconsistencies between rhetoric and action.[27]

There is a further problem with Manners' original model. Manners outlines his 'core' norms and suggests some further 'minor' norms. Applying his conceptualization of normative power, however, does not allow for the development of these norms, or indeed for other, less evident norms to acquire prominence over time. Manners' model may indeed be an accurate analysis of the EU's core norms at one particular point in time. Yet norms and the degree to which they are prioritized can change over time, particularly as an actor adapts to shifting circumstances. The contention of this article is that, in the context of the EU's relationship with Tunisia, stability is a norm given greater precedence than Manners' other core norms. Before addressing the specific case of Tunisia, however, the article considers why the EU assumes that there is a need to promote its norms in the Mediterranean.

Europe as the answer

The EU's decision to promote democracy in the Mediterranean through normative power originates from particular conceptualizations of the region itself. Indeed, the EU's discursive portrayal of the Mediterranean in particular has become the subject of a number of studies.[28] A common theme in the literature draws attention to the representation of the Mediterranean as a violent and conflict-ridden space, or as a space in need of socio-economic development.[29] Illustrative of these perspectives is a document detailing the EU presidency's conclusions for a 2003 conference of Euro-Mediterranean foreign ministers.[30] This conference followed a number of explosions in Casablanca, Morocco, and two earthquakes in Algeria and Turkey. However, rather than recognize the earthquakes as natural disasters and the bombings as isolated incidents in individual Mediterranean states, the conclusions portray the entire region as an area of turmoil. The presidency notes that: 'Violence, destruction, suffering, human rights violations and bloodshed have continued in the *region*, reaching again an alarming level during the last weeks' and that the ministers 'expressed also their concern and eagerness to confront violence and hatred by addressing the very causes of violence, terrorism and dehumanisation in Mediterranean societies'.[31] A further communication stresses the need for the ENP to address the conflicts in the region as 'such conflicts can threaten the Union's own security'.[32] Thus, the Mediterranean as a whole is constructed as a region suffering from instability.

To address this instability, the EU advocates a belief in the utility of democracy promotion as a means of ensuring security. The European Commission, for example, argues that:

> Concerns with security and the fight against terrorism have tended to dominate international agendas, but they have also begun to highlight root causes of violence and the importance of ensuring human rights, rule of law and inclusive democracy to avoid alienating communities and creating conditions of insecurity. Conflict prevention has thus added a new dimension to development strategy and work with civil society.[33]

Here, the EU clearly links the lack of political opportunity and socio-economic deprivation issues with international terrorism. Democracy becomes a weapon in the arsenal of those wishing for the elimination of terrorism. Democracy is therefore constructed as a means rather than as an end. Yet in the context of the normative power debate, democracy is relegated to a level below that of security.

Indeed, the EMP itself can be seen as an exercise of EU normative power, with democracy central to the values it seeks to promote.[34] These values follow directly from the so-called 'Copenhagen Criteria', the criteria setting the political and economic standards necessary for EU membership.[35] Further documents also illustrate the role of normative power in the Mediterranean. The 'Common Strategy on the Mediterranean' (2000), for example, explains that the EU will 'take measures to persuade all Mediterranean Partners to abolish the death penalty *in accordance with agreed EU guidelines*'.[36] It is envisaged that Mediterranean partners are to be brought into line with European behaviour and the belief in EU policy circles that the 'European way' provides the answers to the region's problems. The use of normative power in this context appears to show little regard for values which are not part of a European way of behaviour.

This emphasis on the primacy of European values is also present in EU texts relevant to Tunisia. Romano Prodi, then President of the European Commission, stated in November 2002 that 'The Agadir initiative – the decision by Tunisia, Morocco, Egypt, and Jordan to speed up the liberalisation of trade between them – must be seen as a very positive step [of them becoming more like us]'.[37]

Under its economic section, the EU–Tunisia Association Agreement (1998) talks little of developing common approaches. Rather, it states that: 'Cooperation shall be aimed at helping Tunisia to bring its legislation closer to that of the Community in the areas covered by this agreement.'[38] Never is a state's association with the EU portrayed negatively: it is assumed that this can only be positive. An official from an EU member state claimed that due to the extent of the economic relationship between the two actors, Europe is Tunisia's *only* hope for comprehensive development.[39] The official argued that whatever carrots are being dangled by Washington and other interested parties, nothing can replace those offered by Europe. The EU believes that its neighbours can only 'benefit from the prospect of closer ... relations with the EU'.[40] As Ulla Holm argues, 'humanity, universalism and European values are thus constructed in a chain of equivalence whose opposite is terrorism identified with anti-democracy, and destruction of humanity'.[41] Repeatedly, therefore, one finds a conviction among EU policy makers that Europe's way is best.

This is in keeping with the core tenets of normative power Europe, that is, to promote European norms as a means of developing non-European societies. This position is unreflective and the confidence in the morality of the European message is reminiscent of nineteenth century, (particularly, but not only) French colonial expansion in the Mediterranean. The *mission civilisatrice*, as it came to be known, was based on similar, essentialist understandings of the potential of Europe to benefit the non-European world. Unlike normative power, military force played a major role in the nineteenth century. However, the *mission civilisatrice*'s objective of spreading the benefits of French culture and values was founded upon a similar understanding of the primacy of French-European values over non-European values. It was believed that French culture was progressive and possessed 'unquestioned supremacy of knowledge, technology and prosperity'.[42] The colonized peoples would be offered the very best educational and cultural education and facilities, providing these peoples renounced their own culture and religion.[43] Interestingly, the architects of the *mission civilisatrice* often presented their culturalist project of imperialism as an alternative to the unpopular notion of the military conquest of North Africa. By employing Enlightenment egalitarian arguments, its advocates hoped to challenge liberal opposition to colonialism based on economic and financial reasoning.[44]

Within the frameworks of multilateral policy initiatives, Tunisia is associated with signifiers which, on closer inspection, may only be of relevance to other parts of the region. Furthermore, central to the response advocated by the EU to challenges that are allegedly endemic to the entire Mediterranean region is a greater commitment to European values. Democracy is one of these values and is clearly advocated as a solution to the instability which is attributed to the region by the EU. Yet, as the next section explores, efforts to tackle supposed region-wide problems often have very particular local-level consequences.

Political Islam: a study in shared values

Studies of the local level politics of Arab Mediterranean societies often highlight the importance of Islamist political actors. Indeed, the contributions by Francesco Cavatorta, Are Hovdenak, and Eva Wegner and Miquel Pellicer-Gallardo to this special issue emphasize their role in the politics of Morocco and the Palestinian Territories in particular. In Tunisia, both the principal incarnations of political Islam since the 1970s – the Mouvement de la Tendence Islamique (Movement of Islamic Tendency or MTI) and its successor, the Nahda (Renaissance)

Movement – have arguably offered a more comprehensive challenge to the rule of Presidents Bourguiba and Ben Ali than other opposition movements in the last 30 years.[45] Indeed, François Burgat and William Dowell, and Mohammed Elihachmi Hamdi have all suggested that Nahda developed into a viable democratic political party by the early 1990s.[46] In theory, a Tunisian Islamist movement presents an actor that could be supported by the EU as part of a democracy promoting strategy. Yet, as this section argues, evidence suggests that the EU's actual position on Islamists is closer to that espoused by the Tunisian government.

Tunisian generalizations

The various incarnations of political Islam in Tunisia have regularly been suppressed by the authorities, usually in the context of a larger debate over Tunisian identity.[47] Michael Willis observes that while states such as Morocco have tended to include 'moderate' Islamists within the political process as a means of moderating their demands and isolating more extremist elements, Tunisia is notable for the exclusion of its Islamists as a means of containing radicalism.[48] Despite a brief respite following Bin Ali's takeover of the Tunisian presidency in 1987, the Nahda party was hounded with such vigour by the security forces in the 1980s and 1990s that its leadership is now either in exile, in prison, or executed. Indeed, Christopher Alexander argues that battling Nahda became the greatest preoccupation of the Bin Ali government during its first decade of rule.[49]

Part of this campaign has involved the 'securitization' of Islamist political movements;[50] Bin Ali in particular fostered a 'security doctrine', securitizing Islamist actors to strengthen his own position.[51] Furthermore, Tunisian officials are keen to emphasize how both Tunisia and the EU share a common threat and a responsibility to 'fight terror'.[52] The Tunisian government frequently includes references to Islamists in its security discourse. In the early 1990s, for example, the Bin Ali regime used the notion of security to discredit Nahda following the breakdown of talks between the government and the Islamists. On 28 September 1991, the government revealed details of an Islamist plot to assassinate the president by firing a Stinger missile at his aircraft. The government newspaper *Al-Hurria* claimed that the Islamists had 'sick minds' and 'criminal hands' and were enemies of the Tunisian people.[53] In a later interview, Bin Ali attempted to essentialize the Islamists, claiming that 'there is not much difference between what you call "moderates" and "extremists." Their final goal is the same, to form a theocratic and authoritarian state . . . I do not fear Algerian contamination, Tunisia is a safe body'.[54]

Whilst the Islamists in Tunisia have virtually disappeared as a coherent political force following government clampdowns in the 1990s, official suspicion of public displays of religiosity remains. A recent illustration of the Tunisian government's position *vis-à-vis* public displays of faith was an argument over the wearing of headscarves. Echoing similar moves in France, in October 2006 the Tunisian authorities sought stricter imposition of Law 108 forbidding the wearing of headscarves in the workplace. When implemented by Bourguiba in the early 1980s, pre-dating a similar French ban by some two decades, it was welcomed in France and the United States as a 'liberal' reform.[55] Figures from Islamist *and* secular groups have criticized this as an attack on basic human rights.[56] The recent clampdown was in response to a noticeable increase in the wearing of the headscarf among young Tunisian women, in part due to the popularity of Saudi teen soap operas on satellite channels.[57] The row worsened following comments by Hédi Mhenni, General Secretary of the ruling Rassemblement Constitu- tionnel Démocratique (RCD), or Democratic Constitutional Rally party, who declared that wearing the headscarf was a practice not 'of Tunisian origin', and timed his comments to coincide with the start of Ramadan.[58] Bin Ali also claimed that the headscarf was not a traditional Tunisian garment; it was in fact 'foreign' and did 'not fit with Tunisia's cultural heritage'.[59]

Whilst a row over headscarves might not appear overtly anti-democratic, it is a continuation of the government's drive to stifle any possible opening for Islamists in Tunisia. Indeed, it is the Islamists that have represented the greatest threat to Bin Ali's hold on power during his two decades at the helm.[60] This practice brings with it new exclusions and creates new divisions within societies.[61] What remains largely unexplained in the Tunisian government's discourse are reasons *for* wearing the headscarf. In Tunisia the headscarf represents a plethora of issues, from tradition and religion to simply an act of teenage devotion to their Saudi heartthrobs.[62] Instead, the regime has attempted to associate the headscarf and any explicitly religious behaviour with 'backwardness', attempting to distinguish between the 'modern' secular and the 'traditional' religious.[63] Yet by doing this, the Tunisian government not only denies the expression of religious identities of its population, but also reasserts its position within Tunisian society as sole guarantor of Tunisianness.

European contradictions?

There is ample proof of EU concern over radical, political Islamist organizations. For example, general discussion of more Islamist or religious violence can be found in two key documents addressing EU security policy. The 2003 *European Security Strategy* (ESS), for instance, identifies religiously inspired terrorism as one of the principal security threats to the EU.[64] The *European Union Strategy for Combating Radicalisation and Recruitment to Terrorism* (2005) concurs with this analysis, stating that the 'terrorism perpetrated by al-Qa'ida and extremists inspired by al-Qa'ida has become the main terrorist threat to the Union'.[65] The same document also argues that this violence is the product of 'the pressures of modernisation, cul- tural, social and political crises, and the alienation of young people living in foreign societies'. Therefore al-Qa'ida is repeatedly identified as a perpetrator of such acts.

Nevertheless, through the EMP and ENP policy frameworks in place in the Mediterranean, the EU proposes the promotion of democracy as a means of avoid- ing future violence. Indeed, the EU directly links democracy with security issues.

The EU believes that fostering democracy and participation by civil society in the democracy transformation process is the most successful way of dealing with extremist religious movements.[66] The *Strategy for Combating Radicalisation* explicitly outlines the usefulness of democracy promotion initiatives: 'Outside Europe, we must promote good governance, human rights, democracy, as well as education and economic prosperity, through our political dialogue and assistance projects'.[67] Moreover, the EU recognizes that such initiatives should avoid engaging government elites alone at the expense of engagement with the wider population, claiming that 'Addressing this challenge is beyond the power of governments alone. Al-Qa'ida and those inspired by them will only be defeated with the engagement of the public, and especially Muslims, in Europe and beyond.'[68]

On paper therefore, the promotion of democracy, albeit as a response to security threats, remains consistent with Manners' conceptualization of 'normative power Europe'. Yet the fact that little has apparently changed in Tunisian political life since 1995 suggests that other norms might also play a part in determining the vigour with which the EU promotes this particular norm.

However, none of these texts infer a connection between violent extremist groups and popular, political Islamist movements, either in Tunisia or the wider Mediterranean. This is supported by member state diplomats, who expressed their belief that whilst the largely Algerian Salafist Group for Preaching and Combat (GSPC) may indeed have penetrated Tunisian society, there is little evidence to link Tunisian Nahda members to al Qa'ida or other violent organizations.[69] The British government, for example, receives regular demands from the Tunisian government for the extradition of Nahda leader Rachid Ghannouchi from his exile in London on 'terrorism' charges. However, British officials reiterate that they have no firm evidence linking Ghannouchi with such activities.[70] Indeed, in stark contrast to the Tunisian perspective on Tunisian Islamists, there is little in EU discourse to suggest any link between Nahda and violence. Furthermore, even general references to Islamist violence are absent from Tunisia-specific EU texts.

In fact an antipathy towards Islamist violence at the Mediterranean regional level appears to have manifested itself as hostility towards anything vaguely related to Islamism in Tunisia itself. Despite a decade and more of democracy promotion within the EMP framework, Commission officials, member state diplomats, and European and Tunisian NGO representatives stated that the EU never engages Tunisian Islamist political or civil society organizations.[71] This also extends to bilateral policies by member state governments, some of which hold regular meetings with secular parties.[72] Moreover, this phenomenon is apparently not constrained to Tunisia. Elsewhere in the Mediterranean, at the time of writing, no Brussels-related funding has reached Islamist political organizations.[73] Youngs also observes this practice in the Palestinian Territories. In this example, EU funding is denied to NGOs which are critical for the Middle East peace process. Instead, its financial support was concentrated on former President Yassir Arafat's administration, with Hamas-affiliated organizations particularly ignored.[74] Thus, the EU often appears more partial than impartial during processes of promoting political reform in the region, preferring to back its favoured actors rather than support a democratization process *per se*.

This, however, contradicts the founding principles of the EMP itself. The Barcelona Declaration, primarily through its cultural pillar, calls for the support of religious freedom, demanding a greater understanding of different cultures in the Mediterranean.[75] Nevertheless, there is also a dislike of any religious fundamentalism, including a suspicion of religious-political groups, and particularly Islamist groups.[76] Moreover, no recognition is made of the diversity of Islamist political organizations in the region. There is considerable evidence suggesting that, rather than being a single monolithic entity, political Islam in the Mediterranean is in fact a collection of numerous groups and organizations, which adapt and respond to the political conditions particular to the state that they challenge for power.[77] Nevertheless, for the EU, Islamism is 'the product of sick, social, political and economic systems that need a long-term process of healing'.[78]

This raises the question why Islamist movements might not, in the eyes of the EU, be desirable actors in the democratic transformation process. The EU's *2007-2013 Regional Strategy Paper* for the Mediterranean suggests an answer. It portrays political Islam as a threat to its strategic ambitions in the region, stating that:

> The Mediterranean region is of strategic importance to the EU, in both economic (trade, energy, migration) and political (security, stability) terms. The political situation in the region is characterised by persistent tensions due to the Middle East conflict, the war in Iraq and its spill-overs [*sic*] to other countries, regular upsurges of terrorist activity, and in some countries domestic political tensions, lack of political openness and increasing popularity of political Islam movements.[79]

Intriguingly, democracy or political reforms are not considered; the 'political' component focuses solely on security and stability. Moreover, political Islam is portrayed somewhat negatively alongside lack of openness and political tensions as problems for the region's states. Furthermore, the issue of stability also emerges elsewhere in EU texts. The Barcelona Declaration itself made much of the need for stability in the Mediterranean.[80] In a revealing speech, Commissioner Ferrero-Waldner has also claimed that:

> The Mediterranean and Middle Eastern region is undergoing fundamental shifts – economically, politically and socially. In an interconnected world, these developments have an impact on the European Union. Europe cannot be an 'introspective bystander'. On the contrary, we are and must remain a *key actor* in the region; a political and economic partner who supports and manages change and who helps reap the opportunities that flow from it. This is not just a political imperative, but a *matter of self interest*. If Europe did not 'export' stability, it would import 'instability'. The European Union is neither an island nor a fortress.[81]

This demonstrates that in normative power terms, stability is established as a norm to be exported, whilst political Islam stands in opposition to this norm. Indeed, were an act of terrorist violence to be committed, the act would not only be considered as a material strike on EU territory. Rather, as the 'Declaration on Combating Terror' states, 'acts of terrorism are attacks against the values on which the Union is founded'.[82] Violence is portrayed as an assault on what is fundamentally European, and those who commit such acts are Europe's enemies.

The failure to engage with Islamists has meant that there is little understanding among EU officials of Islamism in Tunisian politics or civil society.[83] EU support for Mediterranean civil society organizations (CSOs) includes initiatives such as the Anna Lindh Euro-Mediterranean Foundation, the Euro-Med Civil Forum, and its successor the Euro-Med Non-Governmental Platform. Whilst the Anna Lindh Foundation seeks to 'promote dialogue between cultures and contribute to the visibility of the Barcelona Process through intellectual, cultural and civil society exchanges',[84] participating Tunisian NGOs are limited to 'official' organizations with links to the government, such as the Union Nationale de la Femme Tunisienne (National Union of Tunisian Women) and the Bin Ali Chair for the dialogue between cultures and civilisations.[85] Meanwhile, a number of 'independent' Tunisian NGOs participate in the Euro-Med Platform, namely the Association Tunisienne des Femmes Démocrates (Tunisian Association for Female Democrats), the Conseil National pour les Libertés en Tunisie (National Council for Liberties in Tunisia), the Ligue Tunisienne des Droits d'Hommes (Tunisian League for Human Rights), and the Comité pour le Respect des Libertés et des Droits de l'Homme en Tunisie (Committee for the Respect of Freedom and Human Rights in Tunisia). The Non-Governmental Platform is an attempt to formalize the relationship between civil society organizations throughout the Mediterranean region based on very similar principles to those upon which the relationship between the EU and the partner state governments is founded. Thus, it establishes an ideal institutionalized framework within which norms and values may be diffused, effectively extending the practice of socialization to the non-governmental level. Yet neither the Foundation nor the Platform includes any Islamist organizations amongst their Tunisian members.

Indeed, when the issue of Islamist civil society or political activity is raised, EU officials express a fear of 'another Algeria' or a 'Mediterranean Taliban', invariably associating the concept of an Islamist government in Tunisia with that of an extremist Islamist administration.[86] This fear of anything Islamist also extends to the European NGO sector: many NGO representatives admit that their organizations' policies limits cooperation to secular Tunisian NGOs only.[87] According to one NGO official, Islamist organizations are simply 'not to be trusted'.[88]

Additionally, the sidelining of Islamist movements concurs with the Tunisian government's position. Moreover, from a normative perspective, it suggests that a democracy that is inclusive of Islamist movements is undesirable, and should not therefore be promoted. In Tunisia at least, EU democracy promotion clearly favours secular groups. This practice is exclusive and conditions the type of democracy which is being promoted. William Connolly argues that secularism's conception of morality is remarkably close to that proposed by Christianity, the faith that originally established the space of the *seculere*.[89] To promote secularism alone is to promote a limited and particularly Christian-European understanding of society. Doing this in Tunisia is to promote a Christian-European world-view in a country steeped in Arab-Islamic heritage.

The stability complex

If Islamists are not considered to be part of the democracy agenda of the EU, the EU cannot avoid contact with the representatives of the Tunisian state. It is after all these representatives, politicians and diplomats alike, who physically represent Tunisia at the negotiating table. It is these individuals who have the most direct contact with EU officials, and, of course, constitute part of a regime which, as the Freedom House report mentioned earlier suggests, remains undemocratic. It is these officials who, in theory at least, might be the first representatives of the Tunisian state to be socialized within the institutional frameworks of the EMP and the ENP.

However, the inseparability of the ruling RCD and state in Tunisia poses a problem for the EU. The separation between members of the government, the regime and state officials is obscure; one who is not an RCD member or who opposes the regime will not obtain a position of seniority in public service.[90] Moreover, most members of the Tunisian government originate from a particular bourgeois cultural background, educated within the *franciste* education system developed under Bourguiba. The same applies to many in the official NGO sector.[91] Consequently, those individuals who argue for Tunisia's case with the EU are in fact arguing from the particular perspective of the *franciste* elite. Tunisian negotiators, so familiar with the intricacies of European thought, are also backed by an impressive economic record, a history of successful security cooperation with Europeans, and the advantage of simply not being one of its 'troublesome' neighbours, such as, for example, Algeria or Libya. They are able to assume the role of the 'self' in negotiations, confirming European understandings that their values are universal.

Tunisian officials echo many of the trends in EU discourse. In a speech addressing the 2005 EuroMed summit in Barcelona, Minister for Foreign Affairs Abdelwaheb Abdallah (speaking Bin Ali's words in the president's absence) noted Tunisia's conviction of the need for the 'partnership to make a quantum leap ... which will offer promising prospects that meet our peoples' aspirations for further solidarity and progress'.[92] Tunisia also strongly supports the notion of solidarity and 'shared ownership of the Partnership'.[93] Indeed, the emphasis on partnership was one of the most appealing elements for the Tunisian government in the framework of the Barcelona Process.[94] The engagement of non-EU states as 'partners' within a region-wide policy initiative offered a break from the traditional bilateral arrangements in which the greater resources of the EU or certain member states would be allowed to dominate proceedings.

Officials stress the importance of stability for Tunisia's continuing development.[95] To this end, both the EMP and the ENP are welcome initiatives if they succeed in delivering regional stability. Within Tunisia, however, preserving stability is the role of the regime and the ruling party, *de facto* guaranteeing the country's future. Bin Ali is explicit in this assertion. He states in a speech to RCD activists that: 'I ... appreciate the diligent efforts exerted by the RCD structures, at the grassroots and local levels, in order to protect the country's gains and preserve its stability'.[96] The party thus becomes a tool of the state, able to control the local level to preserve national 'gains' and 'stability'.

There is also an implication that the RCD is responsible for progress. In the same address, Bin Ali distinguishes the RCD from others in the Tunisian population on the basis of tradition and its 'civilised' nature. He claims that:

> The RCD, which has always served as a school for the education of successive generations, instilling in them the sense of patriotism and allegiance to Tunisia alone, as well as ... [a] commitment to the rules of civilised behaviour, is now called on to step up its efforts in this field.[97]

This rallying call for RCD members to intensify their efforts to spread civilized behaviour indirectly criticizes those who oppose Bin Ali's message and labels them as uncivilized. Indeed, not only do Bin Ali and the RCD stand for civilization, but they are also eager to emphasize Tunisia's commitment to 'universal values'. Whilst these values are often obscure in nature, the *changement* of 1987 is portrayed as a step towards their realization. Bin Ali declares in a speech to commemorate the forty-ninth anniversary of the Tunisian Republic that:

> Since the change, we have emphasized that our people is [*sic*] eligible for a developed and organized political life, based on reference concepts and values that are essentially national in character. We have worked to fashion a model that embraces common universal values, deals wisely with events and developments, anticipates the future and its challenges, and endeavours to acquire the mechanisms and means of the time; our constant motto, in this regard, being exclusive allegiance to Tunisia.[98]

Thus, according to the president, Tunisia is being shaped to be an embodiment of 'common universal values', providing an ideal partner for the EU in the region. By advocating a model of development that applies wisdom and organization in the face of challenges, Bin Ali appears to discourage any overly radical measures. In addition, Bin Ali elsewhere states how Tunisia is attempting to 'join the ranks of developed nations',[99] thereby expressing the belief that development depends on a commitment to the modernist cause. This is found in a speech to commemorate the fiftieth anniversary of Tunisia's independence. Later in the same speech, he states that: 'The battles of today are not the battles of yesterday; and victory is now won only by those who master sciences and knowledge.'[100]

This extract challenges promoters of democratic transformation in the region. Whilst Bin Ali refers to an 'organized political life', he does not elaborate on its meaning. However, other officials are more forthcoming. Certain Tunisian officials are very keen to stress how 'desirable' democracy may be as an ideal, often quoting the work of Western political thinkers during the discussion, yet they also stress that one needs stability before democracy can take place.[101] The closing reference to an 'exclusive allegiance to Tunisia' suggests that Bin Ali suspects a foreign incubator of instability, a source whose identity is confirmed once more by other Tunisian officials. In their eyes, providing political Islamists remain a political force, there can be no stability.[102] Moreover, Bin Ali does not distinguish between different 'knowledges' but rather champions *the* sciences and knowledge, which are also associated with the notion of civilization. Thus, there is no space for those who disagree with either his knowledge or his way of doing things.

Thus, similar to the trend found in EU texts, political Islam is once more constructed as a threat to stability. This construction appears to take precedence over attempts to include Islamists within the democratic transformation process. It is clear, therefore, that both the EU and the Tunisian regime are constructing Tunisian democracy along similar lines which are perceived to embody 'universal' values.

Conclusion

The EU's relationship with Tunisia challenges the conceptualization of the EU as a normative power, particularly if that conceptualization demands that a normative power is one that includes democracy among the values it seeks to promote. As this article has contended, whilst the EU may claim that promoting democracy is a desirable policy goal in Tunisia and the Mediterranean, evidence suggests that security and stability are of greater importance to EU policy-makers. Yet security and stability do not feature in Manners' original list of core and secondary values of the EU's foreign policy. Indeed, where the democratic transformation process 'risks' opening the door to political Islam, as in the Palestinian Territories, and as discussed in Hovdenak's contribution to this special issue, the EU retreats from supporting such governments. In Tunisia, this antipathy leads to a complete EU neglect of political or civil society initiatives that may involve Islamist groups or organizations. This is particularly important as it was Tunisia's Islamists who posed the greatest challenge to Bin Ali during his presidency, and who appeared to be the only political force capable of achieving the levels of organization required to mount such a challenge. However, the EU has been reluctant to explore the potential of Tunisian political Islamists during its support for the democratization process in Tunisia, despite the previous popularity of Islamists as actors within Tunisian politics. That public support for political Islamism was at its peak in the five years before the launch of the EMP suggests a clear missed opportunity by the EU to engage with the last organized political opposition seen in Tunisia in the last two decades.

Furthermore, both the EU and the Tunisian government advocate and prefer a discourse of stability, which is not necessarily compatible with a rapid democratic transformation process. Thus, the official discourses of the two actors converge to exclude commitments to democratization from their relations with each other. Bin Ali legitimizes this discourse by associating it with Tunisia's national character, civilization, and a commitment to development along exclusive lines. Consequently, non-regime Islamist actors or discourses are de-legitimized by being constructed as un-Tunisian and as a threat to the nation's stability. Even the public expression of Islamic religiosity in the form of the wearing of a headscarf has been targeted by the Tunisian authorities and constructed as a threat to Tunisian identity. Yet, as was the case with the colonial power in Fanon's day, the EU chooses to engage with the regime and secular Tunisian civil society actors while ignoring bolder and perhaps, at times, unpredictable engagement with Tunisian Islamism. Not only does this echo the EU's attitude towards other Islamist political actors in the Mediterranean, it also suggests that any conceptualization of the EU as a normative power seeking to promote democracy amongst its international partners is flawed, with EU actions in Tunisia suggesting instead a commitment to security and stability rather than to more emancipatory ideals. This has further implications not only for the role of the EU as a democracy promoter in the region, but also for the nature of the EU's conceptualization of democracy which it attempts to promote in its foreign policy.

Acknowledgements

The author would like to thank two anonymous reviewers, along with Michelle Pace and Peter Seeberg, the guest editors of this special issue, for their hard work, helpful comments, and significant patience during the writing of this article.

Notes

1. Fanon, *The Wretched of the Earth*, 34.
2. Ayubi, *Over-stating the Arab State*, 134.
3. Murphy, *Economic and Political Change in Tunisia*, 43.
4. Sadiki, 'The Search for Citizenship in Bin Ali's Tunisia'.
5. European Union, *Barcelona Declaration*, 1995.
6. EU, *Official Journal* L097: 2–174.
7. Commission of the European Communities, *Wider Europe – Neighbourhood*. For a more detailed outline of the EMP and the ENP, see the Introduction to this special issue.
8. European Union, *EU/Tunisia Action Plan*.
9. King, *Tunisia*.
10. However, there is little evidence of collaboration between the EU and the partner states over the actual content of the declaration.
11. Interview with an official from the Tunisian Ministry for Foreign Affairs, Tunis, April 2006.

12. It is worth noting that a 'Mediterranean Union' was initiated (largely by France) in 2008, after this article was written. This seeks to compensate for the failures of European policy in the region, albeit without including the EU or northern European EU member states within its members.
13. Duchêne, 'Europe's Role in World Peace', 43.
14. For a summary of this debate, see Bretherton and Vogler, *The European Union as a Global Actor*, 37–61; and Pace, 'The Construction of EU Normative Power'.
15. Manners, 'Normative Power Europe'.
16. Bicchi, 'Our Size Fits All'; Diez, 'Constructing the Self and Changing Others'; Manners, 'Normative Power Europe Reconsidered'; Pace, 'The Construction of EU Normative Power'; and Sjursen, 'The EU as a "Normative" Power'.
17. Manners, 'Normative Power Europe', 242.
18. Sjursen, 'The EU as a "Normative" Power', 243.
19. Bicchi, 'Our Size Fits All', 292.
20. See for example Flockhart, 'Complex Socialization', and the various contributions in Flockhart ed., *Socializing Democratic Norms*.
21. Flockhart, 'Complex Socialization', 291; Diez, 'Constructing the Self and Changing Others', 630.
22. Bicchi, 'Our Size Fits All'.
23. Youngs, 'Normative Dynamics and Strategic Interests'.
24. Smith, 'The EU, Human Rights and Relations with Third Countries', 193–8.
25. Ibid., 196–8.
26. Interview with an official from the Tunisian Ministry for Foreign Affairs, Tunis, March 2006.
27. See also Diez, 'Constructing the Self and Changing Others', 615–16; Sjursen, 'The EU as a "Normative" Power', 239.
28. See for example Holm, 'The EU's Security Policy'; Malmvig, 'Cooperation or Democratization?'; Pace, *The Politics of Regional Identity*.
29. Pace, *The Politics of Regional Identity*.
30. Commission of the European Communities, *Mid-Term Euro-Mediterranean Conference*.
31. Ibid., 2.
32. Commission of the European Communities, *On Strengthening the European Neighbourhood Policy*, 9.
33. Commission of the European Communities, *Thematic Programme*, 4.
34. See for example Bicchi, 'Our Size Fits All'; and Diez, 'Constructing the Self and Changing Others', 230–2.
35. Diez, 'Constructing the Self and Changing Others'.
36. European Council, *Common Strategy*, 3, emphasis added.
37. *EuroMed Report*, no. 52, 28 November 2002. Romano Prodi, President of the European Commission, *Europe and the Mediterranean: Time for Action*, speech given at Louvain-la-Neuve: Université Catholique de Louvain-la-Neuve, 26 November 2002. Cited in Pace, *The Politics of Regional Identity*, 105.
38. EU, *Official Journal* L097: 14.
39. Interview with an official from the Tunisian Ministry for Foreign Affairs, Tunis, March 2006.
40. Commission of the European Communities, *Wider Europe – Neighbourhood*, 4.
41. Holm, 'The EU's Security Policy', 12.
42. Young, *Postcolonialism*, 88.
43. Ibid., 30.
44. Ibid., 89.

45. See for example Alexander, 'Opportunities, Organizations and Ideas'; and Hamdi, *The Politicisation of Islam.*
46. Burgat and Dowel, *The Islamic Movement in North Africa*, 234–7; Hamdi, *The Politicisation of Islam*, 67–70.
47. Sadiki, 'The Search for Citizenship'.
48. Willis, 'Containing Radicalism'.
49. Alexander, 'Back from the Democratic Brink', 37.
50. For an outline of the concept of securitization, see Buzan, Wæver, and de Wilde, *Security.*
51. Bensedrine and Mestiri, *L'Europe et ses Despotes*, 49.
52. Interviews with officials from the Tunisian Ministry for Foreign Affairs, Tunis, March and April 2006.
53. Hamdi, *The Politicisation of Islam*, 72–3.
54. Quoted in Hamdi, *The Politicisation of Islam*, 73.
55. Sadiki, *The Search for Arab Democracy*,183.
56. Interviews with Tunisian NGO activists, Tunisia, July 2005 and April 2006.
57. Interviews with former state employees, NGO activists, and artists, Tunis, La Marsa, and Sousse, April and August 2005, April 2006.
58. Magharebia, 'Headscarf Controversy In Tunisia Heats Up'.
59. Magharebia, 'Tunisian President Speaks Against Wearing of Headscarves'.
60. See for example Alexander, 'Back from the Democratic Brink'; Hamdi, *The Politicisation of Islam*, and Murphy *Economic and Political Change in Tunisia.*
61. Biswas, 'The "New Cold War"', 200.
62. Interviews with 18 Tunisian citizens, Tunis, Sousse, Nabeul, and Sousse, 2005 and 2006.
63. Interviews with 14 Tunisian citizens, Tunis, La Marsa, and Sousse, March, April, and August 2005, and April 2006.
64. EU, *European Security Strategy*, 3.
65. EU, *The European Union Strategy for Combating Radicalisation.*
66. See for example Volpi, 'Regional Community Building'; Panebianco and Attinà, 'Security Cooperation in the Mediterranean'; and Silvestri, 'EU Relations with Islam', 390.
67. EU, *The European Union Strategy for Combating Radicalisation.*
68. Ibid.
69. Interviews with representatives of EU member state governments, Tunis, August 2005, March and April 2006.
70. Interviews with British Foreign Office officials, Tunis, March 2006 and an official from the Tunisian Ministry of Foreign Affairs, April 2006.
71. Interviews with European Commission officials, member state diplomats, and representatives from Tunisian and European NGOs, Tunis and Brussels, 2005 and 2006.
72. Interviews with representatives of EU member state governments, Tunis, July 2005 and March/April 2006. The UK government, for example, regularly invite representatives from secular opposition parties and human rights organizations to the British embassy.
73. Bicchi and Martin, 'Talking Tough or Talking Together?', 197.
74. Youngs, 'Normative Dynamics and Strategic Interests', 424.
75. European Union, *Barcelona Declaration.*
76. Önis and Keyman, 'A New Path Emerges', 106.
77. For a discussion on the origins of, guiding influences on, and differences between various Arab Islamist movements, see Ayubi, *Political Islam*; or Ismail, 'Being Muslim'.
78. Silvestri, 'EU Relations with Islam', 390.

79. Commission of the European Communities/European Neighbourhood and Partnership Instrument, *Regional Strategy Paper*, 3, emphasis added.
80. European Union, *Barcelona Declaration*.
81. Ferrero-Waldner, 'The EU, the Mediterranean and the Middle East', original emphasis.
82. EU, *Declaration on Combating Terrorism*.
83. Interviews with Commission officials, member state diplomats, and representatives from Tunisian and European NGOs, Tunis and Brussels, 2005 and 2006.
84. Anna Lindh Euro-Mediterranean Foundation, 'Mission and Values'.
85. For a full list of participating Tunisian organizations, see http://www.euromedalex. org/Tunisia/EN/MembersList.aspx
86. Interviews with EU officials, Brussels, July 2006.
87. Interview with a representative from a European NGO, Brussels, July 2006.
88. Interview with a representative from a European NGO, Brussels, July 2006.
89. Connolly, *The Ethos of Pluralization*, xiii.
90. Interviews with a former government employee and with a human rights activist, Tunis, March 2005 and April 2006.
91. Interviews in with Commission officials, Brussels, July 2006, and with Tunisian officials and Tunisian NGO representatives, 2005 and 2006.
92. Abdalah, 'Address before the Euro-Mediterranean Barcelona Summit'.
93. Interview with an official from the Tunisian Ministry for Foreign Affairs, Tunis, April 2006. Also see Abdalah, 'Address before the Euro-Mediterranean Barcelona Summit'.
94. Ibid.
95. Ibid.
96. Bin Ali, 'Address at the Close'.
97. Ibid.
98. Bin Ali, 'Speech on the Forty-Ninth Anniversary', emphasis added.
99. Bin Ali, 'Speech on the Fiftieth Anniversary of Independence'.
100. Ibid.
101. Interviews with officials from the Tunisian Ministry for Foreign Affairs, Tunis, August 2005 and March 2006.
102. Interviews with officials from the Tunisian Ministry for Foreign Affairs, Tunis, August 2005 and April 2006.

Bibliography

Abdalah, Abdelwaheb. 'Address before the Euro-Mediterranean Barcelona Summit'. Speech, Barcelona, 27 November 2005, http://www.carthage.tn/en/index.php? option=com_events&task=view_detail&agid=3754&year=2005&month=11&day=27&Itemid=90
Alexander, Christopher. 'Back from the Democratic Brink: Authoritarianism and Civil Society in Tunisia'. *Middle East Report* (October–December 1997): 34–8.
Alexander, Christopher. 'Opportunities, Organizations and Ideas: Islamists and Workers in Tunisia and Algeria'. *International Journal of Middle East Studies* 32 (2000): 465–90.
Anna Lindh Euro-Mediterranean Foundation. 'Mission and Values', 2008, http://www. euromedalex.org/AboutUs/EN/MissionValues.aspx
Ayubi, Nazih. *Political Islam: Religion and Politics in the Arab World*. London: Routledge, 1993.
Ayubi, Nazih. *Over-Stating the Arab State: Politics and Society in the Middle East*. London: I.B. Tauris, 1995.
Bensedrine, Sihem, and Omar Mestiri. *L'Europe et ses Despotes: Quand le Soutien au «Modèle Tunisien» dans le Monde Arabe fait le jeu du Terrorisme Islamiste*. Paris:

Éditions la Découverte, 2004, [Europe and its Despots: Supporting the 'Tunisian Model' of Autocracy to Combat Islamist Terrorism in the Arab World].

Bicchi, Federica. 'Our Size Fits All: Normative Power Europe and the Mediterranean'. *Journal of European Public Policy* 13 (2006): 286–303.

Bicchi, Federica, and Mary Martin. 'Talking Tough or Talking Together? European Security Discourses towards the Mediterranean'. *Mediterranean Politics* 13, no. 2 (2006): 189–207.

Bin Ali, Zine el Abidine. 'Address at the Close of the Seventh Ordinary Session of the Central Committee of the RCD', 16 June 2007, Carthage.

Bin Ali, Zine el Abidine. 'Speech on the Fiftieth Anniversary of Independence', 20 March 2006, Rades.

Bin Ali, Zine el Abidine. 'Speech on the Forty-Ninth Anniversary of the Proclamation of the Republic', 25 July 2006, Carthage.

Biswas, Shampa. 'The "New Cold War": Secularism, Orientalism, and Postcoloniality'. *Power, Postcolonialism and International Relations: Reading Race, Gender and Class*, ed. Chowdhry Geeta and Nair Sheila, 184–209. London: Routledge, 2004.

Bretherton, Charlotte, and John Vogler. *The European Union as a Global Actor.* 2nd ed. London: Routledge, 2006.

Burgat, François, and William Dowel. *The Islamic Movement in North Africa.* Austin, TX: Centre for Middle Eastern Studies, University of Texas at Austin, 1997.

Buzan, Barry, Ole Wæver, Jaap de Wilde. *Security: A New Framework for Analysis.* Boulder, CO: Lynn Rienner, 1998.

Commission of the European Communities. *Mid-Term Euro-Mediterranean Conference (Crete, 26-27 May 2003): Presidency Conclusions.* 9890/03 (Presse 151).

Commission of the European Communities. *On Strengthening the European Neighbourhood Policy.* COM(2006) 726 final.

Commission of the European Communities. *Thematic Programme on the Promotion of Democracy and Human Rights Worldwide under the Future Financial Perspectives.* COM(2006) 23 final.

Commission of the European Communities. *Wider Europe – Neighbourhood: A New Framework for Relations with our Eastern and Southern Neighbours.* COM(2003) 104 final.

Commission of the European Communities/European Neighbourhood and Partnership Instrument. *Regional Strategy Paper (2007–2013) and Regional Indicative Programme (2007-2010) for the Euro-Mediterranean Partnership.*

Connolly, William. *The Ethos of Pluralization.* Minneapolis, MN: University of Minnesota Press, 1995.

Diez, Thomas. 'Constructing the Self and Changing Others: Reconsidering "Normative Power Europe"'. *Millennium* 33, no. 3 (2005): 613–36.

Duchêne, François. 'Europe's Role in World Peace'. *Europe Tomorrow: Sixteen Europeans Look Ahead,* ed. Richard Mayne, 32–47. London: Fontana, 1972.

European Council. *Common Strategy of the European Council on the Mediterranean Region* (2000).

European Council. *European Security Strategy: A Secure Europe in a Better World* (2003).

European Union. *Barcelona Declaration* (1995). http://www.eu-delegation.org.eg/en/eu_and_country/4.pdf

European Union. *Declaration on Combating Terrorism* (25 March 2003): Brussels.

European Union. *The European Union Strategy for Combating Radicalisation and Recruitment to Terrorism* (24 November 2005): DOC 14781/1/05.

European Union. *EU/Tunisia Action Plan,* http://ec.europa.eu/world/enp/documents_en.htm#2

European Union. *Official Journal* (30 March 1998): L097.

Fanon, Franz. *The Wretched of the Earth*. London: Penguin, 2001.

Ferrero-Waldner, Benita. 'The EU, the Mediterranean and the Middle East: A Partnership for Reform'. (2 June 2006): Speech, German World Bank Forum, Hamburg.

Flockhart, Trine. 'Complex Socialization: A Framework for the Study of State Socialization'. *European Journal of International Relations* 12 (2006): 89–118.

Flockhart, Trine. *Socializing Democratic Norms: The Role of International Organizations for the Construction of Europe*, ed. Trine Flockhart. Basingstoke: Palgrave Macmillan, 2005.

Hamdi, Mohammed Elihachmi. *The Politicisation of Islam: Essay on Democratic Governance*. Boulder, CO: Westview, 1998.

Holm, Ulla. 'The EU's Security Policy Towards the Mediterranean: An Impossible Combination of Export of European Political Values and Anti-Terror Measures?'. Danish Institute for International Studies, 2004, Working Paper no. 2004/13.

Ismail, Salwa. 'Being Muslim: Islam, Islamism and Identity Politics'. *Government and Opposition* 39 (2004): 614–31.

King, Stephen. *Tunisia*, Freedom House Country Report (2007). http://www.freedom house.org/template.cfm?page=140&edition=8&ccrpage=37&ccrcountry=172

Magharebia. 'Headscarf Controversy in Tunisia Heats Up'. http://www.magharebia.com/cocoon/awi/xhtml1/en_GB/features/awi/features/2006/10/27/feature-01

Magharebia. 'Tunisian President Speaks Against Wearing of Headscraves'. http://www.magharebia.com/cocoon/awi/xhtml1/en_GB/features/awi/newsbriefs/general/2006/10/12/newsbrief-04

Malmvig, Helle. 'Cooperation or Democratization? The EU's Conflicting Mediterranean Security Discourses'. Danish Institute for International Studies, 2004, Working Paper no. 2004/8.

Manners, Ian. 'Normative Power Europe: A Contradiction in Terms?'. *Journal of Common Market Studies* 40 (2002): 235–58.

Manners, Ian. 'Normative Power Europe Reconsidered: Beyond the Crossroads'. *Journal of European Public Policy* 13 (2006): 182–99.

Murphy, Emma. *Economic and Political Change in Tunisia: From Bourguiba to Bin Ali*. Basingstoke: Macmillan, 1999.

Önis, Ziya, and E. Fuat Keyman. 'A New Path Emerges'. *Journal of Democracy* 14 (2003): 95–107.

Pace, Michelle. 'The Construction of EU Normative Power'. *Journal of Common Market Studies* 45 (2007): 1041–64.

Pace, Michelle. *The Politics of Regional Identity: Meddling with the Mediterranean*. Oxford: Routledge, 2006.

Panebianco, Stefania, and Fulvio Attinà. 'Security Cooperation in the Mediterranean: EMP Instruments to Mitigate Divergent Security Perspectives'. *Euromesco Research Papers* July (2004).

Sadiki, Larbi. *The Search for Arab Democracy: Discourses and Counter-Discourses*. London: Hurst, 2004.

Sadiki, Larbi. 'The Search for Citizenship in Bin Ali's Tunisia: Democracy versus Unity'. *Political Studies* 50 (2002): 497–513.

Silvestri, Sara. 'EU Relations with Islam in the Context of the EMP's Cultural Dialogue'. *Mediterranean Politics* 10 (2005): 385–405.

Sjursen, Helene. 'The EU as a "Normative" Power: How Can This Be?'. *Journal of European Public Policy* 13 (2006): 235–51.

Smith, Karen E. 'The EU, Human Rights and Relations with Third Countries: "Foreign Policy" with an Ethical Dimension?'. *Ethics and Foreign Policy*, ed. Karen E. Smith and Margot Light, 185–204. Cambridge: Cambridge University Press, 2001.

Volpi, Frédéric. 'Regional Community Building and the Transformation of International Relations: The Case of the Euro-Mediterranean Partnership'. *Mediterranean Politics* 9 (2004): 145–64.

Willis, Michael J. 'Containing Radicalism through the Political Process in North Africa'. *Mediterranean Politics* 11 (2006): 137–50.

Young, Robert J.C. *Postcolonialism: An Historical Introduction*. Oxford: Blackwell, 2001.

Youngs, Richard. 'Normative Dynamics and Strategic Interests in the EU's External Identity'. *Journal of Common Market Studies* 42 (2004): 415–35.

Index

For Product Safety Concerns and Information please contact our EU
representative GPSR@taylorandfrancis.com
Taylor & Francis Verlag GmbH, Kaufingerstraße 24, 80331 München, Germany

www.ingramcontent.com/pod-product-compliance
Lightning Source LLC
Chambersburg PA
CBHW070411270326
41926CB00014B/2782

* 9 7 8 0 4 1 5 8 4 7 5 1 3 *